FROM THE
TEMPLE OF ZEUS
TO THE
HYPERLOOP

FROM THE
TEMPLE OF ZEUS
TO THE
HYPERLOOP

University of Cincinnati Stories

Edited by Greg Hand

To Jim Luken,
who lit a fire
& launched a journey
12/26/18

University of
CINCINNATI | PRESS

About the University of Cincinnati Press

The University of Cincinnati Press is committed to publishing rigorous, peer reviewed, leading scholarship accessibly to stimulate dialog between the academy, public intellectuals and lay practitioners. The Press endeavors to erase disciplinary boundaries in order to cast fresh light on common problems in our global community. Building on the university's long-standing tradition of social responsibility to the citizens of Cincinnati, the state of Ohio, and the world, the press publishes books on topics which expose and resolve disparities at every level of society and have local, national and global impact.

The University of Cincinnati Press, Cincinnati 45221
Copyright © 2018

Published with generous support from Patti and Buck Niehoff, and Betsy and Peter Niehoff for the University of Cincinnati Bicentennial.

ISBN 978-1-947602-04-5 (hardback)
ISBN 978-1-947602-05-2 (e-book, PDF)
ISBN 978-1-947602-06-9 (e-book, EPUB)

Names: Hand, Greg, editor.
Title: From the Temple of Zeus to the Hyperloop : University of Cincinnati
   stories / edited by Greg Hand ; with a foreword by Buck Niehoff.
Description: First edition. | Cincinnati : University of Cincinnati Press,
   [2018] | Includes index.
Identifiers: LCCN 2018008574| ISBN 9781947602045 (hardback) | ISBN
   9781947602052 (pdf) | ISBN 9781947602069 (epub)
Subjects: LCSH: University of Cincinnati--History. | University of
   Cincinnati--Alumni and alumnae.
Classification: LCC LD983 .F46 2018 | DDC 378.771/78--dc23 LC record available at
https://lccn.loc.gov/2018008574

Designed and produced for UC Press by Orange Frazer Press, Wilmington, Ohio
Typeset in: Wilmington, Ohio
Printed in the United States of America

First Printing

*In memory of Bob Dobbs (1953–2017),
among the Spirit of History Committee's
founding members and inspiring contributors.*

Contents

Foreword
Five Presidents 1984–2016
Different Styles, Different Times
by Buck Niehoff   pg. ix

Introduction
How a Dedicated Crew of Bearcats
Assembled This Book, with the Help
of Willie Nelson, the *New York Times*,
and the Good Folks of Granville, Ohio
by Greg Hand   pg. 1

Books, Bricks—and 'Potencie'
by Kevin Grace   pg. 9

It Started with a Valentine
Archaeology at UC, Carl Blegen,
and the Department of Classics
by Jack L. Davis   pg. 16

**William Howard Taft and
the UC College of Law**
by Bob Taft   pg. 30

**No One Has Ever Come
For Dean Loueen Pattee**
by Anne Delano Steinert   pg. 35

On Hazel's Diary
by Janice Currie   pg. 43

A Force for Nature
E. Lucy Braun
by Meg Hanrahan   pg. 50

Presidential Politics
Raymond Walters, Franklin D. Roosevelt, and
the Photo Op That Never Developed
by Robert Earnest Miller   pg. 57

**A Brief History of Computing
at the University of Cincinnati**
by Russell E. McMahon   pg. 67

My University of Cincinnati Journey
by Clark Beck   pg. 73

UC Engineering
A Cauldron for Personal Transformation
by Donald L. Vieth   pg. 82

Jazz in the Workshop
The Story of the "Queen City Suite"
by Steven Lawrence Gilbert   pg. 95

Reflections
by John Bryant   pg. 99

**The Provost Doesn't
Call There Anymore**
by Jon Hughes   pg. 105

For the *Record*
by Judy McCarty Kuhn   pg. 109

Where It All Began
A Very Short Play with Some Music, Wherein
the University of Cincinnati Is Revealed to Be
the Most Unlikely Place for the Nation's First
Musical Theater Program
by Jack Rouse with Helen Laird   pg. 124

Introduction to UC and Cincinnati
The 1972 New Faculty Orientation
by Edna S. Kaneshiro   pg. 143

Working with Warren Bennis
by Bill Mulvihill   pg. 148

Introductions
My UC Story 1973–1979
by Julia Montier-Ball   pg. 153

RAPP
Changing Attitudes—
One Mind at a Time
by Marianne Kunnen-Jones   pg. 161

Memories of David Blackburn
by Sarah Jessica Parker   pg. 167

A Celebration of the Arts in Cincinnati
by Jim Cummins   pg. 169

My Quest for a Just Community
by Mitchel D. Livingston   pg. 171

**Of Structures and Spaces
and Structural Spaces**
DAAP's Genesis of New Architecture
at UC and Cincinnati
by Jay Chatterjee   pg. 179

UC
An Urbanist University
by Terry Grundy   pg. 191

**Confessions of a
Famous Jingle Scientist**
by James J. Kellaris   pg. 199

My Search for H. M. Griffin
by Paulette Penzvalto   pg. 212

Cincinnati Storystorm
by Julialicia Case   pg. 219

Serendipity and Stewardship
The Preservation Lab
by Holly Prochaska   pg. 224

**The Challenges of Creating the
Bearcat Transportation System**
by Jerry P. Tsai   pg. 229

**From International Student
to Bearcat for Life**
by Sid Thatham   pg. 234

**Vignettes from a Corner
of Café Momus**
by Vidita Kanniks   pg. 239

DAAP Slapped
by Victoria Fromme   pg. 242

Embracing the Uncertainty of Life
by Faith Prince   pg. 244

The Ultimate UC Trivia Quiz
by Kevin Grace and Greg Hand   pg. 247

Our Contributing Authors   pg. 266

Foreword

Five Presidents 1984–2016
Different Styles, Different Times

by Buck Niehoff

In the course of one year, 2009, I served as chair of the UC board of trustees with three presidents—Nancy Zimpher, Monica Rimai, and Greg Williams. That's a record number. At no time in the two-hundred-year history of the university has there been so many in such a brief period. I had worked as a volunteer on a number of projects with Joe Steger, who preceded Nancy, and with Santa Ono, who followed Greg. As a result, over three decades or so, I have become an amateur presidential observer, deeply appreciative of their diverse contributions to the university and fascinated by their charming quirks.

Of the group, Joe was probably the least presidential in the traditional sense. But, in many ways, he was the most effective. After all, he lasted in the job for nineteen years (1984 to 2003), far longer than any of the others. Only one UC president, Raymond Walters, outdid him, serving twenty-three years, from 1932 to 1955.

Joe's easygoing attitude, quick jokes, and humorous comments gave an impression more of an insurance salesman than the head of a major university. Once, at a dinner party, I introduced him as the president of UC to an out-of-towner, who looked at me in confusion and said, "You're kidding."

For Joe, jocularity leveled the playing field, put people at ease and empowered them. He especially enjoyed teasing his friends. Because he did it with warm-hearted intelligence, you felt complimented and understood, rather than embarrassed or put out. His humor made everyone comfortable around him, even though he might be their boss, or their boss's boss.

He encouraged you to express your ideas and was willing to support you if your suggestions made sense for the university. Of course, the best idea he embraced was the signature architecture program that transformed UC into one of the most beautiful urban campuses in the world.

I always admired his commitment to this plan. Although he knew a great deal about many things, he knew very little about architecture. Actually, nothing.

I got a sense of his ignorance on this topic once when he and I were having lunch together at the Maisonette, Cincinnati's former five-star French restaurant. As we were studying the menus, trying to decide about a wine, I began chatting, to make conversation, about architecture, a particular passion of mine.

I said, "You know, I really like Le Corbusier. Really wonderful." Looking up from the wine list, Joe said, "Oh. That's good. Le Corbusier is one of my favorites, too. Let's order a bottle of it." To this day I don't know for certain if he was kidding.

In the history of the university, Joe's legacy is the rebuilding of the campus, transforming it from asphalted acres of surface parking lots, surrounded by mundane, uncomfortable structures, to an interconnected pattern of world-class buildings, designed by the most accomplished architects of our time.

But, for me personally, his true legacy is the humanity that he brought to the university, expressed by his friendly humor and intelligent wit.

If Joe was a bit laid back, his successor, Nancy Zimpher was nearly the opposite. A dynamic extrovert, she exploded with more energy than she could use up in any given day. But her gregarious enthusiasm was exactly what the university needed, from 2003 to 2009, to propel it to the next level academically and enable it to evolve as a leader in our region.

At the beginning of her administration, she collaborated with many stakeholders to create a plan known as "UC|21: Defining the New Urban Research University." It got everyone focused on quality in our academics and teaching. Along the way, admission standards were raised and enrollment increased substantially.

She initiated the Proudly Cincinnati Capital Campaign, which had an initial goal of raising $700 million. But her energetic vision demanded a larger objective and she encouraged the campaign leadership, including me as one of the co-conveners, to increase it to $1 billion, making it the largest campaign for any organization in the history of the Greater Cincinnati region.

When the higher goal was announced, I remember thinking that we might get to that amount eventually but not within the period of time we had set for the campaign. I was wrong. Not only did we reach the goal within the timeframe but we exceeded it by $90 million. As Nancy often said, "Make no small plans."

She also became a leader in the community, improving UC's visibility and connection with the region. She co-founded StriveTogether, an innovative "birth to career" educational initiative, which has spread to other communities across the nation. She chaired the Uptown Consortium, responsible for much of the development in the neighborhoods adjacent to the university.

Her extroverted energy was one source of her success. She came alive in a crowd and the more input she had, the more outgoing she became. Once, at the end of a long day crowded with several difficult meetings about various matters at the university, she and I went to a retirement party for a beloved staff member. I remember she was so worn out that she could barely drag herself into the party. But as the excitement of the gathering hit her, her face relaxed, and she started to smile and banter. People energized her.

Another example of her outgoing nature was her plan to revive the Commencement ceremonies by shaking hands with each graduate. If you think about it, that is the sort of thing only an extrovert would want to do.

With this change, students and their families for the first time in decades enthusiastically enjoyed the ceremonies. They liked the personal connection with the president. Attendance skyrocketed and students looked forward to walking across the stage and being congratulated by the president.

As a member of the board of trustees, I sat through many of these Commencements and watched her joy in greeting each graduate. With not much to do during the hour or two of hand shaking, I passed some of the time by counting how many she would do in a minute. She was pretty good at it. As I recall, she managed as many as thirty-five, or one graduate every two seconds.

Sometimes I think that her famous, highly patterned stockings were another aspect of her gregarious personality. They were part of the electricity that surrounded her.

Once they played a small part in her unsuccessful attempt at jogging. After she was at UC for a few years, she mentioned one day at a meeting that she wanted to start an exercise program. "I have time now to get in shape," she declared. I couldn't imagine how she handled half of what she was already doing. But I picked up on her comment and volunteered to help her start jogging. We agreed to go for a run early one morning. On the day we selected, I ran the two miles from my house to her building. I found her in the lobby and suggested that we run for about a mile and a half. She was dressed in shorts, a bulky Bearcat sweatshirt, and her trademark fancy patterned stockings. "Usually," I mentioned, "people consider socks are more comfortable to run in than stockings."

"I always wear stockings," she gruffed. She seemed unhappy, almost sullen, which was very unusual for her. "Let's get started," she sighed. We jogged out the door and headed down the long driveway at a slow but steady pace. When we reached the street, about 250 yards from where we had started, she stopped suddenly. Turning to me, she smiled politely and said, "That was great. I really enjoyed it. Let's do it again sometime."

With that she spun around and went back toward the building. At first, I worried that my sock comment had discouraged her in some way. More likely, though, she probably just didn't like exercise. Anyway, we never ran again.

Just over a week after I was elected chair of the board of trustees in late January 2009, she resigned. But I was not the cause of that. She had been offered a major promotion, to become chancellor of the State University of New York system. With 460,000 students, it is the largest university system in the country. It was a job as large as her energetic personality.

Nancy was almost a walking billboard for UC, usually wearing the university's colors of red or black or both. As she often said, "Vision trumps everything." She inspired us all to dream, to think of the university as better than great—to envision it as premier. She encouraged us to believe that we could pretty much accomplish anything, and during her presidency we did a lot.

By contrast our next president, Monica Rimai, was a nuts-and-bolts pragmatist, who kept the ship running smoothly from March to November 2009 through the chopping waters of selecting a new president and transitioning to new leadership.

Whereas Nancy enjoyed leading the parade, like a high-stepping drum majorette, Monica focused her energy more in the background, making certain that everything was in good order. She had served Nancy as senior vice president for administration and finance, and had helped to organize and push through many tough decisions, such as performance-based budgeting for the academic departments.

While Nancy inspired change through excitement and bold vision, Monica relied on steadfast tenacity, hard work, and thorough research. At every meeting I attended with her, Monica knew the facts about the issues better than anyone in the room. She simply out-prepared everyone else.

Even her leisure activities involved hard work and tenacity. She often "vacationed" by mountain climbing and long-distance bike riding—two interests we shared. We swapped tales about her climb to base camp on Mount Everest and my summiting Mount Kilimanjaro, and on many Sunday mornings we rode with the head of the UC Recreation Center on the Little Miami bike path. Invariably, those rides, which started pleasantly enough, turned into all-out, exhausting, competitive races.

For me the visual image of Monica's focused dedication was, surprisingly, her car, a Mini Cooper. I will always recall seeing it on McMicken Circle one morning as I drove up Clifton Avenue about a half hour before a meeting that she had scheduled with me for 7:00 A.M. Hers was the only car I saw. The sole person working at that early hour was the top leadership of the university.

I think that her behind-the-scenes nature was challenged when it came to Commencement. Before the ceremony, she looked stressed. I sensed that being center stage as president and having to connect with several thousand graduates as they "walked" did not appeal to her.

But she was determined to do her duty and she soldiered on. During the ceremony, when I counted the number of handshakes per minute that she was doing, I was astounded. She reached as high as sixty, one graduate per second. I turned to another trustee sitting next to me on the stage and asked, "How come she is going so fast?"

"None of the students know her," was the response. "They just walk past and don't really notice her."

Being unnoticed was, I suppose, an important aspect of her leadership style. Her primary tools were discipline, keen analysis, and solid dedication, exactly what the university needed at the time as we transitioned to a new president.

If you were casting a president for a Hollywood movie, your choice might well be Greg Williams, who led UC from 2009 to 2012. With classic good looks, he not only looked the part but, with a reserved, scholarly demeanor, he acted it, too.

Typical of many academics, he was thoughtful and sensitive to others, but perhaps a bit remote. As a scholar, he wrote four books and earned four advanced degrees, including a Juris Doctor and a PhD, as well as five honorary degrees. For him the life of the mind was part of his personality and was central to his leadership style.

It was natural for him to use the power of reasoning to influence decisions. Unfortunately, not everyone was on his wavelength. Many people were unable to grasp the complexity of what he was saying. His cerebral approach probably was out of step with our current personality-oriented society.

But he was extremely sensitive to people's feelings. This awareness probably resulted from his difficult childhood in Muncie, Indiana, which he described in his award-winning memoir, *Life on the Color Line: The True Story of a White Boy Who Discovered He Was Black*. Instead of becoming bitter about his early life experiences, he became compassionate and determined to help others transform their lives.

In the hundreds of speeches that he gave each year to groups on campus and to organizations within the community, he emphasized the transformative value of education. As well as encouraging diversity and access for first-generation students, he developed a program to help gifted students and distinguished faculty to receive well-deserved recognition through seeking national awards and grants.

During his tenure, he enhanced the national stature and academic reputation of the university. He helped to create our current athletics conference, the American Athletic Conference, and he developed a plan, UC2019—Accelerating Our Transformation—that expanded Nancy's UC|21 agenda.

His primary gifts to UC were this focus on excellence in academics, and more importantly, encouraging us to believe that our job was to help transform and improve lives through everything that we do at UC. He was a good judge of character and he filled many of the senior positions and deanships with some outstanding picks, including the provost, Santa Ono, who succeeded him in 2012 and led the university until 2016.

Without question, Santa was UC's most student-oriented president. He simply loved being with students and he enjoyed interacting with them in many ways. He embraced their preferred method of communication—social media—and became known, nationally, for using his tweets to give a human voice to the UC president.

His Twitter account, which gave birth to the hashtag #HottestCollegeInAmerica, had more than 77,000 followers. He was famous for responding, almost immediately, to emails, posting photos of his daily activities, and tweeting about everything from the best doughnuts in town to his favorite Taylor Swift songs.

He was willing to try anything that the students were doing. Once, when he practiced with the football team, he learned to catch a pass if it was lobbed very gently in his direction. Another time, he sweated through a hot yoga class with thirty students.

Perhaps the most visible evidence of his student interaction were the bowties which he wore nearly every day and which became part of his identity. He started wearing them after having dinner at a fraternity house, where he became aware of their popularity. At first, like most people, he had trouble tying them. Several times, as someone who has worn them since the 1970s, I had to help him, until he finally got the hang of it.

Because he believed in putting students first, he chose not to live in the president's official residence. Instead, he urged the university to sell it and to use the proceeds for scholarships. As many as forty students each year were able to receive this funding.

However, not all of his student connections were a success. When it came to shaking hands at Commencement, he proved to be much slower than any other president. He could only manage a meager fifteen or so per minute. The problem was he was so popular that many students paused to take a selfie with him. Eventually, the university had to ban these selfies.

While continuing the university's tradition of selecting the best people for the job, Santa also perpetuated our commitment to diversity. Nancy had been our first woman president. Greg was our first African American and Santa was our first Asian American. All three of them contributed to our cultural richness that has helped propel UC to international stature. In this regard Santa supported UC's strategic partnerships with several international universities, including Chongqing University, Hong Kong Polytechnic University, Beijing University, and Botswana International University.

Santa signed on to the establishment of the UC Press, to promote academic scholarship through publication. This plan was advanced by UC Libraries Dean Xuemao Wang, with encouragement from the UC Bicentennial Commission's Spirit of History Committee, which was responsible for creating books about the university's 200-year history. Santa intended that this Bicentennial book of essays would be one of the first produced by the press. He also envisioned that the press would be one of the tangible enduring legacies of the Bicentennial celebration.

Santa's leadership style can be summarized in one word—enthusiasm. He found something positive in nearly every idea that came his way and he was generous in his efforts to give new ideas a chance. As with nearly everyone, however, his greatest strength was also his greatest weakness. The many novel ideas that he embraced sometimes could not be seen through to completion.

His gift to UC was the excitement for learning and passion for college life that he gave to the students. He brought the students to the forefront, where they truly belong.

Each of these five presidents has been, I believe, the right person for the time they served. Their various personal styles helped to provide balanced leadership that propelled UC into one of the great urban research universities in the world.

Introduction

How a Dedicated Crew of Bearcats Assembled This Book, with the Help of Willie Nelson, the *New York Times*, and the Good Folks of Granville, Ohio

by Greg Hand

For more than forty years, across two employers and a dozen job title changes, I consistently reported to the Internal Revenue Service on my annual Form 1040 that my occupation was "editor." There was a logic to this: no matter what it said on my business card, press pass, or office door, "editor" was the most powerful title I ever had, or ever would have.

Editors, you see, control reality. As editor, I could make little events huge when they interested me and I could make great events tiny, buried in the briefs, if they bored me. My opinions ran at the top of the editorial page, while your whiny objections ran in small print among the letters at the bottom. Bwahahaha! (Editors would make great mad scientists.)

In putting this book together, there were quite a few moments in which I wished editors really did have that sort of power. Alas, I discovered this editor could not make manuscripts appear on deadline as if by magic, or inspire contributors to overcome writer's block. I discovered that some authors (gasp!) were unimpressed by my attempts to brighten or tighten their prose.

The long journey to the book you hold in your hands began seven years ago with the first meeting of a dedicated crew officially named the Spirit of History subcommittee of the University of Cincinnati Bicentennial Commission. Chairing the meeting and providing the leadership that has carried us through to publication was Buck Niehoff, just coming off his term as chair of the UC board of trustees. At that first gathering, Buck directed the committee's attention to a pair of books published to mark the bicentennial of Granville, Ohio. Offered in a slipcase, one book contained scholarly histories of the town in chapters ranging from prehistoric times to the present. The companion volume offered an *olla podrida* of brief essays highlighting dozens of aspects of that charming town.

Buck's brief description of those volumes established our goal. Over the years, the Spirit of History team entertained any number of possible projects—websites, videos, architectural timelines and such—but we always circled back to our initial vision: a set of companion books to demonstrate the significance of our university as well as its breadth and diversity.

Our committee itself reflected the breadth of the University of Cincinnati and included, in addition to Buck, Jay Chatterjee, dean emeritus of the College of Design, Architecture, Art & Planning; marketing guru Sean Connell; Dr. Philip Diller of UC's Family Medicine program; the greatly mourned Bob Dobbs, an alumnus whose talents soon got him promoted to co-chair the entire Bicentennial celebration before his untimely death; University Archivist Kevin Grace; Jennifer Heisey and Keith Stichtenoth from the Alumni Affairs office; Marianne Kunnen-Jones, who has managed communication for UC's President's Office through six administrations; Emeritus Vice President for Student Affairs Mitchel Livingston; University Architect Mary Beth McGrew; recent alumnus Jordan Moss; graduate student Peter Niehoff; Senior Planner Marc Petullo; communications maven Jack Rouse; professors David Stradling and Tracy Teslow of the History Department; alumna Miriam West; and the combined MD and JD Frank Woodside.

In short order, the committee extended an invitation to Professor Stradling to research and write the first volume in our duet. Stradling's previously published volumes, including *The Nature of New York: An Environmental History of the Empire State* (2010), *Making Mountains: New York City and the Catskills* (2010), and *Cincinnati: From River City to Highway Metropolis* (2003), are highly regarded among both scholars and lay audiences. At the time he accepted our invitation, he was nearing completion of *Where the River Burned: Carl Stokes and the Struggle to Save Cleveland* (2015) and needed to get that manuscript to press before diving into the UC project.

The second book, which you hold in your hands, took somewhat longer to bring into focus. Over many meetings, the committee suggested a host of potential authors and a veritable encyclopedia of topics. On rare occasions, a suggestion paired an author with a topic, but mostly topics came up without authors and authors got pushed forward without topics. The discussion, however, was far from fruitless because each suggestion carried us closer to understanding what this book would look like. The committee also elected me as editor. I complained about typecasting. My complaints elicited zero sympathy.

A crystalizing moment occurred on August 22, 2014, when the *New York Times Book Review* featured a volume published on the occasion of Brown University's 250th anniversary. One sentence in Amanda Katz's review of this book grabbed our attention: "…the book is likely to be of interest mainly to those with pre-existing ties to Brown." At our next committee meeting, we discussed that review and determined that our book would not suffer the same opprobrium. We agreed to look for content of interest to readers not yet familiar with the University of Cincinnati.

But what would such content look like? For a couple of years, we tossed around the idea that we wanted *New Yorker*–style essays, but we soon discovered that the *New Yorker* intimidated potential writers as much as it inspired them. I have forgotten who suggested we look at Michael Hall's article on Willie Nelson's guitar, Trigger, in the December 2012 issue of *Texas Monthly*. Over the course of about five thousand words, Hall hooked readers on the saga of Willie's much-autographed Martin N-20 gut-strung guitar. After discussion at our next meeting, Hall's article became our model essay. It was personal, specific to a particular object, and interesting to people who didn't think they would be interested in Willie Nelson, acoustic guitars, or country music.

Although our conception of the ideal book was beginning to gel, we realized that we had exactly one manuscript actually in our possession. Marianne Kunnen-Jones had recruited Professor Jack Davis of UC's Classics program to write about the romantic life of the renowned archaeologist Carl Blegen. (Davis occupies the Carl Blegen Chair of Greek Archaeology at UC.)

To generate some additional material, the Spirit of History Committee organized a contest, with financial awards. We invited UC students and alumni, as well as faculty and staff to submit personal reflections on some person, place, or thing that provided insight into the essence of UC. Although we braced for (and would have been thrilled to get) hundreds of entries, fewer than forty arrived. Thankfully the quality far outstripped the quantity. Our contest winners included Julialicia Case's story about the stories that brought her into UC's story, Jon Hughes's revelation that the UC writing program was conceived in a tavern, and Janice Currie's reflections on her mother's diary as a UC student in the 1920s. All of the contest winners appear in this book, but so do many of the entries that did not claim a prize. In all, fourteen of the chapters here started as contest entries.

The contest reinvigorated the committee, who soon brainstormed bunches of additional good ideas. Although it was too late for prizes, we took these suggestions and assigned committee "patrons" to knock on a lot of doors. Another seven or eight chapters came from writers rousted into creative expression by the insistent knocking of the Spirit of History Subcommittee.

Some of our contributors just sort of wandered in. Your editor retired after thirty-six years of employment at the University of Cincinnati on July 1, 2014. On the afternoon of his final day in the office, Judy McCarty Kuhn called to inquire about the University of Cincinnati Press, because she had a book she wanted to publish. Although the UC Press was not yet organized at that point, we invited Judy to adapt a chapter for inclusion in this book and she accepted the offer. Anne Delano Steinert's chapter took root in the sub-basement of Cincinnati's Bockfest Hall as she marshaled rowdy beer fans through her exhibit on Over-the-Rhine history. Steven Gilbert's story about his father's "Queen City Suite" originated at the birthday party at the Montgomery Inn Boathouse for a ninety-year-old geology professor. (Gilbert's wife is a geologist.)

Unfortunately, several good stories got away. It looked like we had a lock on a memoir from one of the founders of UC's Gay Society. We had a staffer lined up to write about the 504 Club, which forced UC to rethink handicap access all over campus. We lost the story of the 925/SEIU union's battle to represent UC's clerical workers when the prospective author stopped answering emails. There were a couple of good prospects to do something involving sports. We really wanted something about UC's faculty union. Despite the formidable application of editorial authority (and charm), none of these ideas progressed beyond initial conversations.

So effective was the intrepid Spirit of History Subcommittee in identifying talent and assigning topics that we ultimately abandoned an idea your editor very much hoped to pursue. Someone suggested that we delve into the archived student publications and pull some student writing from past eras. Your editor is inordinately excited by archival research and had begun assembling an anthology of student writing from the 1890s through the 1960s. Although none appear in this book, most of these old publications have been made available online by the UC Archives and are worth a visit.

The collection here is arranged in mostly chronological order, with representative glances at the university from about 1910 right up until this book went into production.

The autumn of 2016 brought Liz Scarpelli to UC as the director of the new University of Cincinnati Press and as the newest member of the Spirit of History Subcommittee. With her appointment, your editor was presented with the editorial equivalent of kryptonite—a real deadline. In the presence of a deadline, all editors resign themselves to awareness that only real manuscripts can be published, and that potential manuscripts are actually not manuscripts at all. Joining Liz at the UC Press was acquisitions editor Michael Duckworth, who took on oversight of our companion volumes and saw the real manuscripts through to manifestation as the volume you now hold in your hands.

It goes without saying that editors also lack the power to beguile readers to purchase a book, much less read it. That you have done so of your own free will, dear reader, has earned you the gratitude of your editor, the Spirit of History Subcommittee, and the 200-year-old University of Cincinnati.

FROM THE
TEMPLE OF ZEUS
TO THE
HYPERLOOP

Books, Bricks—and 'Potencie'

by Kevin Grace

From mid-autumn to late winter, I come to work in the dark and I go home in the dark. These are my favorite months of the year because the campus is beautiful when nighttime is just hanging onto the edges. There are the glowing colored lights rotating in the dome above Van Wormer Hall, the soft swishing on Clifton Avenue of the early morning cars and bicycles, and the smell of dry leaves and snow. But this is Cincinnati, after all, so often there is damp cold, sleet and drizzle, and odd industrial odors that are as weirdly unidentifiable as they are familiar. Eventually the two dark seasons seem to merge easily into the two light seasons of spring and summer—just with more humidity, I suppose. I take all of this in on my walk from the gatehouse on Clifton into the Carl Blegen Library every workday for the past four decades. Created as the Main Library before the Walter C. Langsam Library was built on the north end of campus, Blegen Library is home to the Archives & Rare Books Library, the Gorno Memorial Library for the College-Conservatory of Music, the John Miller Burnam Classics Library, and the Department of Classics.

I never enter this 1930 Art Deco library on any day without first glancing up to the top right of the building, because it is my ritual to read the words carved there before I go through the front door. Those words instruct and inspire me; they tell me that what is contained in that library is both a legacy and a promise, and that everything held there is essential for understanding ourselves now and for the future: Books. Manuscripts. Documents. Photographs. Music scores. And digitized knowledge. Inscribed in the façade are these words from poet

John Milton's *Areopagitica*, his 1644 polemic against censorship. The University of Cincinnati's excerpt from Milton's speech reads: *"For books are not absolutely dead things, but do contain a potencie of life in them to be as active as those whose progeny they are."* Academic courses generally come to Milton mainly through his epic poem, *Paradise Lost*, a pillar of world literature published in 1667, and that may be the only book of his that is taught to students. But his *Areopagitica* pamphlet should be studied as well because it remains constantly relevant. It was published during the English Civil War in protest against Parliament's "Ordinance for the Regulating of Printing," which mandated that authors have an approved government license before their work could be printed. Milton argued that a free and open society was best served by open discussion and that all books—good or bad—had lessons to impart. The faculty who helped determine the mottos and art for Blegen and who came together from all areas of the University of Cincinnati knew the strength of a university is determined by the strength of its libraries and the freedom to study everything.

The dark seasons of Cincinnati require a considerable pause in front of Blegen Library until the eyes adjust and I can make out the letters. The seven tall, west-facing windows of the building help to illuminate them and before too long so does the growing golden gray (which might be a distinctive Cincinnati color) of the morning light. Milton's words are on the southwest side of the building. On the northwest side are words from Francis Bacon's 1597 *Of Studies*: *"Read not to contradict and confute nor to believe and take for granted nor to talk and discourse but to weigh and consider."* I don't really care for these particular words, perhaps because out of context, they strike me as false. In his essay, Bacon's words continue with: "Some books are to be tasted, others to be swallowed, and some few to be chewed and digested: that is, some books are to be read only in parts, others to be read, but not curiously, and some few to be read wholly, and with diligence and attention." I rather think that one of the purposes of an education is not only to weigh and consider, but to engage in those other activities as well: Talk and discourse. Argument. Counter-argument. Contradiction. Critical thinking and analysis. All good and necessary for an education. However, there is only so much space on a wall.

When it was built as the university's Main Library in 1930, the intent was to employ symmetry in its construction, an ideal superbly executed by Harry Hake, the architect, and the designers who worked in brick, limestone, bronze, and terrazzo. And as part of this symmetry, the decorative elements, most of which were created by sculptor E. Bruce Haswell, were all of a purpose, extolling the heritage of learning and the history of the "book," at least in the Dead White Men/Western Civilization view of the times. Despite this somewhat Eurocentric approach, though, examples from world culture managed to sidle in to give the library more global reach. Because in embracing knowledge from every corner of the world, a good library building enforces two major concepts, both martial in their own way: a library is a fortress in that it physically protects the books and collections therein; and it is a cathedral in which we acknowledge that there is something deeply precious and eternal and inspiring within its walls. To maintain both fortress and cathedral requires constant vigilance against ignorance and corruption. That is a library.

Bacon's words are carved on the left side, Milton's on the right. On either side of the front doors, which are below the library's purpose as "Dedicated to the Advancement of Learning," are six categories of university instruction: Philosophy, Science, Literature, Religion, History, Politics—three to the left, three to the right. Window grilles with the trademarks of printers from the fifteenth century to the twentieth are at both sides. Pylons of notable printers in history range near the top—Benjamin Franklin of America, William Caxton of England, Aldus Manutius of Venice, Christopher Plantin of Antwerp, William Morris of England, and Johannes Gutenberg of Germany. Bas reliefs "Ex Occidente Lux" and "Ex Orientale Lux," light from the West and light from the East, are filled with the prominent figures in the ages of learning: Confucius, Shakespeare, Buddha, Galileo, Jesus Christ, Euclid, Plato, and on, eighteen in all.

The center bronze grille above the door complements the bronzes that depict the evolution of learning from oral history to writing on cuneiform and parchment to printing of books, and the grille is rich with an abundance of traditional symbols of knowledge: Minerva, the goddess of wisdom, dolphins, keys, sunbursts, six-pointed stars, five-pointed stars, and owls, always owls. Dozens of owls are found in the architecture and bronzes of Blegen Library. The owl is Minerva's familiar and, as a bird of the night, represents the hope that in a college education, as one learns, one gains wisdom and is led from darkness to the light of wisdom.

In the lobby of the building, there are large chandeliers with their edges punctuated with proverbs about education, all taken from different cultures. And up the grand staircase into the massive reading room there are more chandeliers. This beautiful reading room with its ceiling soaring above the student tables and with light coming from the western windows once served as the study space for the Main Library and now accommodates the same purpose for the College-Conservatory of Music Library.

The first chandelier in the building carries a Japanese proverb that reads, "There are no age limits to learning. Anyone can learn anything if he studies it a hundred times." In the center chandelier is a proverb in Egyptian hieroglyphics from the philosopher Ptahhotep, "Be not proud because of thy knowledge; be not puffed up because of thy manual skill; no art can be wholly mastered; no man can attain perfection in manual skill." Other chandelier proverbs are in Chinese, Latin, Greek, and Hebrew. But as a graduate student in anthropology in the 1970s, I rather liked the Latin of Terence on one chandelier: *"Humani nihil a me alienum puto,"* or "Nothing human is alien to me."

Other buildings on campus carry other carved words, on McMicken Hall, on Braunstein Hall, inside Swift Hall and Old Chem, for instance. These public words are the physical manifestation of our ideals, meant to lead us to lifelong learning and introspection and to civic responsibility and engagement. How often the proverbs and statements succeed in doing this is anyone's guess, but at least they are there for the taking. Perhaps inscriptions mean a bit more in a library. If a library is both a fortress and a cathedral, does that mean it also provides us sanctuary while girding our loins with knowledge in order to charge the world? Yes, it does. There is considerable heft to the printed word, to a bound codex of accumulated human thought and experience. In the best possible consideration, the library is a place of hope, of anger, of goading, of comfort, of exhilaration, of revelation, of amazement, of indignation, of tears for all reasons, and of reason itself. A teacher once told me that a book is a confluence of endeavors, that the efforts of so many individuals come together to create a book: the author, the papermaker, the ink maker, the printing press maker, the typesetter, the artist, the binder, the editor, the publisher, the bookseller, the READER! Another teacher told me that in a book the only thing you can really depend on is that something happened. So read another book! And another book! And another! Compare versions of what happened and arrive at your conclusions. That is what a library lets us do.

I first stepped into Blegen Library in 1975 when I was a graduate student in the Anthropology Department. It was the Main Library then, and to be honest, I didn't notice the inscriptions and the chandeliers. It was a fairly rundown place. Over forty years of wear had darkened and chipped the black and red tiles. The walls were flaking their pale green paint, the brown metal windowsills were rusted, and the woodwork had lost its varnished sheen to a dull finish. In the summer the air was sticky and stifling. I loved all of it because despite the cosmetic and structural neglect, it was filled with books, and the human possibilities contained in them weren't overwhelming at all, but instead encouraging. Graduate students were permitted to wander in the stacks or, as with undergrads, you could put in a request at the main desk and a dumbwaiter brought your book up from the bowels of the building. You sat at massive oak tables in either Windsor chairs or the stodgily firm straight-backed chairs. You read and read (or you photocopied to read later). When you left the library, a staff member sitting at a high table at the entrance checked your bags—that was the security. The next day and the next week you returned.

Two years later I took my degree and left Cincinnati. Two years after that I came back, this time as an archivist in the Archives & Rare Books Library, though it was called the Special Collections Department then. The main library had shifted to the north in a new structure called Central Library before it was renamed in the years that followed as Langsam Library. Things still looked the same to me in what was now the old library. The same custodian was in the building, a gentle rotund man named Orville Cook who lived down in Camp Washington and came up the hill to campus every day. At the back of the lobby, Mr. Cook had a little room with a hot plate and every morning he made a pot of bad coffee for us and then did his best throughout the hours to keep an aging building clean. The books were still important. The stacks were still fascinating. The promises of enlightenment still grew every day. And change was coming.

In 1983 renovation was completed: new tile floors, new paint, new offices, clean hallways. The building was renamed in honor of the famous archaeologist Carl Blegen. The chandeliers and other bronze elements of the building were polished. The decorative integrity of the building was preserved. Thirty-five years on, there have been some minor renovations, some administrative offices have come and gone, the libraries that share the building have rearranged space and collections. The primacy of the printed word—whether analog or now, digital—has been a mainstay.

This is a place where I learn something new every day, even as various facts of university history, Cincinnati heritage, rare books about this or that, or countless other aspects of the special collections become muscle memory of a sort. Those confluences of human endeavor take a fresh breath every day and that "poten-cie" of life is maintained. I've developed favorites among the holdings, books or photographs I return to time after time because they always have the potential to reveal something new. And as I grow older, emotions run closer to the surface. For instance, I can look at a book of hours in the collection, which is a prayer book from 1475 created in Limoges, France. It has a velvet binding, the pages are vellum—not paper—and the miniature illuminations and calligraphic initials are exquisitely done in gold, blue, red, and green. I read at the pages, pause at the thumbprints in the bottom corners, prints, perhaps, that were made five hundred years ago. I show the book to my students and sometimes tears well up at the sheer beauty of what a human being can make in the world. Or I lift the flaps of an illus-trated book on eye surgery from the sixteenth century and marvel at the intricacy of understanding anatomy that still informs the science of today. I study an old photograph of UC students on campus in 1916 as they commemorated the 400th anniversary of William Shakespeare's death with plays and dances and Elizabe-than markets. They are all dead now, those UC Bearcats. At one time, they came together in celebration of a literary heritage. It was alive to them then and in the way of this photograph, those people are still alive to us today.

This is what a library can do. So I tell my students in class that a book or a manuscript is a sensual object: read it and comprehend what it is telling you, then close your eyes and run your fingers lightly over the page. Do you feel the indenta-tions of the type? Sniff it. Inhale the aroma of paper and ink, let your senses lead you to understanding. And it works for them. Sometimes shock is effective: I take an old book of no value (though there are people, I imagine, who would argue with me that there is no such thing. There is.), and I take a scalpel and I cut through the attached endpapers and toss the binding to them. Some of them gasp and some of them even cry out. But they all pay attention. I cut off the title page and hand it around. I trim away the headband and I slice through one of the gatherings of pages. They get it. They need to know everything that makes a book a precious human commodity, both in its words and in the physical ways those words are presented. They learn the division of endeavors that make the whole.

Nearly forty years have gone by. After all the renovations in Blegen Library, there is one chandelier on the sixth floor that addresses the passion for libraries. That chandelier holds a proverb in Chinese provided by one of the university's in-ternational students when the building was being constructed. It states, "Libraries are valuable to readers because they preserve the riches of the world from which come the beginning of wisdom. Everything in the heavens or upon the earth is for our appreciation."

This is true. In antebellum days, the Lane Theological Seminary existed in Cincinnati, about a mile from our campus. The school was founded in 1829 by the abolitionist minister Lyman Beecher, who brought his family west from Connecticut and built his seminary to preach the equality of all people and equip them for the fight against slavery. One of his sons, Henry Ward Beecher, brother of Harriet Beecher Stowe and Catharine Beecher, attended his father's school and graduated in 1837. The younger Beecher also became an abolitionist and a clergyman. Henry collected books. He had a number of nice thoughts about his books, but one particular sentiment he expressed about them explains libraries quite well: "A library is not a luxury but one of the necessities of life." Libraries come in all forms and sizes, they are personal and institutional and often private. They all contain that "potencie" of life among the bricks and stacks.

In daylight or not, when I walk into Blegen Library to work, I read Milton's words and everything is brought up in light.

It Started with a Valentine

Archaeology at UC, Carl Blegen, and the Department of Classics

by Jack L. Davis

The Department of Classics, established in 1920, is one of the finest in the world. Its graduate and research programs in archaeology are renowned. Sparked by the vision of a scholar in Greek and Roman language and literature, William Semple, the creation of this center of excellence depended on a collaboration with one archaeologist, Carl William Blegen, who would become the first-ever recipient of the Archaeological Institute of America's gold medal for Distinguished Achievement.

Blegen and Semple shared a dream, and over a period of three decades strove to fulfill it. Today a building bearing Blegen's name houses the university's respected John Miller Burnam Classics Library and its Modern Greek Collection as well as the Department of Classics. Yet the fact that Blegen ever came to the University of Cincinnati in the first place was the result of a sequence of coincidences that began as a romance.

It was Saint Valentine's Day, 1923. Ten days earlier, Carl Blegen had posted from Athens a Valentine to his beloved Elizabeth Pierce in Rome. On February 13 he followed it up with a letter:

> *My darling: I love you. My heart is beating very steadily and firmly tonight and every throb says: "Elizabeth, I love you." Just to hear it repeat so regularly that ardent thought makes me more warm and cheerful than I have been all day. For it is a wonderful thought that I love you and you love me...*

A day later he wrote again:

> *Dearest Elizabeth: I love you. All day I've been thinking of you, wondering how you are*
> *and where you are and what you are doing....I would give anything I possess to be with*
> *you Darling, I love you more than words can tell...*

He was a young man in love with a young woman, like any of millions of twenty-year-olds. But this romance, which bloomed so far away, would change the face of the University of Cincinnati forever.

Carl W. Blegen (1887–1971) was of Norwegian American stock, and his family spoke Norwegian at home. Carl's father, John Hansen Blegen, taught Greek at Augsburg College in Minneapolis. Carl himself took degrees at Augsburg, the University of Minnesota, and Saint Olaf College before enrolling at Yale, where he received a BA in 1908. It was at this point that young Carl began to separate himself from the pack. With support from a fellowship he immediately enrolled as a PhD student in Yale's Department of Classical Philology and Archaeology, Indo-Iranian Philology, Comparative Philosophy, and Linguistics. At Yale, he mostly studied Greek and Latin language and literature—except for an elementary course on Sanskrit!

Professors at Yale in those days had close connections to what remains today the premier American archaeological institution in Greece, the American School of Classical Studies, and in 1910 Blegen crossed the Atlantic and discovered what would remain his principal residence for the next sixty years—Athens.

Athens in 1910 seemed primitive by American standards, and the American School was isolated even from what delights existed in its center. Indeed, when the American School opened in its present location in the 1880s, there was debate as to the wisdom of situating it in a monastery's olive grove, twenty minutes by foot from Constitution Square and the Royal Palace, and even farther from the Acropolis.

Blegen described those early days in Athens at the School years later:

> *The School at that time still stood in the very outer fringe of the city. The view in all*
> *directions was open and magnificent. No houses had been built between us and Lyk-*
> *abettos. Toward the east, outside our wall, was a deepish ravine which, despite its*
> *occasional use as a repository for garbage, served to carry off rain water and as a very*

inadequate forerunner of the present Gennadios St.; beyond it rose the monastery—not so large as it is now—but there were no other houses in this quarter—only olive trees—and no buildings except some temporary barracks much further away. We were practically in the country.

He continued:

Life was relatively quiet and peaceful at the old School. By day we were usually prowling about the Acropolis or in the Museum, or exploring Athenian topography. We ordinarily took our meals at restaurants down town, the Averoff when we were feeling flush, or other times the Panhellenion or some smaller place. We learned quite a lot of Greek there. In the evenings, we generally studied in the Library, unless it was too cold. There were no nightclubs in those far off days, no tavernas with a floor show, no Athens Festival, no concerts in the Odeon of Herodes Atticus. Before going to bed, however, some of us, who had a sweet tooth, often wandered down town again to the "Dardanellia" where in a milk and pastry shop called the "Ηνωμένα Βουστάσια"—known to us as the "United Cowstables"—we enjoyed a kataeef or a honeyed Kopenhai, or some such satisfying concoction. The walk down and especially up the hill again always stimulated one's circulation so that we went to bed warm in a chilly, unheated house.

Then, as now, students studied the monuments of Athens and more generally of Greece; as its first director emphasized in 1881, they had come abroad to do things that weren't possible back home in the classroom.

Blegen flourished in this new environment, was appointed secretary in 1913, then in 1920 assistant director, his position when he fell in love with Miss Pierce. Blegen had no inkling someone else was in love with her.

Who was this young woman who had captured his heart?

Elizabeth (Libbie or Lib) Denny Pierce had enrolled as a freshman at Vassar College in 1906, already having studied Latin and determined to learn Greek. But, as Robert Pounder, her biographer, has written: "Little did she suspect . . . on that long ago autumn day, that she would transform the life of one of her professors."

That professor was Ida Carlton Thallon, over ten years her senior. Ida had already traveled to the American School in 1899, then returned to teach at Vassar. The growth of the romance between the two women cannot be documented, but it was profound and meaningful to both. Any letters they may have exchanged have not been found. In any case, by the end of World War I they were a couple, and it had been determined that Pierce would go to Athens in 1922. Thallon would take a sabbatical and join her in the spring of 1923. What had Blegen accomplished in the meantime? Among other things, he had supervised an expansion in infrastructure—no mean feat in early twentieth-century Greece. He later wrote:

A new era was inaugurated on April 8, 1913 when excavation was begun for a much needed addition to the School building. Its primary purpose was to provide room for the growing library, but…at the same time to add more bedrooms and a dining room for students, a Ladies' Parlor, a Common Room, a drafting room and a study or office, and to install modern heating and plumbing throughout the whole structure, old and new…[T]he project was pushed to completion in the spring of 1915. I found that much of my time was taken up by multitudinous minor errands and tasks in connection with the work of construction. But frequently there were more exciting assignments. I remember particularly the many epic battles of facts, figures and works that Stuart Thompson and I together waged from time to time with the general contractor in our heroic struggles—often successful—to pare down his exorbitant estimates and claims. But my greatest tribulation came…when I had to deal with high-powered professional plumbers and a carpenter from New York…who made constant demands for American food and American accommodations, which they insisted were guaranteed in their contracts. I should like to tell you tales about some of the specific problems that came up, culminating in an abortive strike. It was not only, they complained, that the breakfast coffee was undrinkable, the toast inedible, and the bacon burnt to cinders (we ourselves never had bacon), but as a crowning insult the maid who waited on their breakfast table had actually appeared in bare legs without stockings.

In these early years in Athens, Blegen had integrated into Greek society and politics and became entirely fluent in the language—skills that situated him well for the role that he was to play in 1918–1919, immediately after the end of the First World War. Greece had suffered greatly in the war. At first Athens was sympathetic to Germany and refused to aid the Allies. In defiance Eleftherios Venizelos, the prime minister for whom Athens Airport is named, formed a separatist government in Thessaloniki.

Although at the very end of the war Greece did participate in the final victory over the Axis Powers, at the Armistice the country was shattered. Parts of the north had been occupied and, as Bulgarian troops departed, they burnt villages, destroyed crops, slaughtered livestock, and took hostages. In the fall of 1918, these hostages began to return, but faced only starvation with a long, hard winter ahead.

In the midst of this human disaster, Blegen volunteered to serve the American Red Cross, and spent much of 1918 and 1919 in Macedonia and Thrace under extreme conditions —actions for which he was awarded a medal by the Greek state. He delivered needed food and clothing and arranged for shelter. On the front lines of the relief mission, he assessed damage in isolated mountainous villages with names attesting to their diverse histories of settlement. Blegen's diary entry for December 3, 1918, is typical and gripping:

> *Steele and I were taken in Ford to Pravi. Here we found horses waiting for us with an officer as escort and set off at 11 A.M. for Cromista. The officer (name of Liberides) was formerly φρούραρχος at Paleohori and Nikishan and rushed to visit these two villages en route. It was a cold rainy day but we agreed to go by that route with the understanding that we should arrive at Cromista in the evening. Liberides promised this expressly. We reached Palehori in the rain and sat for a while in a house there eating our sandwiches. Heard tale of woe from wife of former schoolmaster (hanged by the Bulgars). Later we rode on in light drizzle to Nikishan over mountain trail where we were obliged to walk part of way leading our horses. Finally reached Nikishan at 4 P.M. in rain. Lt. Liberides wished to stop here for night in house where he lived as φρούραρχος but we reminded him of his agreement to get us to Cromista by evening. He admitted he agreed to go. Distance said to be 2 to 2½ hours. We left at 4:40 P.M. From now on it rained steadily somewhat more than a drizzle. We were wet cold and uncomfortable. At 5:30 it was dark and by 6 it was black as pitch. We couldn't see the ground between our horses. Also the ground was very muddy and wet. We splashed through mud and water from 6 to 11 inches deep. We couldn't see to guide and let our horses go as they wished. The way seemed interminable and there was no light visible save from Drama far away across the plain. At last our horses lost the road and we found ourselves skidding through the mud in a plowed field close to the bank of a foaming stream. The sensation of being lost revived Steele and we expressed our gloomy disgust at the situation. Our journey had now become an adventure. Our Greek friend however fell into a panic from cold and discomfort. He reproached me for having led him out on a night like this. I remarked that he shared the responsibility for having taken me offtrack at Paleochori and Nikishan. But that was an accomplished fact said he. We had already done that. There's no use*

going back to that. I rejoined "well it's also an accomplished fact that we left Nikshan and that we're here now lost in the mud. We've got to make the best of it and find the road again and shelter as soon as we can."

Blegen again offered his services to the public good in the wake of the "Asia Minor Catastrophe" of September 1922, when troops of Ataturk, father of the Turkish state, burned the metropolis of Smyrna (modern Izmir). In the aftermath of this, virtually the entire Christian community of Turkey was expelled and Greece found its population doubled overnight. Blegen traveled widely to assess the magnitude of the refugee problem.

It was in the midst of the chaos of autumn 1922 that Libbie Pierce arrived in Athens—and what a stir she caused in the American community. As Pounder, her biographer, writes: "Her infatuation with Greece, its people, and the antiquities was immediate. No one, it seemed, was immune to her charm, flirtatiousness, and thoughtfulness, including [director of the American School and Blegen's boss] Bert Hill. The one holdout—at first —was Carl Blegen, who treated her with stiff formality, thus alienating her somewhat in the beginning."

Libbie remained deeply in love with Ida and wrote her frequently, although, at some point in the fall, Carl fell madly in love with her. His affections were returned and, when he proposed marriage in January 1923, Libbie accepted.

Ida took the news of the engagement in stride at first, and sent a measured response to Blegen on February 2:

I do not need to tell you that you are going to marry the finest girl in the world, but I do want to tell you that I have known Lib more intimately and closely than anyone else in the world has…I know I can never really lose Elizabeth but I shall miss her constant companionship more than any words can tell, for the last seven years we have been together all the time, but I must warn you…that I shall try often to descend on you at Athens and you will have to think of me as a sort of older sister.

Libbie was in seventh heaven when at first Ida approved of the engagement. She wrote to Carl:

I am so happy. I have just had a splendid letter from Ida written after she got the cables and she is as pleased as can be over our engagement and says mother is, too…I'd like to send you Ida's letter but I can't bear to part with it yet, it is such a nice one. Of course the important fact about this affair is that we love each other so deeply but it does make things happier for both of us to have everyone else pleased over our engagement—Uncle Bert & the others in Athens and now mother and Ida. I know too, dearest, that they will love you when they meet you and we shall all be one happy family! I feel like dancing a jig in the middle of the floor but shall finish this instead and then go out and look for a picture frame for your photograph and have some tea.

A few days later, she replied to Carl's Valentine card with equal enthusiasm:

But now that I have had your letters I am going to stiffen right up again and be a good sport for these last few days have been much harder for you than for me. The one that stays behind always has the loneliest time for he has to go about in the places where they were together! I hope your heart will go on beating "steadily and firmly" and telling you not only that you love me but that I love you also. You are such a darling and I never thought I could love any man as I love you—because, having been brought up with boys, I had always played around with them and been good friends but had never had any deeper feelings for anyone. It is a miracle sweetheart and I am so glad you woke up my "cold storage heart" for the whole world seems brighter and happier now.

But in the spring, the engagement was broken. Surprisingly, though, in summer, all parties reached a remarkable compromise.

From her parents' home on Lake Placid, in New York, Libbie wrote to Carl and Bert Hill, and gradually a solution to their problems emerged. Carl would marry Libbie, Bert would marry Ida, and the four would live together in the same house in Athens. Ida was the last to sign on to this plan, at first bewildered by the suggestion. But a month prior to their weddings in 1924, she proposed in a letter to Bert a sort of contract that would establish the ground rules for their "Pro[fessional] Par[tnership]" or "The Family," as it would be called. There were two weddings in summer 1924—Ida resigned from Vassar, and the quartet moved in together in Athens, first near the National Gardens, then, in 1929, into a Neoclassical mansion nearer the American School, where they would spend the remainder of their lives together.

Meanwhile in Cincinnati, change also was in the air. At about the same time as Libbie was contemplating coming to Athens for the first time, archaeology at the University of Cincinnati hitched its star to the American School. In 1921, William Tunstall Semple and Rodney Robinson, professors of classics at the University of Cincinnati, became known to Edward Capps, chairman of the managing committee of the American School and a professor of classics at Princeton. By 1923, there had been visits to Cincinnati both by Capps and Bert Hill. Hill's visit marked Semple's success in raising funds for a permanent UC membership in the School at Athens. Capps proclaimed that he foresaw "a great deal of kudos and glory in store for Cincinnati and for the Department of Classics."

It was soon arranged that Hill and Blegen would excavate on behalf of Cincinnati in the Sanctuary of Zeus at Nemea, one of the four principal Pan-Hellenic sanctuaries of Antiquity. The excavations were heralded in the *Cincinnati Times-Star*, with news that they were to begin on April 15, 1924, and with the headline: "Distinction Seen for the Queen City." The project found considerable financial support in the community of Cincinnati, and a list of donors was published.

Semple even asked the American School if a number of the larger contributors in Cincinnati might have portrait busts sculpted as adornments in the school! But more significant was the genuine interest expressed by some of these individuals and their families. Capps wrote: "Those Cincinnati people are very enthusiastic about a Cincinnati excavation. One of their number, George Warrington [then chairman of the board of trustees of UC], proposes to go to Greece for next winter with his family with the sole motive of catching up with the school and taking part in the Cincinnati dig."

Semple promoted the project tirelessly in Cincinnati and through ingenious means found financial support that enabled Hill and Blegen to continue their dig. Semple ensured that a steady flow of Cincinnatians would visit the project, as he did himself. He wrote that he considered it to "be of the greatest advantage to us in keeping the matter before the attention of the Cincinnati public to have first hand reports from Cincinnatians concerning the progress of the 'Dig.'" And in 1924 Semple reported to the team in Greece that:

The matter of the Cincinnati Excavation in Greece was given extraordinary prominence before the Cincinnati public during May. The Classical department of the University assumed the responsibility for a lecture by Howard Carter on the Tomb of Tut-ankh-amen. We had the publicity running in all the four local papers every day for ten days,—the announcement being to the effect that the lecture was given under the aus-

Howard Carter brought the Cincinnati audience near tears with his account of the discovery of a bouquet of flowers left by King Tut's young widow in his tomb. The excavations at Nemea were an enormous success. Three annual campaigns of large-scale excavation were conducted within the Sanctuary of Zeus at Nemea in 1924, 1925, and 1926–27. Special attention was given to the Temple of Zeus. Fallen debris was cleared away from its foundations, exposing for the first time the crypt in the rear part of the interior of the temple and the long altar to the east of it. The Cincinnati team also determined the location of the stadium and a basilica.

Capps praised UC's efforts: "The University of Cincinnati was the only American university, with the exception of Harvard, which was in Greece conducting an excavation sustained by its own funds." The entire Warrington family came to Greece to camp at Nemea and participate.

Such an active presence in Greece sprung from the head of a visionary, William Semple. In 1910–11, Semple (PhD, Princeton) was hired in UC's Department of Greek, after he had completed supplemental graduate studies in Rome and at Halle, in Germany. In 1917, he married Louise Taft, a niece of William Howard Taft, a U.S. president and chief justice. Then, after the death of John Miller Burnam, for whom UC's Classics Library is named, Semple in 1920 became head of the newly constituted Department of Classics. With the help of his wife, Semple embarked on a lifelong mission to create, through the investment of their own personal fortune, an academic department that, in the words of Blegen's student John Caskey: "saw the study of classical antiquity as a single undertaking, not to be divided sharply into separate compartments. The historical and archaeological approaches to the subject were not less important than the linguistic and literary and not ancillary, but integral components of the classical discipline."

Semple soon enticed renowned scholars to Cincinnati, and the addition of new faculty made it possible for the first time in 1924–25 to offer a separate curriculum in each of four subfields: Greek, Latin, ancient history, and archaeology.

But, as Semple was building his ideal department in Cincinnati, the world of the American School that Blegen had known for some two decades began to be destabilized. The American School, a consortium of American and Canadian universities, is governed by a managing committee and its chair holds ultimate authority over the director in Athens. Thus, when Edward Capps had assumed the chairmanship in 1921, he became Hill and Blegen's boss. Soon after that sparks began to fly.

From the start of his reign Capps had a clear vision for the school and a strategic plan to realize his goals. He saw the school's highly visible archaeological fieldwork and the regular publication of the results as crucial to shoring up its shaky financial foundations. The director of the school was at the nexus of both activities. Hill's attention to detail and pursuit of perfectionism, however, did not result in publications appearing in quick succession. As early as 1922, Capps had already become frustrated with Hill's lethargy, which, as he saw it, was blocking much-needed progress.

In the spring of 1923, Capps wrote candidly to Hill about the school's affairs. He concluded his four-page, single-spaced letter as follows: "So far, we have been working at cross-purposes, to a greater or lesser degree, since I became chairman. I hope that in our conferences next summer we shall be men enough to face this situation frankly, and settle it."

This did not happen.

By May 1924, Capps's impatience with Hill and Blegen reached a breaking point. In a long letter, he castigated Hill and stated bluntly: "Our present condition is intolerable, as I suppose you and Blegen realize quite as well as I do."

Despite constant warnings, Hill continued to run the school as he had done before. His procrastination and unwillingness to cooperate vexed Capps greatly.

Thus, as a consequence of Hill's unwillingness to reform his ways, Capps took punitive action against him in June 1925. Hill reacted angrily and Capps finally had had enough. By late spring 1926 he had maneuvered Hill into accepting a "voluntary leave of absence" for 1926–27, after which he would resign from his position. Blegen was appointed as acting director for 1926–27.

All-out war ensued, as Ida Thallon, now three years Mrs. Bert Hill, mounted a spirited, but ultimately unsuccessful, campaign against the decision to remove her husband as director, and against Capps personally. Ida wrote venomously to her husband on December 30, 1926:

> But at any rate there are some people who have sense enough to realize what it means, and archaeologists all over the world to whom Edward Capps is less than a worm...

As I never had any training as how to deal with the insane or am I accustomed to a sewer such as is Capps' habitat… the filthy slime of that reptile is now smeared all over the School and it will take longer than his lifetime to get it clean again. Lady Macbeth was a parlor pet in comparison. The damned spots will never be washed out until an entirely new generation grows up. I agree it would be a waste of time to try anything more with this bunch of crooks.

Ida was saddened greatly that Capps had been able to marshal so many allies within the school against her husband, men whom they had considered friends. She argued that "the sooner we cut loose from such a bunch, the better. So now for a free and unnagged life in the future."

And so it was that after Blegen's brief tenure as acting director in 1926–27 ended, the Hills and the Blegens, "The Family," withdrew from the American School and set up an independent salon in their shared quarters in Athens. Their alliance paved the way for Blegen to consider new opportunities.

If he wanted to pursue his archaeological ambitions, Blegen now enjoyed limited options—the best being employment at UC. How odd that step must have seemed to some, but in the logic of the times it made sense, and in retrospect one can see clearly how events in the previous half-dozen years had paved the way for his arrival in Cincinnati. But it was by no means easy to seal the deal when the time came to offer Blegen a job. By 1927 he had become something of a superstar and was prepared to bargain hard. He knew what he needed to continue to enjoy success and was prepared to risk all to obtain it. Blegen received his offer from UC in a letter dated March 2, 1927, typed on Department of Classics stationery. Semple wrote:

[T]he interest in Classical archaeology has so increased during the past four or five years in Cincinnati that the standard of excellence to be expected in the presentation of Archaeology in the University has risen greatly. Our supporters now demand a full time man and this man they wish to be the foremost representative of this branch of learning among American scholars.

The offer was a full professorship at a salary of $5,000. Although the post was envisioned as serving the graduate program of UC, the expectation was that Blegen would initially teach an undergraduate course in archaeology.

The following day, in a supplemental letter to Blegen, Dean Louis T. More of the Graduate School added that, at UC, "I am sure that you would have much more time for productive work than you could find in most universities. I feel sure that the policy permitting field work will be most liberal."

Still, Blegen was cagey when he replied to Semple, asserting that to complete the program of research in which he was already involved in Greece would:

> … necessitate my presence in Greece at least during half of each year to study the material on the spot and to conduct further exploration and excavation of the many sites which are still awaiting examination. This is the determining consideration which is governing my decision as to the acceptance or not of a new position upon leaving the School at the end of the present term.

Dean More dug in his heels and refused to agree to Blegen's terms except for an initial two-year appointment. George Warrington supported More:

> It is wholly without precedent here to make a permanent arrangement with a professor that under no circumstances will he be expected to devote more than one-half his time to residence at the University, and I am sure that the Board would be loath to set such a precedent by making such an agreement in advance…This really means that you would never be required to spend more than a third of the year in Cincinnati: that there would be no inducement for you and Mrs. Blegen to establish a permanent residence here and to become a part of the University life.

But it came to pass that Blegen struck a deal with UC that had no precedent. He would never teach in Cincinnati except for autumn term and neither he nor Mrs. Blegen would settle in the Queen City.

However odd an arrangement, it came to benefit both UC and Blegen over more than forty years. In Cincinnati, Blegen would train graduate students who, in turn, became leaders in their field. He was a figure in the community, not least through his close friendship with socialites Marion and Dorothy Rawson, both of whom became trusted assistants in the field; and he was chosen as one of the elite hundred members of the Literary Club of Cincinnati. At the same time, Blegen had time not only to conduct excavations, but to publish his discoveries—in so doing escaping the curse of so many archaeologists and spreading the fame of the Cincinnati program far and wide, both among scholars and laity.

Blegen's extraordinary accomplishments were recognized in 1965 when he was chosen by the Archaeological Institute of America to receive its first gold medal for Distinguished Achievement. With customary modesty, he emphasized in his acceptance speech that:

> *Field archaeology—i.e., excavating—is an uncertain and fickle mistress. In addition to work, application, and perseverance, many other factors are necessary for success: among the most important may be counted good luck and good comrades. Most of my failures resulted from the lack of one or both of these two elements; and most of my enterprises that somehow turned out reasonably well owed it to my able colleagues.*

With the addition of Blegen to the faculty in 1927, Semple's vision had been nearly complete. Blegen now had access to the personal wealth of the Semples. He was able to launch landmark expeditions to Troy and to Pylos—thus inaugurating a tradition of research programs abroad that continues to this day.

Not only did archeology at UC start with a Valentine. That same Valentine launched an "uncommon arrangement" that persisted for four decades until the last of the quartet, Blegen, passed away in 1971. Their marriages, their relationships, although of an uncommon character, were no less for that—full of love and devotion.

Libbie ministered to the daily needs of Bert Hill and cared deeply for him. In 1936, when Bert was summoned to an audience with Prince Paul of Greece, she wrote to Carl:

> *You would have died laughing seeing Bert get off—his afternoon clothes had not been worn for so long that his vest was too tight and had to be ripped out at the side seams and hastily sewn up. He took one look at his top hat and decided not to wear it—his old dark gray or "black" as he called it—felt it was in an awful state. I had to trim off the ends of the ribbon and coat spots on it to make them match the rest in color!*

Ida died peacefully and suddenly in 1954, while crossing the Atlantic to return to Greece with Libbie. She was lying in bed as Libbie read to her. Still after that, taking care of domestic needs for Bert and Carl could be a community affair, responsibilities now shared between Libbie and Marion Rawson. In 1956, Libbie could write to Marion that "I have Carl's belt—Has he any decent jacket to wear in case we should have to go to the opening of the new hospital in Pylos?"

But the world that the Blegens knew in Athens changed radically after World War II. In the 1950s, the tranquility of their neighborhood of stately mansions was shattered by incessant noise from the construction of apartment houses. The wildflowers they both so cherished in their garden would be covered with cement dust. And their personal lives were irrevocably altered by a massive stroke that Libbie suffered in Cincinnati in December 1956, one that first consigned her to a walker, then a wheelchair.

Libbie's Valentine to Carl in 1957 consisted of nothing more than her name scrawled on a store-bought greeting card. In April, the Blegens returned to Greece. Libbie did regain her ability to speak, and managed to type letters. Carl's archaeological discoveries at Pylos continued, sometimes with her, sometimes without her. But, whatever the case, Carl was loyal to her and solicitous of her needs, whether they were together or apart.

A letter from Pylos in 1957 is characteristic:

My wonderful Mibsie [as he called Libbie]:

How are you today? I've been thinking of you nearly all the time and hoping that you've quite recovered from that tummy upset of the other day. Have you taken your exercises today, and have you had a little walk with the walker? I hope you've managed another little practice session with the typewriter, too? You see I'm pushing you to keep going until you're all well again.

Bert Hill died in 1958. Libbie survived a full decade after her first attack, suffering a fatal stroke in 1966. Carl lived until 1971, completing his excavations at Pylos and publishing his results with Marion Rawson's help. Today the Blegens and the Hills rest side by side in the Protestant section of the First Cemetery of Athens, an enduring monument to the love of four remarkable individuals who not only changed UC, but also the archaeological world in Greece.

William Howard Taft and the UC College of Law

by Bob Taft

Upon enrolling in the UC College of Law in the fall of 1973, I attended classes in Alphonso Taft Hall, named after my great-great-grandfather. Nine years later, Alphonso Taft Hall was no more, the exterior columns removed and the former building gutted, remodeled, and encased in a new, bigger, better home for the law school. In its place, a statue of William Howard Taft, Alphonso's son, was erected just to the east of the law school where, I understand, it is sometimes humorously attired by students.

On a personal note, I am glad to have been able to attend UC Law School in Alphonso Taft Hall. Alphonso is the member of my family whom I perhaps admire the most. He was self-made, leaving New England after college to settle in Cincinnati and establish the family tradition of public service.

Alphonso Taft had a distinguished career. He served as an Ohio judge, U.S. ambassador, attorney general, and secretary of war. He taught at the Cincinnati Law School and served as president of the board of trustees of the University of Cincinnati. Nevertheless, his son William Howard Taft's current prominence on campus is fitting in view of his long association with the law school and his ascent to the pinnacle of the legal profession as chief justice of the U.S. Supreme Court.

After completing Yale in the 1870s, William Howard returned home and attended the Cincinnati Law School, which later merged with UC. Apparently, law studies in that era were not too burdensome, consuming two hours a day and allowing Taft to pursue outside employment as a court reporter. Alphonso was not pleased with his son's work ethic, however, complaining that school and a reporter's duties "allowed too much time for leisure and the pursuit of wicked pleasure." In his remarks to the 1905 UC Law graduating class, William Howard, then U.S. secretary of war, admitted: "I am sorry to confess it, but the truth is that the amount of law I learned as an instructor was far greater than that which I learned as a student."

Taft served as dean of the law school at UC from 1896 until 1900, when President William McKinley appointed him president of the Philippine Commission after the Spanish-American War. In 1896 Taft was only thirty-nine years old, but he had already been an assistant county prosecutor, a state court judge, and U.S. solicitor general. At the time of his appointment as dean, he was already a judge on the U.S. Court of Appeals for the Sixth District, but he managed to perform both jobs without difficulty. "The deanship is going to involve considerable work," he told his wife, Nellie, "but I think I can systematize it."

While he was dean, Taft was also professor of property law and taught two separate courses, one to first-year students and one to second-year students. His students remembered his energy and the many questions he put to them. He was protective of the school's reputation; according to his biographer, when a local newspaper published a drawing of students playing poker on top of professors' desks, he was furious and told the students he would expel any of them caught playing cards during school hours. He pounded his desk for emphasis, frightening his students out of their wits.

Taft's first challenge as dean was to seek a merger of the independent Cincinnati Law School with the University of Cincinnati. The Cincinnati Law School, which Taft attended, was the last remaining educational offering of Cincinnati College. It was the oldest law school west of the Alleghenies, the first in Ohio, and the fourth oldest in the United States. It had an endowment, facilities, faculty, and a library in downtown Cincinnati. Across the country, however, many law schools were beginning to affiliate with universities, and the UC trustees proposed such a merger to the trustees of Cincinnati College. After their offer had been rejected on several occasions, the trustees were able to get a state law enacted in 1892 to force a union by providing that UC's board would henceforth serve also as the board of Cincinnati College.

The Cincinnati College trustees were not amused by this takeover plan, opposing the law in court, and when the Ohio Supreme Court overturned the law as an unconstitutional taking of private property, UC decided to establish its own

Department of Law in 1896. Judge Taft and other prominent leaders, including prior U.S. Attorney General Judson Harmon and former U.S. solicitor general Lawrence Maxwell, were recruited to serve on the faculty of the new school. There were now two competing law schools in Cincinnati, one with the advantage of an established reputation and history and the other with the benefit of a university affiliation and some prestigious faculty members.

As dean, Taft succeeded in negotiating a merger of the two schools in 1897 for a term of ten years. The new faculty consisted of UC's law faculty plus two faculty members from Cincinnati Law School. The Cincinnati Law School provided lecture rooms and a law library at their downtown location, and the combined school was to be funded by tuition dollars, the Cincinnati Law School endowment, and $1,000 a year from UC.

This initial merger lasted until 1911 when Cincinnati College decided to break away and restore the independent status of its law school. Fortunately, under Dean Alfred Benedict, in 1918 a permanent merger was achieved, and even to this day the president of UC is the president of Cincinnati College, and the dean of UC's School of Law annually reports to the Cincinnati College board, now made up of the university's vice presidents.

The second major change introduced under the leadership of Judge Taft was an entirely new approach to the teaching of law. Traditionally, instruction had been "philosophical," based on textbooks, treatises, and lectures. Now the law school's faculty adopted the "case method" which had been introduced at Harvard Law School by Dean Christopher Columbus Langdell and Professor James Bar Ames. Law was viewed as a "science" with instruction to be based on actual cases. In his address at the dedication of Alphonso Taft Hall in October of 1925, then Chief Justice Taft described the benefits of the case method:

> [A]s common law and English and American law is established by precedents, the proper method of its study was the application by the students of law to the original sources from which the law was drawn. It thrusts the student into the atmosphere of the controversy which each case presents and enables him in a concrete way to trace from one case to another general principles, the distinctions in their applications, their variations and exceptions, and thus in a dramatic and effective course to possess himself of the judge-declared law…It trains students…in the mental processes

they must exercise in the practice of their profession in the consideration of the actually decided cases where they must find the law.

This innovation was one that has stood the test of time. In fact, much of my own instruction at UC Law School in the 1970s was based on the case method.

At the time of Taft's deanship, legal education was undergoing a period of "professionalization." Also in his 1925 remarks Taft stated: "It is the higher and purer atmosphere of a university in which young men shall acquire the right to become members of the bar that will keep them constant in the knowledge that the practice of law is profession which exists for the benefit of society."

In that later speech Taft even recommended that a bachelor's degree should be required for admission to law school and that more instructors should be full-time. Significantly, it was in 1900 during his deanship that the American Association of Law Schools was formed, with UC Law as a charter member, for the purpose of advancing excellence in legal education.

The final contribution of the Taft family to the law school came in 1923. At the time, the school was housed in what was supposed to be a "temporary location," the old McMicken House at the top of Clifton Avenue hill. The long-range plan was for a building to be constructed on the main Clifton campus.

This step was made possible in significant part by a $75,000 contribution from Charles P. Taft and his wife, Anna Sinton Taft, who lived then in what is now the Taft Museum. Charlie was an older brother of William Howard and had attended UC Law before going into business. The university agreed to name the new building in honor of their father, Judge Alphonso Taft, who had taught at Cincinnati Law School, served as president of UC's board of trustees, and three of whose sons had attended the law school.

As noted, former president William Howard Taft, then the chief justice of the United States, delivered the address at the dedication of Alphonso Taft Hall on October 28, 1925. This milestone event was also attended by Vice President Charles G. Dawes, Speaker of the U.S. House Nicholas Longworth, and former Speaker of the House "Uncle Joe" Cannon, all of whom were UC Law alumni.

However, it was his son William Howard who had the closest and most influential relationship with what has become the University of Cincinnati School of Law. My great-grandfather had a lifelong passion for the law, in sharp contrast to his feelings about politics. After serving as president, he said, "politics when I am in it makes me sick." And in a speech in Idaho when he was president, Taft declared: "I love judges and I love courts. These are my ideals, that typify on earth what we shall meet in heaven under a just God."

His mother, Louise, knew him best. When asked what she thought of his candidacy for president, she responded: "A place on the Supreme bench, where my boy would administer justice, is my ambition for him. His is a judicial mind, you know, and he loves the law."

So it is altogether appropriate that William Howard Taft should be standing tall in his judicial robes just outside UC's College of Law, with an inscription that reads "Chief Justice, 1921–1930."

Author's Note: As I was preparing this account, by total coincidence I had the opportunity to acquire an original letter written by then-Chief Justice William Howard Taft to Edwin Gholson, Librarian of the Cincinnati Law Library Association, seeking information about the early history of Cincinnati Law School. The letter was dated October 12, 1925, and clearly was sent to help Taft prepare the Alphonso Taft Hall Dedication Address he delivered on October 28, 1925, to which I have referred.

No One Has Ever Come for Dean Loueen Pattee

by Anne Delano Steinert

Loueen Pattee was the dean of women at the University of Cincinnati from September 1917 until her sudden death from pneumonia in 1921.

I first ran across Loueen Pattee in 2016 when I was researching a Cincinnati playwright and poet, Mary MacMillan, as a PhD student in the history department. In the 1920 census MacMillan was listed as head of household in apartment number 7 of the Delmoor Flats on Telford Avenue in Clifton. Loueen Pattee was listed as her "partner."

I have often imagined the day the census taker, Elizabeth Roberts, came to enumerate 3414 Telford. It was January 10, 1920. I picture her knocking on the door of apartment number 7, and Mary MacMillan answering. It was a cold day, so I imagine MacMillan invited Miss Roberts in to sit with her and Loueen Pattee in their crowded living room. It was a Saturday, so both MacMillan and Pattee were home. They might have been going over last-minute details for a visit by social reformer Jane Addams, whom Pattee was to host at UC six days later, or planning out details for poet Edna St. Vincent Millay's visit with them as a part of an event for the Ohio Valley Poetry Society the next month. Whatever they were working on, they would have set it down to welcome the enumerator.

The census lists MacMillan first as "head of household." When they got to Pattee, I imagine the census taker asking, "How are you related to her?" and I imagine Loueen Pattee answering, "I am her partner." Partner is what was written down by that enumerator, though it was later crossed out and replaced with "bdg" (for boarding).

Though it is difficult to know exactly what "partner" meant to this couple, it is clear from MacMillan's later poems and a letter MacMillan wrote about Pattee to Edna St. Vincent Millay, that they had both a romantic and domestic relationship. Today we would call them lesbians, though this was not likely to be the term they used to describe themselves as this term was just beginning to be used—and pathologized—during the time MacMillan and Pattee spent together.

Neither Mary MacMillan nor Loueen Pattee, nor their siblings, left any descendants. As their friends and colleagues passed away, there was no one to remember the amazing lives they had lived. Rediscovering Loueen Pattee and her connection to UC feels like unearthing some forgotten treasure. She left just enough scraps of her story scattered in published works and archives, from the Webster City Public Library, to the Library of Congress, and from university libraries from UC to Grinnell and Virginia Tech (home of Lillian Weaver's papers), that I was able to reconstruct some of Pattee's now-forgotten, but totally remarkable life.

Loueen Pattee (sometimes known as Lulu or Lou) was born on January 23, 1874, in Buda, Illinois, the middle child of three. Her father was a traveling salesman, so the family moved around at first, but eventually settled in Webster City, Iowa. Pattee's uncle Ed Brown was the town photographer. She was educated in the public schools there and there met life-long friend and colleague Lillian C. Weaver. Pattee lost her father when she was twelve. As the sheriff knocked at his hotel room door to arrest him for failure to pay his debts, Harry Pattee put a gun in his mouth and pulled the trigger. Her mother died just a few years later, leaving Pattee in the care of her Webster City relatives. In her teen years, Pattee's uncle seems to have indulged his niece by taking photos of her clowning around with her friends. Many of these images also feature Lillian Weaver.

Soon after her mother's death Pattee spent two years at Grinnell College in Grinnell, Iowa, then called Iowa College. After beginning at Grinnell, she went off to Europe in 1894 to study in Hamburg, Germany. Between 1894 and 1907 she bounced between teaching in high schools in Dubuque, Iowa, and Oak Park, Illinois, and studying at German universities in Heidelberg and Berlin. Her loves were foreign languages and art, and at the time of her death she spoke five languages and had sculpture on display in galleries in the United States and Europe. She spent five years as the chair of the foreign language department in Oak Park, where she reconnected with old friend Lillian Weaver who taught math and English there. Together they made plans to go to Europe in the fall of 1907.

In 1907 Loueen Pattee and Lillian Weaver founded the Munich School for Girls, a boarding school for wealthy American girls, at Friedrichstrasse 9 in Munich. More than one newspaper report referred to the school as a place where Americans could leave their daughters while they toured the continent, although Weaver recalled their more ambitious intention had been to send "American girls to college with a richer background." The school welcomed between four and twelve students at a time and combined traditional academic courses with daily outings and an immersion in the arts and culture of Munich. It nurtured the once-sheltered girls' intellect and sense of independence and it gave Pattee a way to sustain herself within Munich's flourishing world of arts and culture. Pattee was remembered as a "remarkable teacher" whose "standards inspired the girls." Also during this time Pattee was awarded an AB from Grinnell based on the submission of her credits from abroad, and translated the German play *Agnes Bernauer* for publication in *Poet Lore Magazine*, where it claimed the first sixty pages of the January/February 1909 volume.

At least two outlandish stories about the Munich School for Girls made it back to the American press. In one tale, a group of four girls, including Chicago meatpacking heiress Ida Swift, had to dig themselves out of a snow drift while hiking in Switzerland. Another story described the girls hiking four hours up a Bavarian peak to a mountaintop watering hole and returning in a giant sled in a half-hour's time. A 1912 photograph of the Munich School girls shows them lounging together on a long couch, hands entwined, heads resting on shoulders and knees. There is a clear connection among them. Lillian Weaver later wrote, "The experiment was so successful that Lou would have been happy to stay there all her life." Sadly, the outbreak of World War I interrupted their plans.

When World War I broke out in the summer of 1914, Weaver was in the United States recruiting girls for the school, while Pattee remained in Munich. Though they didn't expect the war to last long, Pattee cancelled the fall term and opened the school as a center for women and children whose husbands and fathers were away at the front. The American community in Munich quickly banded together and opened an American Hospital, where Pattee took on the role of assistant director and secretary. In this capacity, she published articles about the hospital's work in the American Red Cross magazine and in a local publication called *American Notes* in Munich. Her writing is flowery but factual as she describes the hardships faced by the hospital, frankly to solicit American support. She stopped short of describing the horrors she and other nurses witnessed in their work, but wrote, "We have grown familiar with all phases of suffering," and noted that "one of the attendant nurses quietly slipped from the room," to convey that the horror was too much for that nurse to bear. In one article from October 1915, she wrote about "baffling nerve shocks" and went on to offer description of what we would call PTSD. There are photos of her at the hospital receiving a much-envied "giant dray load" of supplies, and posing with foreign dignitaries or other nurses.

As the war wore on, American support for the Red Cross dried up and German troops began to block delivery of supplies, so by the end of 1915 the American Hospital was forced to close. Loueen Pattee left Munich in the spring of 1916. She spent the summer with her brother Fred outside of Chicago, and in August accepted an appointment as dean of women at the University of Cincinnati, to replace Emilie Watts McVae, who became president of Sweet Briar College.

When I compare the photo of McVae in the 1916 *Cincinnatian* to the one of Pattee in the following year's annual, the difference is striking. McVae was a buttoned-up older woman, posing stiffly, while Pattee appears to be just barely suppressing a grin. Her warm eyes convey a youthful energy, and she is dressed in what must have been the latest fashion.

Loueen Pattee took UC by storm. The *University News* story introducing her was titled, "New Dean, Miss Pattee Arrives at Varsity," an expression of both the quality of her credentials and the first impression she made. Her arrival was reported in the national magazine of Kappa Kappa Gamma, *The Key*, where the UC correspondent reported, "Women's convocations are unusually interesting this year, conducted by the charming new Dean of Women, Miss Loueen Pattee." The role of dean of women was what we know today as student affairs or student life. The dean oversaw social events, extracurricular activities, student conduct, and disciplinary action. In addition to her responsibilities of dean of women, Pattee taught courses in art history and French. She was a driving force in many campus fundraising and war-relief efforts, and helped lead a drive to provide scholarships for five French women to attend UC during the war.

She was the first dean of women to occupy the new Women's Building (later renamed Beecher Hall), where her first-floor office was described as an "attractive sanctum, with its flowering plants, its books and reproduction of many of the masterpieces which the world of art affords." The Women's Building, designed by Lincoln Fecheimer, gave campus women spaces equivalent to those the men enjoyed. It included study rooms, a large reception area, domestic science labs, classrooms, offices, and a gymnasium, pool, and women's lockers.

Pattee was well known to students for her political views, so much so that a cartoon of her in the 1918 *Cincinnatian* yearbook features a "votes for women" pennant held by a well-dressed Dean Pattee standing on a soapbox.

Pattee was remembered on campus for her boundless energy, and her social calendar was staggering. In just the five-week period between March 23 and April 27 of 1919, in addition to her routine teaching, administrative, and household responsibilities, she also managed to lead citywide classes on suffrage, attend a meeting of the Association of Collegiate Alumnae in St. Louis, take in a choral program given by the Clifton Musical Club, read and offer analysis on several poems at the Ohio Valley Poetry Society meeting, and score an appointment to the Women's City Club board.

Beyond her work at UC, Loueen Pattee was deeply involved in Cincinnati's civic and cultural life. She served on the board of directors of the Women's City Club, and the nominating committee of the Ohio Valley Poetry Society, where she nominated Mary MacMillan as president. She was a member of the Cincinnati Women's Club, the College Club, L'Alliance Française, and nationally was a member of the American Association of Collegiate Alumnae, now known as the Association of University Women. In 1920, she traveled to London for the American Association of Collegiate Alumnae as an alternate on the American delegation to a convening conference for the creation of an international association of college-educated women. For the Women's City Club she acted as a hostess of the Chamber Centennial Festival at the Cincinnati Zoo in which more than four thousand youth members of the Civic and Vocational League were invited to explore the zoo and given a pamphlet on the history of Cincinnati, partially written by Mary MacMillan, as a souvenir.

While I don't know how MacMillan and Pattee first met, many of their civic and cultural activities overlapped. By 1918, Pattee is listed at MacMillan's house in Mount Auburn, and by 1919 the pair had moved together to Clifton's Delmoor Flats. Perhaps the most telling document of their relationship is a poem by Mary MacMillan published in 1927, six years after Loueen Pattee's untimely death. It is entitled "After Reading Thomas Hardy's Poems."

What shall I do to-morrow?
I must not go to her grave
And stand six feet above
The lips I crave.
What shall I do to-morrow?
I cannot stay indoor
And see beside the bed
The shoes she wore.
What shall I do to-morrow?
For if I am there or here
Her ghost is beside me
Year upon year.

The death that MacMillan was lamenting came about unexpectedly in March of 1921. In February, UC authorized Loueen Pattee to attend the national conference of deans of women in Atlantic City. I have to admit that I have daydreamed more than once of traveling back in time to beg her not to go.

Before Loueen Pattee left for the conference, she arranged to give a lantern-slide presentation at the public library entitled "Spring in Florence" on March 17. It was a talk she would never give.

After the conference in Atlantic City, Loueen Pattee stopped off in New York. Her death certificate reports that she died of pneumonia, with a contributory factor "influenza contracted in N. York." Newspapers reported that immediately upon her arrival at the train station, she placed herself under a doctor's care. She lingered a few days, but passed away the afternoon of March 7, 1921. A small memorial service was held at the Cincinnati Crematory where she was incinerated on March 9, and a UC memorial on March 15 attracted over five hundred attendees. Memorials praised Pattee as "nationally known as an instructor," having lived a life "more cosmopolitan than that allotted to most of us," "a woman of great intellect and high ideals, and one whose place in the community can not easily be filled," "having the welfare of the city always at heart," and a lover of "the joyous things of life, [whose] very presence bespoke sunshine, radiance, warmth, love." Astonishingly, she is all but unknown today.

During the summer of 2015 I taught a summer course entitled "The History of American Cemeteries." As a part of this course my students and I visited the

Hillside (formerly Cincinnati) Crematory, so I knew about the rows and rows of beautiful urns and niches there. When I read that Loueen Pattee had been cremated at the Cincinnati Crematory (now Hillside), I wanted to go see what records they had of her incineration, and see if she might still be there somewhere in a beautiful Rookwood urn.

The folks at Hillside were easily able to find a file card for Pattee. It was dated March 19, 1921, and under niche it said "Section Com S., Tier Bottom, No. 19." While this seemed like great news (yay, she is in a niche there somewhere!), no one in the organization knew what the code on the card meant. The current owners had taken over recently and weren't familiar with the old abbreviations on the card.

An elderly employee and I spent almost an hour counting nineteen from everything we could think of. We looked through the niches in three different rooms, and still no luck. He said he couldn't really think of anywhere else she could be. I was discouraged. But then he said, "Well, she could be in the closet."

Yes, the closet.

This weathered old white-haired man took me to a small dark room full of floor-to-ceiling metal cabinets. He opened one and showed me shelves chocked full of ceramic urns and metal tins much like those chrome kitchen canisters from the 1950s. These, it seems, were the people who had never been claimed.

After getting my bearings, I saw that the cabinets were numbered. I found cabinet 19. I had to stand on a chair to reach it, and when I opened it I saw that there was a list on the inside of the cabinet door. This was the inventory of everyone in that cabinet. I looked down the list and was discouraged not to see "Loueen Pattee." But I looked at a few of the tins in the cabinet and realized that they were in the right date range. She just had to be in here. I looked back to the inventory again and found, with a jolt of recognition, she was listed last. I had quit looking before I got to the very last name. I was both completely excited to finally have found her, and mildly outraged that she was here in a dark backroom closet.

I removed tin after tin, looking at yellowed name tags, until there, in the far back corner of the middle shelf, I found all that remains of Loueen Pattee.

After learning so much about this woman I was deeply moved to be holding her remains in my hands. I was excited to have found her and yet sad that she was nothing more than a sandy, rattling dust inside a tin can. I spoke to her like she was there with me in the room. I think I said something like "Oh my goodness, it's you! I'm so glad I found you." The staff of the crematory who had gathered to share my excitement quietly slipped from the room.

On the tin is a tag written in a curly script that lists her date of death (March 7), her date of incineration (March 9), and the date she was put into the storage closet (April 25). I wonder about those six weeks when she must have sat in the office waiting to be claimed until they finally realized that no one was coming. Mary MacMillan had no legal right to claim Pattee's ashes, and her brother didn't get them when he came for her memorial service on March 15.

No one has ever come to claim UC's beloved dean of women, Loueen Pattee.

On Hazel's Diary

by Janice Currie

One little book sheds unexpected light on my mother's life—her diary. She wrote it as a sophomore at University of Cincinnati in 1927. I love the feel of the diary's soft cover. Although hidden for years, the tan leather with gilded inlay has weathered well. Only the brass clasp is damaged. When my niece, Jamie, gave it to me in 2010, it had no key. Picking the lock with a hairpin, I felt like an intruder. Did my mother want her four daughters to know about her secret loves and the romance that blossomed with my dad?

I imagine my mother, Hazel Heintz, a twenty-year-old with wavy hair and hazel eyes, sitting at her desk. She picks up a fountain pen to write in her tiny, cursive script. In chronological order, her thoughts and feelings flow quickly. Remarkably, there are no mistakes in the diary, no cross-outs, no attempts to erase. She records her anxiety about exams, her intimate feelings about her boyfriends, and discussions with girlfriends about love, morality, and friendship. With many different suitors, she goes dancing at the Alms Hotel and Castle Farm, and to the Shubert Theater for plays and the Capitol for silent movies. Doug, my dad, is obviously her favorite. She teases him by reading passages written about her secret love, Vince.

At the top of each page, Hazel notes the weather and date. The first page:

Snowy, bright. Saturday, January 1, 1927. She starts with curiosity: All these blank pages makes one wonder what can be in store for the coming days. Since it must go day by day, I'll start with the first day of the New Year of 1927.

In 1926, Hazel's family had moved to a home on Erkenbrecher Avenue near the zoo. In a few words, she gives us an idea of her social milieu: "Mother and father gave a tea as a housewarming, and we were all busy preparing the food. The tea went off beautifully, and we served about 100 guests." The *Cincinnati Enquirer's* society section describes this New Year's Day celebration: "Mrs. Heintz received her guests in black velvet and ecru lace, assisted by her two daughters, Marie and Hazel, both of whom are students at the University of Cincinnati. Miss Marie's frock was of king's blue crepe combined with silver lace, while Miss Hazel wore a Chanel dress with collar and cuffs of seal" (January 2, 1927).

Later on the night of this housewarming, Hazel parties on:

Had a date with Dick Cunningham for the Princeton–UC game. We went with Al and Sal of course. Varsity won 27 to 25. Best of all I saw my secret love, "Vince." After the game we went downtown to Caproni's and tried our hands at spaghetti. It was Sal's last night in Cincy. Tomorrow will see her in Pittsburgh. We had so much fun together this Christmas. I hated to see her go.

Hazel, her older sister Marie, and their mother Edith all studied at UC in 1927. They became members in different societies/honorary fraternities: Hazel in Papyrus, the women's journalism fraternity; Marie in Pi Chi Epsilon, an engineering fraternity; and Edith in Blue Hydra, a botany society. Edith became one of the first graduates in UC's landscape architecture program and developed a landscaping company.

On March 27 Hazel writes in her diary about one of the dilemmas she wrestles with—whether or not she should kiss a man. She starts with a playful incident: "Coming home Doug flipped a glove in my face, so I challenged him to a duel in the kitchen. We failed to have a duel with each other, but I had one with myself. I had been letting Doug kiss me whenever he wanted to, and I was getting a guilty conscience about it." Later in life she recalled: "My mother had tried to instill in me the idea that I should kiss only the man I intended to marry." Hazel wasn't sure about this, as her diary indicates:

Sal and I went down to a show today and saw Children of Divorce. It was mainly a story of two love affairs. In both of them, after the heroes had kissed the girls, the men said that it was practically a promise, but both girls replied that a kiss didn't mean that much to them. That's just the way it is with all of us. The boy who kisses us expects to marry us. We each like them a whole lot, but none of us is even contemplating marriage.

The diary reveals only a few times when her mother gave her moral guidance. Once her mother reprimanded her for being out too late at night. Another time she put her foot down, refusing to allow Hazel to go to a Sigma Chi party in Indiana. Hazel writes in a sarcastic tone about this incident: "Got a letter from Doug and he asked me definitely for the Sigma Chi party at Rising Sun, Indiana, but Mother won't let me go, because she thinks it's too far for her little daughter to go."

However, in a newspaper article, "Mother and Two Daughters Are University Students," a reporter asked my grandmother what she thought of the modern flapper. She offered this praise: "They are always active, doing things. They love the outdoors and sports" (*Daily Enquirer*, June 1, 1926). Flappers pushed the boundary of what it was to be a modern woman. Movies from the 1920s show flappers in loose-fitting dresses and their hair cut short in bobs. This is an apt description of my mother. I have some of her 1920s dresses with beads, hemlines just below the knee, and plunging necklines—rather daring!

Flappers demonstrated independence by driving machines. The three Heintz women drove a Dodge sedan to campus while my grandfather, Michael Heintz, walked or rode the trolley three miles to his downtown law office on Fourth Street. (He graduated in the UC law class of 1890. Two of his brothers also graduated from UC: one in law and one in engineering.) I am struck by how attractive my mother was in her 1929 yearbook photo. In the Roaring Twenties, she was probably called the "bee's knees" or the "cat's meow" with her sparkly eyes, high cheekbones, and long neck. She was confident and full of energy. She had the silent movie actress Clara Bow's "It." Hazel recounts, "'It' is certainly causing a commotion around the university. In the Commons today seven or eight of us started talking about sex appeal or 'it.'" When she was sixty, I saw her dance the Charleston with as much liveliness as any young girl could. As Virginia Woolf described *Mrs. Dalloway* (1925), my mother "never lounged in any sense of the word." She once said to me: "It's not how clever you are that matters; rather it's how much energy you have that decides whether you succeed or not." My mother's role model was my grandmother—never idle.

At UC, Hazel expressed her love of writing by joining the editorial teams of the *Cincinnatian* and the *Cincinnati Bearcat*. At the *Cincinnatian*, she was women's athletics editor, and humor editor at the *Cincinnati Bearcat*. In one of her humor pieces, she writes about her friend, Erma Pfleger, who later married Dick Farrell:

June 20: "Farrell forgets McCue long enough to be ensnared by Pfleger."
May 30: "The affair of Pfleger and Farrell assumes alarming proportions!"

Along with Jane DeSerisy, Hazel was a sophomore commissioner at UC. In that role, she also served on the Honor Court and records a difficult case in her diary:

I had to serve on the Honor Court today and we tried one boy. His case was pathetic. Snooks Fabing talked to us and told us we were going about it in the wrong way, and he said he could get a confession out of the boy in 3 words. The boy was brought in and all Snooks said was, "Did you crib?" The silence was terrible and then the boy answered, "I did." I never felt such a tension before. I was weak; I could have cried. We dismissed the boy and we had to adjourn the meeting to relieve the strain. I never felt so low in my life—and that poor, desperate boy must have been miserable.

During the spring of her junior year, Hazel was initiated into Mortar Board and Mystics 13, and Cincinnatus in her senior year—honorary scholastic and leadership societies. When the thirteen women were inducted into Mystics in 1928, they walked across campus between the senior Mystics who were dressed in black robes with cone-shaped hoods that covered their faces, except for tiny eyeholes. Hazel is in the very middle of the photo, the seventh from the right. As a child, I looked at this photo and thought these thirteen women were Ku Klux Klan members in their black hoods.

Later, the Mystics women of 1928 dined together for many years at each other's houses. When they met at our house, my sisters and I helped our mother set the table. We pulled out the heavy, walnut table to full length and placed the sterling silverware on fancy placemats. Our mother chose a deep red set of dishes for the evening with matching goblets.

Two of the women stood out to me. Jane Early, later to become a UC trustee, arrived in a fur coat and spoke in the deep, gravelly voice of a New York debutante. I imagined her with a long-stemmed cigarette holder, leaning against a Cadillac. She oozed sophistication and wealth. Jane was married to Dan Early, a heart surgeon, who appears in Hazel's diary as one of her secret loves.

I was helping Jane DeSerisy (later Early) decorate the Commons for the basketball banquet, when Dick Cunningham came along. Therein lies my tale, because Dick asked me out for the Ulex Party. I didn't hesitate in accepting because it's the most sought-for occasion of the social life here, and I was scared to death that I wouldn't go although I did hope that Dan Early or Tom would ask me.

The other woman who impressed me was Erma Farrell, then president of the National Girl Scouts. She always came over to chat with us in an engaging manner. She was thin but full of energy. In a diary entry, Hazel describes how she differed from Erma Pfleger (later Farrell): "Went to a meeting at Pfleger's. Every nook in their house speaks wealth—the lucky girl. I wouldn't mind having even half of what she has."

Although my mother envied the wealth of Erma's family, she was in no way deprived. She was solidly middle class with all the cultural benefits it bestowed. My father was from the working class and had to earn money to go to college. He enrolled in UC's co-op program and sandwiched courses in commercial engineering between internships in Dayton where his father was a mechanic. In contrast, Hazel received a generous allowance from her father. For graduation presents, their Uncle Walter gave Marie and Hazel a trip to Europe.

Even though they were different in many ways, my parents were alike in others. They enjoyed dancing, sports, and playing pranks on each other. To meet my dad, my mother threw a firecracker at his feet at a July Fourth picnic. Once she had got his attention, he wooed my mother intensely and believed she was the only one for him. She was clearly smitten by him but still dated other boys. Her diary reveals her ambivalence about whether to marry Doug.

Got a box of Maud Muller's [candy] from Doug for Valentine's Day. Doug is awfully sweet to me. All Mother said was "Poor Doug. He spends all his money on you and you don't like him." But I really do like him—I'm not in love with him, but he is the one that occupies most of my thoughts. I do think about Dan, Tom, and Vince but none of those think much about me.

The August 30, 1927, entry was the last. Hazel and Marie were dropped off at a Kappa Delta camp not far from Cincinnati. Their mother and father were on their way to Canada. Hazel writes:

Of course, it rained just to spoil our breakfast hike, but the food tasted awfully good anyway. It cleared up later in the morning but just after swimming, it poured again. Doug was due today, but I thought the rain might delay him. It didn't—he came in all his glory, bearing a wooden heart he had swiped in Michigan and a comb and case from Canada—all for me. Doug told me all about his trip, and then we went down to Hamilton for supper. We met Barney down there—he went back to camp and got Rose, and we all took a ride. We stopped at a fortuneteller on the Dixie, but she didn't tell us a thing worthwhile. There wasn't anything to do, so we went back to camp. Doug and I...

I stare at the words: "Doug and I..." She came this far and stopped, deliberately leaving what follows to the imagination. It would be six years before they married. The Depression intervened. Perhaps she wasn't certain that he was the one for her. My grandmother predicted he would never make "a splash" in business and he didn't. Nevertheless, he remained gainfully employed until his retirement.

Hazel majored in political science, went to Chase Law School, and passed the bar. However, she never practiced law (a family mystery); instead, she became a secretary (to Dr. Albert Sabin) and then a teacher. After the last of her daughters was in school, she earned a master's degree at UC in elementary teaching, a profession her mother hated but one that fit in with raising four girls. Later, she used her legal skills as chief negotiator for Cincinnati's teachers' union.

At her ninetieth birthday party, Marie confessed she had always wanted to be a teacher. However, her mother had other plans for her. In 1925, after hearing on the radio that UC wanted more women in engineering, Edith enrolled Marie in chemical engineering without consulting her. Later Edith told Marie to switch to medicine because she wasn't doing well in mathematics. My grandmother was rather domineering.

Marie's internship at Christ Hospital coincided with Dr. Clarence Gamble's initiative in supporting family planning. He was heir to the Procter & Gamble soap company and had the resources to establish the first maternal health clinic in Cincinnati in 1929. While raising two sons, Marie worked for thirty-nine years at that clinic (later to become a Planned Parenthood clinic). The diary gave me a fleeting glimpse of my mother's life when she turned twenty—moving from adolescence to womanhood. With the death of my parents, many questions remain unanswered, especially the most perplexing one: what was their relationship really like?

At the age of seventy-one, breast cancer took my mother. What was her legacy to her four daughters? She gave them curiosity and a love of nature. All of her daughters attended college and followed in their mother's and grandmother's footsteps: Joel majored in zoology and English, earned a PhD in science education and became a principal; Susan graduated in fine arts and flourished as an artist and decorator; Maryan studied horticulture and established a landscaping company; I majored in political science and became a professor of education.

Hazel embodied the spirit of the twenties when the role of women began to change: a university degree, a professional career, civic leadership, and motherhood. She had it all. Her daughters, who grew up in the second wave of feminism, became confident, spirited women just like their mother.

A Force for Nature

E. Lucy Braun

by Meg Hanrahan

"And then, ahead, rises the majestic column of the 'big poplar'—straight, sound, and perfect, towering eighty feet to the first branch, lifting far aloft its crown. In reverence and awe we stood and gazed upon this tree, the largest living individual of its kind in North America."

Lucy Braun wrote about her first visit to "the big poplar of Perry County" in an article published in *Nature* in 1936. She was deep in the fight to save it. It wasn't just one tree at risk, but a noteworthy stand of virgin timber that had survived earlier destruction because it was so hard to get to in the rugged terrain of southeastern Kentucky. In the interest of preserving what she determined to be the most remarkable forest she'd ever seen, she helped to start the Save Kentucky's Primeval Forest League with garden club members in Lexington.

In articles that Lucy Braun wrote for *Nature* and other national publications, she lobbied for the establishment of National Primeval Monuments "as a means of preserving for all time some of the few remaining areas of primeval vegetation." She wanted the area of the big poplar, called Leatherwood of Lynn Fork, to become the first designated site if the campaign was a success.

Braun typed and sent letters to "one to four selected persons in each state," instructing them to write Washington in support of the idea, then to "pass on this request to ten more people…who can in turn pass it on to others." Then she traveled to Washington, meeting with National Park Service representatives with whom she pleaded their case. On February 28, 1936, Braun received endorsement of her idea from Acting Secretary of the Interior Charles West: "It is recommended by the National Park Service that this area be given national monument status if, and when, it can be secured and tendered as a donation to the Federal Government."

"If, and when" proved to be a challenge. Regardless, it was a huge accomplishment to get the National Park Service to buy into her plan, one that had required massive amounts of time, especially considering the full teaching load she maintained at the University of Cincinnati. The story is one of many that reveal Braun's determination, focus, and devotion to a cause. Repeatedly, she showed her mettle, plowing ahead with projects that showed merit, despite apparent challenges.

E. Lucy, as students called her, became a faculty member at UC immediately following completion of her doctorate in 1914. She climbed the ranks to assistant professor of botany in 1923, associate professor of botany in 1927, and full professor of plant ecology in 1946. Her official teaching career lasted thirty-four years; though, in actuality, she taught all her life.

Lucy wasn't the only family member to make her mark at UC. Her sister Annette, five years older, was the first woman to receive a PhD from the university in 1911. Following her sister's footsteps, Lucy became the second woman to earn the degree. These were rare achievements at a time when women didn't even have the right to vote. By 1900, only a few more than two hundred women in the United States had PhDs, with only about fifty earning doctorates in the sciences by 1920.

The focus on academics came from parents who were both educators. George Frederick Braun was a German immigrant who became a Cincinnati public school principal, and the girls' mother, Emma M. Wright, had been an elementary school teacher before leaving to raise her family. Mother Braun passed on her love of natural science, her artistic inclinations, and the careful attention to detail that became the hallmarks of both Lucy's and Annette's scientific accomplishments.

Lifelong residents of Cincinnati, the Braun sisters started classifying different orders of life at young ages. The family collected and pressed plants, then systematically arranged them for study in their Walnut Hills home. As a young teen, Annette focused her interest on insects, leading her to the PhD in zoology, with a dissertation on the moth genus *Lithocolletis*. She became recognized around the world for her work as a micro-lepidopterist, studying tiny leaf-miner moths.

Lucy had received a master's in geology in 1912 before she entered the emerging field of plant ecology, which made use of her combined interests and expertise in geology and botany. Ecology was a new science, and Lucy became known as one of its pioneers. For the PhD in botany, she wrote her dissertation on the physiographic ecology of the Cincinnati Region, riding Cincinnati's streetcars to natural areas around the city in order to conduct fieldwork for the study.

Many stories attest to her encyclopedic knowledge of plants and her gifts as an educator. One student told how they tested her knowledge of a standard reference work for botanists: "The students would try to trick her by opening *Gray's Manual* to a certain page and asking her, by judging about where the pages were, to tell what family they were looking at. She knew the book so well that she was usually correct!" One biologist who went on field trips with E. Lucy emphasized that she had "compassion" for those she taught. Friend and naturalist Elizabeth Brockschlager commented that Lucy had a "contagious enthusiasm."

Concurrent with teaching, Braun engaged in ongoing research and writing. By 1916, only a few years into her teaching career, she was already on the map with botanists in the State of Ohio, having identified numerous new species listed in the *Catalog of Ohio Vascular Plants*, published by the *Ohio Journal of Science*.

An interest and activism in preservation that eventually propelled her into the fight to save Leatherwood started early too. In 1917, as a member of the Ecological Society of America (ESA), she joined the Committee for the Preservation of Natural Conditions, a group whose efforts were "directed toward the preservation of natural areas with original flora and fauna."

The organization published *Naturalist's Guide to the Americas* in 1926, a book that provided listings of "preserved and preservable areas in North America." E. Lucy Braun is given credit on the title page for her contributions in having assembled and edited the section on US National Parks and Monuments, and Victor Shelford, chairman and editor, made special note in the preface of her editorial contributions. Braun also coauthored the section on Ohio.

Simultaneous with her involvement in the ESA, Lucy motivated the creation of the Cincinnati Wildflower Preservation Society, an organization still in operation that celebrated its 100-year anniversary in 2017. The group started *Wild Flower*, a magazine that Braun used to educate and lobby for conservation in over a hundred signed and unsigned articles.

The first issue describes the local chapter's beginnings: "In the Spring of 1917, at the instance of Dr. E. Lucy Braun, several individuals, herself included, enrolled as members of the Wild Flower Preservation Society of America." Five members were needed to form a local chapter.

A group of seventy-two charter members held their first meeting in the Botany Rooms of the University of Cincinnati on April 25, 1917. The group's first objective was "To encourage by every possible means the preservation and protection of native plants." Along with Braun, the Advisory Council included Irwin M. Krohn, Alice Betts, Mrs. William T. Rowe, and others. Using the motto "Enjoy: Do not destroy," the group promoted adult outdoor education and taught conservation to children in area schools.

Lucy began exploring areas of southeastern Ohio early on. "In the 1920s, I became very interested in the Adams County Ohio area near Mineral Springs and began an extensive study of soil and vegetation. Some of my students assisted in the survey taking samples of soil at different depths and listing all the plants from trees to mosses." Thomas J. Cobbe, a botanist from Miami University who earned his MA under Dr. Braun, related that "she and her students would walk along through forests for miles, and while she yelled out the names of trees they were passing, the students would record the data."

Through the 1920s and into the 1930s, she published regularly in a variety of scientific journals. E. Lucy Braun quickly became a respected name, though not without occasional confusion. In a letter to her friend and colleague, Margaret Fulford, written October 6, 1930, she relates the story of being invited to a meeting of the Ohio Valley Section of the Association of American Foresters. "I've decided to take it all in—suppose I'll be the only woman, for the Association is all men of course." She adds that the invitation came when "they 'thought Dr. Braun was a man,'" and ends the story by expressing some doubt as to how she'll be received: "I'm just wondering how the most of this gathering will take the invasion by a woman."

Being a woman in a male-dominated field didn't slow her down. But it probably did have an impact on her personal life. Female faculty members at colleges and universities and successful women scientists usually remained single, as merging the responsibilities of career and family life presented challenges that were difficult to overcome. Both Lucy and Annette remained single throughout their lives.

Lucy worked and provided income, while Annette supported life at home. After teaching for a short time, Annette had returned home to care for their mother and to cook, clean, and keep an orderly household. The sisters maintained their respective roles as breadwinner and homemaker throughout their lives, though Annette did not give up on her scientific studies. She continued her research, raising moths "in jelly jars with close-fitting lids," and used a hand lens and microscope to discern details for the pen-and-ink illustrations she drew of the tiny creatures.

Annette and Lucy were companions not just at home, but in the field, and on travels near and far, including trips across the country on at least a dozen occasions. In the early days, they traveled by train to Adams County to do their research, hiring a horse-pulled buggy and driver to take them as far as roads allowed.

In the 1930s, after the purchase of their first car, research in eastern Kentucky resulted in many adventures. On one occasion, after an overnight stay in the Natural Bridge area and a mile-plus walk, they had car trouble. The temperature had dropped and they learned from the "mountaineers" that the radiator was frozen. The delay got them home after dark. "Lights on for the first time. Speedometer 894 mi," Lucy wrote to her friend Margaret. "I'm getting to feel like an 'experienced driver,' even went 38 mi. per hr."

Traveling in Kentucky brought the sisters into contact with locals who lived in the hills and hollers they explored. The mountain folk came to know them as the plant ladies, and became their friends, though Lucy and Annette still had reason to proceed with caution. Moonshiners didn't like surprise visits. The Brauns learned to check in with landowners before trespassing, and to look for signs that indicated where stills might be hidden.

It was through her research in the forests of eastern Kentucky that Lucy became involved in efforts to save Leatherwood. Her activism for the cause is revealed in an extraordinary record of personal correspondence that she wrote and received between 1934 and 1936. The success of the campaign hinged on raising funds for purchase of the property that was owned by a lumber company. But money was slow to come. Mr. Savage, a representative of the National Park Service, called Lucy with news that signaled their defeat. "The lumber road is built all the way up Lynn Fork and now goes within one-half mile of the big tulip tree. There is a force of 22 men working, and it will take only two weeks more to complete the logging road to the big tree."

It was a major blow. But Lucy picked herself up and went back to the research projects that had been languishing while her attention had been diverted.

She received a Guggenheim Fellowship in 1943, and retired from teaching in 1948, at age fifty-nine, to devote more time to research. The university awarded her the title professor emeritus of plant ecology. Though only making $4,000 a year at the time, the title marked a significant achievement, one that was especially rare for a woman.

Braun's magnum opus, *Deciduous Forests of Eastern North America*, was published in 1950. She traveled 65,000 miles to acquire material for the book. In the dedication, she acknowledged Annette, "who has shared the joys and hardships in the field." Providing original theories and detailed documentation of trees all the way from Florida to Canada, it is still hailed as groundbreaking. Botanist Francis Fosberg said the book "reached a level of excellence seldom or never before attained in American ecology or vegetation science."

Her decades of involvement in preservation finally coalesced and came to fruition in the 1950s too. The Nature Conservancy was a key player. Scientists with the Ecological Society of America formed an organization called the Ecologists Union in 1946; the group incorporated as the Nature Conservancy in 1951. In May 1958, the Ohio chapter was formed. With support from Cincinnati's Town and Country Garden Club and members of the Cincinnati Wildflower Preservation Society, the Ohio chapter made its first purchase in Adams County near the village of Lynx. Braun had helped to identify the dry prairies of Lynx as a prime site for preservation as early as 1933, and it had been a favorite area for her research for decades. Lynx Prairie was designated the E. Lucy Braun Preserve in her honor.

The acquisition of other sites in Adams County soon followed. Braun was again instrumental in the Ohio chapter's purchase of Buzzardroost Rock in the spring of 1960 as it faced destruction by "pulp wood cutters." Hundreds came together to celebrate when the two properties, Lynx and Buzzardroost Rock, were awarded National Natural Landmark status in 1967. Lucy was seventy-eight years old.

Another property in Adams County, called The Wilderness, was added in 1968. Once again, acquisition became urgent when Lucy discovered that lumbering was destroying the area's pristine woods and rare plant communities. With resources and strategies for fundraising in place, quick action produced successful results.

It was during that time that Richard and Lucile Durrell also became involved in preservation in Adams County. The Durrells had been students of Braun's, and Richard was a geology professor at UC. He became a prominent figure for his work with environmental organizations in Cincinnati and across the State of Ohio.

The Ohio chapter of the Nature Conservancy deeded Lynx and Buzzardroost Rock to the Cincinnati Museum of Natural History in 1961. Over time, The Wilderness and other sites were added and became known as the Richard & Lucile Durrell Edge of Appalachia Preserve System. E. Lucy Braun is credited for her leadership role at what is commonly called the Edge. One of the most successful preservation projects in the country, it currently contains over 16,000 acres in eleven preserves.

Her honors and awards are many: first female president of the Ohio Academy of Science (1933–34), first female president of the Ecological Society of America (1950), winner of the Mary Soper Pope Medal (1952), and first woman listed in the Ohio conservation Hall of Fame (1971), to name a few. The University of Cincinnati awarded her an honorary doctor of science degree in 1964.

Emma Lucy Braun died on March 5, 1971, and is buried next to Annette, under the low, spreading branches of the oldest oak tree in Spring Grove Cemetery and Arboretum. The sisters maintain a status as role models for women, especially women of science.

Lucy couldn't save Leatherwood, but her work to save areas of ecological significance inspired countless others and resulted in a legacy of preserved spaces that continues to thrive and grow. Her status among botanists, plant ecologists, and conservationists is legendary for her many outstanding contributions.

Presidential Politics

Raymond Walters, Franklin D. Roosevelt, and the Photo Op That Never Developed

by Robert Earnest Miller

On October 29, 1937, University of Cincinnati president Raymond Walters noted in his diary that a *Cincinnati Enquirer* photographer had taken a picture of him as he was seeing off his overnight guest, noted author H. G. Wells, at a local train station. Walters speculated with pride that the photo would someday prove to his children that he had the opportunity to "hobnob with greatness."

Over his many years as UC's longest tenured president (1932–1955), Walters, in his official capacity, attended countless commencement exercises and other academic functions. Throughout his time at UC, Walters maintained a daily diary. One of the constants in his many entries was the way he delighted in nonchalantly mentioning the notable individuals—from authors and aviators to poets and politicians—that he hosted as president of the university. He relished being in the spotlight, especially when that publicity worked to the benefit of UC.

Walters's eagerness to perform his ceremonial duties during the Wells's visit stands in marked contrast to his curious behavior on October 16, 1936, when President Franklin D. Roosevelt visited the UC campus. On that day, the state party chairman of the Ohio Democratic Party had convinced FDR to come to Cincinnati to make a campaign speech just a few weeks prior to Election Day. Local party officials invited Roosevelt to inspect public works projects that had been funded by his New Deal. Among those projects on the president's itinerary was Nippert Stadium, where the Bearcats football team played. Works Progress Administration crews had renovated the stadium and doubled its seating capacity from 12,000 to 24,000. While the advance publicity for his trip assured that the president's remarks would be "nonpolitical," FDR was actively campaigning for reelection. His campaign stop was designed to remind Cincinnatians that the New Deal had put many of them back to work.

When FDR arrived on UC's campus, numerous local dignitaries were on hand, including Cincinnati Mayor Russell Wilson, City Manager Clarence Dykstra, and the governors of Ohio and Indiana, to welcome the president. Walters decided to absent himself from the festivities. Why would he deprive himself of a perhaps once-in-a-lifetime opportunity to introduce the president of the United States to a crowd of 15,000 well-wishers? Why would Walters shy away from a public relations event that placed UC in the best possible light? Why had Walters, who cared so deeply for the athletic program at UC, publicly opposed the renovation of its football stadium? The answers can be found in the pages of Raymond Walters's diaries.

PARTISAN POLITICS OF A PRIVATE NATURE

As president of a large municipal university, Walters learned quickly to get along with whoever controlled city hall. Under the city's bylaws, the mayor appointed members of the university's board of directors, the people to whom Walters reported directly. By all outward appearances, Walters was "the ideal university president," in the words of one colleague. He was beloved by students, passionate about advocating for the growth and best interests of the university, a patron of the arts, and an all-round pillar of the community. During his tenure, he developed good working partnerships with Charterite, Republican, and Democratic mayors. With few exceptions, he also maintained a cordial and productive partnership with his board. In terms of his political views on national and global matters, Walters remained circumspect. As much as possible, he projected an amiable, apolitical image in public. Maintaining that public persona came at a cost. It meant that Walters had to keep part of his identity hidden away.

In private, when he penned his nightly diary entries, Walters felt unshackled and allowed himself to voice his true feelings. His most common topic was politics. He was never shy about expressing his well-informed opinions. Before settling into his career in academia, Walters had worked as a newspaper reporter for the *Philadelphia Daily Ledger*, and he never lost his nose for news. Walters had an insatiable appetite for current events and was an avid consumer of all forms of mass media. He read up to three newspapers and he also tuned into daily radio broadcasts. By the late 1920s, Walters mainly used his diary to digest and recap the events of the day.

No one showed up in the Walters diaries more than Franklin Roosevelt. Even though he never voted for Roosevelt, Walters felt that a special bond existed between himself and the new president. Part of that feeling obviously stemmed from the fact that Roosevelt was president longer than any other individual during Walters's life. But Walters's sense of connection to Roosevelt ran deeper than that. Both men were elected in 1932 and both came to power at a time when the downward spiraling economic situation posed seemingly overwhelming threats to their leadership. Each was charged with the herculean task of restoring faith among their respective constituents. Roosevelt was tasked with restoring faith in capitalism and representative government to workers and citizens. Walters had to steady the nerves of his board of directors, his faculty, and his student body.

During the election of 1932 Walters had supported President Herbert Hoover's bid for reelection. At first, he was despondent when Hoover lost. In the months leading up to Roosevelt's inauguration, as the Great Depression worsened, Walters's views of FDR began to change. Over the next four years, from FDR's election in 1932 to his campaign stop in the Queen City in 1936, Walters's attitudes about the nation's thirty-second president evolved dramatically, from high praise and optimism to pointed criticism and skepticism.

At the time of FDR's inauguration on March 4, 1933, Walters appeared ready to give the new president a chance to succeed. He and his wife listened to the president's inaugural address, in which FDR summoned the American people to maintain its faith in its government and its economic system. Walters observed, "[T]he public mood is rife for a change. His smile and his courage may do the trick of turning the national spirit back to confidence. Here's hoping."

Two days later, the Walters listened in again, along with millions of other Americans, to the president's first fireside chat, in which he declared a bank holiday. According to Walters, the speech "was an admirable exposition and it was in addition, an effective piece of persuasion. Delivered in the President's manly, cheery voice, this address must be coming to millions everywhere, as it did to us, as a mighty counsel of confidence and courage. We Americans may thank God for Franklin D. Roosevelt."

The following week, as FDR's New Deal began to take shape, Walters enthused: "There is a new spirit abroad. Having scraped bottom, our economic and financial ship is starting upward, I believe." Walters, of course, was not alone in his favorable views of the president. The inauguration had stirred a bandwagon effect among many Americans who welcomed a change of leadership. Many Republicans and business leaders supported the early years of the New Deal. Walters, the old English professor, seemed to have been particularly impressed with Roosevelt's ability to deliver a rousing and well-timed speech, a skill Hoover most certainly lacked. Walters remained optimistic about President Roosevelt's leadership and the overall nature of the nation's economic recovery until 1936, which was, not coincidentally, the year FDR stood for reelection.

On May 1, 1936, Walters was lucky enough to meet President Roosevelt in person, as part of a delegation from the American Council of Education that traveled to Washington, DC. At a White House reception, Walters met the first lady and the president. Later that day, he recorded a very favorable impression of the visit and its host. "I had abundant chance before and after his talk to observe Mr. Roosevelt. He is very tall and now [a] very heavy man. Despite the thinning of his gray hair and heavy facial lines, he is still a handsome man…His voice is vibrant, his diction and pronunciation wholly admirable."

On May 27, 1936, less than a month after his White House visit, Walters's confidence in the president had noticeably waned. On that day, FDR accepted the nomination of his party for a second term. Walters decided to "take in a movie" instead of listening to the president's address on the radio. That night, he noted: "Well, I hold only good will to Mr. Roosevelt personally but I have lost faith in his judgment and in his administration's policy. I don't want to see this country subject, as it is now, to domination from Washington."

After the conventions ended, the gloves came off for the partisan Walters, who had thrown his support behind Republican candidate Alf Landon. Walters objected to the president's methods—the so-called "Alphabet Soup" of relief and recovery agencies funded by the federal government—more than the president's overall results. By 1936, President Roosevelt's New Deal had helped reduce unemployment and restored a measure of confidence that had been lost, facts that even Walters could not dispute.

Yet even after the nominating conventions, Walters continued to express an inner conflict about the message and the man when he wrote in private about FDR. After listening to Roosevelt's 1936 Labor Day fireside chat, Walters concluded: "It was Roosevelt at his best…While I admire the rhetorical efficiency of the address, I remain unimpressed so far as my own vote is concerned. I still think Mr. Roosevelt a well-meaning idealistic man but [I] have lost confidence in the men in whom he places confidence and in the plans he has devised."

To suggest that Walters's ongoing assessments of Franklin Roosevelt were complicated was an understatement. Walters's comments about Roosevelt could, and often did, run in contradictory directions. As a partisan critic, Walters's disdain for New Deal policies made it easy for him to love to hate Roosevelt, or at least his policies. On the other hand, as someone who appreciated a well-delivered speech, Walters's begrudging respect for the silver-tongued president meant that he ended up hating the fact that he loved, or at least admired, FDR at times.

ALL POLITICS ARE LOCAL

Walters's partisan politics offer, at best, only a partial explanation for his decision to snub President Roosevelt when he came to town in October. As UC's president, Walters had become all too conscious of the New Deal's centralizing tendencies when he tried to work with the federal government to improve the university's infrastructure. By the early 1930s, Walters and the board were having conversations about seven possible construction projects that would involve federal construction crews. Between the launching of the New Deal in 1933 and Roosevelt's reelection in 1936, federally funded works projects had shifted away from the auspices of the Civilian Works Administration (CWA, 1933–1935), which coordinated efforts between state and federal officials, to the more familiar Works Progress Administration (1935–1943). WPA officials in Washington, DC, eventually took a more active role in staffing and directing public works projects in states and localities.

Of the seven proposed projects, only three came to fruition. By May 1935, the university had agreed to move forward on the construction of a new student union in the basement of McMicken Hall, and the construction of a "Greek out-of-door theater." Walters expressed jubilation over the two projects, which he supported for two reasons: they improved the quality of student life on campus, but equally important to Walters was the fact that the Student Activity Council had agreed to finance a portion of the construction costs, thereby reducing the contribution of the federal government. Walters liked the way the student body had agreed to become stakeholders in the process of improving their university.

A third project, the proposed renovation of the football stadium, proved more contentious. In January 1934, innovative plans surfaced in which stadium seating at Nippert Stadium would be increased by digging twelve feet below the present level of the field to build more seats. This type of excavation was known as the "Yale method," as it had been carried out successfully at that school. The initial plan, factoring in assistance by CWA workers, seemed appealing and affordable. The projected $95,000 project would only cost the university about $38,000. Walters expressed confidence that gate receipts would easily cover the costs of the construction. When the CWA was disbanded, all discussions about the stadium were put on hold. It looked as if UC would fall victim to the growing pains of the New Deal. For several months, there was little discussion about the project. Then in late October, a surprised (and erudite) Walters wrote in his diary, comparing the stadium project to a pivotal character from Shakespeare's *Macbeth*: "Like Banquo's Ghosts, the stadium project bobbed up again today. It appears that the W.P.A. people think the enlargement [of the stadium is] an advantageous work relief job and [they] are making a very good offer. The details remain to be definitely ascertained."

Eventually, the WPA came up with a plan to renovate the stadium. When Walters learned it would cost twice the amount of the original projected budget, he withdrew his support for the renovation. He wrote members of the board of directors in October 1934, saying: "It is a project to which I consented, but as about $70,000 is now called for, I am opposed to it." From that point forward, Walters continued to object to the federal funding of the stadium project.

MORE PRESIDENTIAL POLITICS

A third possible reason for Walters's passionate objection to the stadium renovation can be found in the pages of Walters's diaries that predate his arrival in Cincinnati. Before coming to UC in 1932, Walters first taught English courses for several years at Lehigh University, his alma mater. In 1921, Walters's career received a boost when he was recruited by Frank Aydelotte, a dynamic pioneer in higher education. Aydelotte, the president of Swarthmore College, a small, Quaker, liberal arts school just west of Philadelphia, hired Walters to perform administrative work and to teach. During his twelve years at Swarthmore, Walters taught English courses for Aydelotte's innovative Honors Program, he worked as the college registrar and the dean of men, and also served as President Aydelotte's personal assistant.

In addition to revolutionizing the undergraduate curriculum, Aydelotte fought to take back control of college athletics from overzealous coaches. The 1920s had seen the explosion of team sports on college campuses—with radio broadcasts, Bowl games, pampered student athletes—that distracted from the mission of higher education. Aydelotte stripped Swarthmore's athletic department of its independence, integrated its coaches into the faculty, and deemphasized the role of sports in general. Much to the chagrin of the Swarthmore alumni, the level of athletic competition that resulted from Aydelotte's efforts was only a step above intramural play.

As second in command, Walters had little choice but to support Aydelotte's athletic reforms. Yet, Walters's diary entries about the proper balance of sports in college life, like most other topics, reveal a tension between his public actions and private thoughts. Outside of work, Walters enjoyed listening to boxing matches and baseball games on the radio or attending a tennis match. Walters recorded his secret rapture about a dramatic 1925 come-from-behind football victory over Swarthmore's arch-rival, Haverford:

> *A splendid day and a glorious victory over Haverford. I fear I share in the rejoicing of our dyed-in-the-wool alumni in the discomfiture of the Orthodox. Malicious joy! Haverford astounded everybody by 15 minutes of splendid play which produced two touchdowns. Struck two sharp blows…[After the slow start, Swarthmore] swept up and down the field, executing every type of play, especially aerial, and the sum of their efforts was 70 points, the greatest total in the history of the rivalry. Great rejoicing, not intemperate. Mass meeting; bonfires; dances in the gymnasiums.*

This private, guilty pleasure stands in stark contrast to a very public statement issued by Walters as UC president nine years later. Walters carried many of Aydelotte's ideas about achieving the appropriate balance of athletics and academics into his new job. When the CWA funding fell through for Nippert Stadium in 1934, Walters took the extraordinary step of reaching out to the student body directly through its student-run newspaper, the *News Record*. Walters wrote a lengthy, page-one editorial explaining his views about where sports should rank on any college campus. The sentiments voiced by Walters were vintage Aydelotte:

> *When I came to Cincinnati two years ago I was pleased with the spirit shown in regard to football which, I am told, marked a considerable improvement over preceding years.*

I am against commercialization of college athletics, with the evils of subsidizing and of emphasis away from the real purpose of college and university training.

I don't want a world beating football team in the University of Cincinnati, no roving-press-agented aggregation of stars. I do want a team that truly represents the city and our University.

In the same editorial, Walters acknowledged that federal funding for the stadium renovation no longer seemed viable. In its place, he came up with a home-grown solution. The Bearcats were scheduled to play Kentucky and Vanderbilt at Nippert Stadium during the 1935 season. It was anticipated that both teams would be accompanied by record numbers of alumni and fans eager to see the contest in Cincinnati. Walters appealed to the UC student body to surrender their seats for those two games and allow them to be sold to the visiting fans. The gate receipts, he believed, would generate enough revenue to help fund the necessary renovations at Nippert.

The board of directors, perhaps doubtful of Walters's calculations, eventually overruled their president and allowed the WPA to guide the stadium renovation through to its completion. In the end, it turned out that both Walters and the board had pinned their hopes on unrealistic formulas to fund the stadium project. Even after the work was complete, the university still owed more than $30,000 for the work. The debt was finally settled on December 12, 1941, when George French, a board member, presented Walters with a personal donation to pay it off.

CONCLUSION AND POSTSCRIPT

Three days after FDR delivered his October 1936 speech at UC, President Walters walked from his office on the west side of campus, in the Van Wormer building, down to Nippert Stadium to watch his football team practice their drills. Despite his dramatic absence at Nippert Stadium when FDR was on hand, Walters had developed a reputation, over the years, of supporting his teams through winning and losing seasons. He relished attending games in the president's box seats and inviting local dignitaries as his guests. On occasion, he would make congratulatory visits into the team clubhouse. He even went as far as to visit injured players in the hospital. In short, he was fan of his school's athletic pursuits. It is ironic, then, that he, of all people, would end up protesting the long overdue renovation and improvement of the university football stadium. Clearly, Frank Aydelotte's ideas about maintaining an academics-first environment had made a long-lasting impression on his protégé.

Walters's objections to the centralizing tendencies of the New Deal and his distrust of Roosevelt as an effective architect of economic recovery neatly dovetailed and overlapped with his attitudes about the sanctity of higher education. When Washington policymakers proposed jobs programs that would benefit college campuses, Walters supported public works projects, like a new student union, that improved the overall quality of student life, and he ultimately objected to others, like Nippert Stadium, that seemed to benefit a select few. The day that Roosevelt came to visit must have been especially painful to Walters. It represented a celebration of an economic policy that was anathema to him. Moreover, the day's festivities represented a rare rebuke from the board of directors, who ultimately supported the federally funded renovation.

Walters's 1936 boycott of FDR's visit did not make headlines in the local newspapers. In fact, it wasn't even reported or mentioned. Walters, it is likely, was fine with that. He had managed to keep his partisan views private up to that point and would endeavor to continue that practice moving forward. He was angry enough on the evening of the visit to leave the page of his diary blank.

While he never again spoke about the events of October 16, 1936, his opposition to FDR certainly did not end on that day. Walters had thrown in his lot with the Republican candidate, Kansas governor Alf Landon. Writing from Austin, Texas, on November 1, just days before the election, Walters observed:

> *The sky is overcast. I am not feeling cheerful. It isn't the weather, however, but the morning newspaper reports indicating a Roosevelt victory. I fear the President will consider himself endorsed in policies which, as a liberal, I consider dangerous for America. The argument that great social good can be more quickly accomplished by a strong central government does not impress me. The same centralization can quickly wipe out the gains which liberalism has slowly built up.*

Four years later, Walters predictably found himself at odds with yet another campaign to reelect President Roosevelt. Some things remained the same—Walters still considered FDR a dangerous demagogue, even a threat to the traditions of representative democracy. But in many other ways, the world had undergone several profound changes. After several long, tense years, Europe and Asia had plunged into a world war. In the aftermath of the Roosevelt victory in 1940, Walters took stock of the situation and realized that Adolf Hitler and his Nazi regime represented a far greater threat than FDR ever could to the traditions and values he held most dear. Walters, the old anti–New Dealer, found himself supporting many of the president's actions, from the passage of the Selective Service Act, to the president's "Arsenal of Democracy" speech (Walters hailed it as "an excellent exposition of the situation, admirably delivered"), to the passage of the Lend-Lease Act (1941). When America did enter the war, the partisanship that had defined Walters's core beliefs during the 1930s bowed to the higher order of patriotism.

During the war years, Walters worked closely with federal officials to transform the University of Cincinnati into a training camp for aviators. Moreover, he supported the war effort in the Queen City as one of three citizen judges on the Alien Enemy Hearing Board, in which he determined whether persons of Italian and German birth or descent should be interned or not. He also made almost weekly trips to the nation's capital to coordinate the efforts of higher education to support the war effort. On a personal level, he watched with a combination of pride and anxiety as all three of his grown sons enlisted in the armed forces.

Walters happened to be boarding an eastbound train for Washington, DC, on April 12, 1945, when he was jolted with the news that President Roosevelt had died of a cerebral hemorrhage in Warm Springs, Georgia. The next day he described the somber crowds milling around the nation's capital and the flags, flown at half-staff, adorning the federal buildings. Walters offered this generous assessment of the fallen leader: "Agree or disagree with Franklin Roosevelt (in recent years I largely disagreed), he was a figure of such power and vitality as to merit the designation: a great American."

Clearly, time had allowed the differences that had once separated the two presidents to be forgotten. When Walters retired as UC president in 1955, he was credited with overseeing much of the heavy lifting that brought the university into the modern age. The student body had grown exponentially, in large measure because of the GI Bill of Rights in 1944, which helped returning servicemen to attend college. When Raymond Walters died in 1970, the enlargement of the footprint of the university, the number of its colleges, and other physical improvements, including the student union and football stadium, both of which had undergone subsequent renovations since the 1930s, all become a part of his enduring legacy at the University of Cincinnati.

A Brief History of Computing at the University of Cincinnati

by Russell E. McMahon

While digital computers have been around for a while, they are still relatively young compared to UC as it celebrates its 200th birthday. The first functioning digital computer used outside of a lab in the United States was the Electronic Numeral Integrator and Computer (ENIAC), which went online in 1946 just after World War II. UC can claim to be a grandfather of the ENIAC, as John Mauchly, co-inventor of the device, was born in Cincinnati, the son of a UC graduate, Sebastian Mauchly, who received his PhD in physics in 1913.

Since the advent of computers, UC alumni, faculty, and staff have distinguished themselves in the computer field and have been deeply involved in its evolution as computers went from behemoths to fitting in the palm of one's hand.

I started at UC in the fall of 1972 with a dream of becoming a science and math teacher. In 1975, I took my first programming class at UC. The course was on FORTRAN, and I remember going to the basement of Beecher Hall to fight for a keypunch machine in order to type up my program on cards that then had to be fed into a card-reader upstairs. Normally, I would submit my job in the morning, go to class, come back in the afternoon, pickup my output, fix the typos and bugs, resubmit the job, and return in the morning to start the process over again. Little did I know at that time that I was using a computer that was a part of the Southwest Ohio Regional Computer Center or SWORCC. I discovered that UC and Miami University had entered into an agreement in 1972 that constituted one of the largest university computer centers in the country. Although there were other college computing centers, SWORCC was highly unusual. Over its brief lifespan, from 1972 to 1975, it had only one director but it handled both administrative and academic computing, a merger all but unheard of at that time.

Besides enjoying those subjects, I found that I also loved the history about the men and women who played important parts in the advancement of their discipline. I often would intertwine some of these historical discoveries into my teaching to show my students that the subject they were learning was really about people like us. I was able to take this even further in 2005 when I began to research UC's own computing history and discovered that many Bearcat achievements have helped make this university a leader in the field. This is a story of pivotal events showing UC's advances in the computer field, long forgotten by many, but the foundation for today's IT@UC.

UC's first computer nerd was Viola Woodward, who cut her teeth programming on the ENIAC when this computer was moved to the Aberdeen Ballistic Research Laboratory. Woodward attended Walnut Hills High School and graduated from UC in 1943 with a degree in math and education. Instead of becoming a teacher, she decided to join the Navy to help support our troops. Upon completing her service and obtaining a master's degree from Stanford, one of her professors mentioned that the Army was looking for programmers to write code for the ENIAC. After the ENIAC was replaced with the next-generation computer, the ORDVAC, she was eventually promoted to the section head of the computing center. She knew John Mauchly, because he would visit the Aberdeen Lab to see how things were going since it was his company's computers that were being used. This Bearcat clearly demonstrated that women could tame these beasts as well as anyone.

One of Viola's classmates from high school married another Bearcat who also blazed a trail in the computer field, Arnold Spielberg, who could be called the grandfather of E.T., because he is the father of Steven Spielberg. Arnold was a 1934 graduate from Hughes High School (now Hughes STEM High School) in Cincinnati, but did not start college immediately. Instead, he worked in his family's retail business located in Cynthiana, Kentucky, until the start of World War II. He was an electronics tinkerer and ham radio operator much of his young life, once the war began, he served in the Pacific where he was responsible for radio communications. After the war, he enrolled in UC's electrical engineering program, going through the coursework and co-ops in four years. One of his co-ops was with the Crosley Radio Corporation. His son, Steven (director of *E.T.*, *Jaws*, *Jurassic Park*, and many other movies), was born in Cincinnati. Upon Arnold's graduation in 1949, the Spielberg family moved to the East Coast where Arnold took a job with RCA. In 1954, he developed the first computerized point-of-sale system, which was tested in Higbee's Department Store (seen in the movie *A Christmas Story*) in Cleveland. For this work, he received the IEEE 2006 Computer Pioneer Award. He later went to work for the GE Computer Department designing their computers.

Many other Bearcat alumni were early computing pioneers as well. Richard Canning created systems analysis consulting. Tom Nies helped create the software industry. Everett Yowell advanced the concept of numerical analysis computing. Bill Uttal was at the forefront of human factors and user experience in computing. Donald Shell who wrote a sort routine that bears his name, still studied by all computer science majors. Saul Rosen helped create the first computer science degree program in the United States while at Purdue University. Robert Hahn brought together computers and machines to create a new era of industrial manufacturing. John Blatt helped develop the first computer in Australia called the SILIAC. Roland Roessner experimented with one of the first computer-aided learning systems while a professor of architecture at the University of Texas.

The first computer in the Cincinnati area arrived in 1953 and was housed at the GE Aircraft Division located off of I-75 in Evendale. The company employed, among others, a recent PhD graduate from UC named Donald Shell. But it would be five years before UC would have its own computer, and it was due in part to Paul Herget, a world-renowned astronomer and UC graduate who was head of the Cincinnati Observatory and the Minor Planet Center. Herget distinguished himself for his ability to accurately calculate the orbits of the minor planets, which eventually translated to calculating the orbits of satellites and manned spacecraft and even to today's GPS devices. He became an accomplished computer programmer and was very involved with both the Vanguard and Mercury space programs. Through his tireless work, an IBM-650 computer was delivered to UC in May 1958 and UC's computing history began. The computer was housed in an annex that was built onto Braunstein Hall. I actually took a class in the room where the first computer was located and remember someone mentioning to me that a computer had been there at one time. Little did I know that I would be researching that computer forty years later!

Faculty members also became very involved with computers at UC. Carl Evert worked tirelessly in those early years to promote the use of computers at

UC, and eventually became the director of the academic computing center. Bob Howe taught the first specific programming class for engineering undergrads; before that computing had been mostly used by graduate students and their advisors. Hans Jaffe advanced the field of chemistry through the power of the computer, which allowed him and his graduate students to complete their related computations in hours versus weeks. Alex Fraser used computing to advance the field of genetics by building simulations that modeled group interactions. Ron Huston and his assistant Mark Harlow wrote some very complicated and resource-intensive simulations of the human body for NASA. At one time his applications were using more than 50 percent of the computing resources available at the university. Walter Baude developed an application to predict the stock market, which is something that people are still trying to do today. Robert Cook was a lawyer who saw the need for computing power to help in tracking information on real estate, thus saving time on title searches. Jerry Paul was one of the primary persons who led the creation of a computer science department in the 1970s and became its first head in 1984. George Shields led the development of medical informatics and his work motivated a young nursing student, Diane Domonkos, who become an expert in the field.

In the 1960s computers found their way into the medical field and UC was at the forefront of this as well. A program to teach visually impaired and blind persons was started by Ted Sterling. The program started with twelve persons (eleven men and one woman). One of the first students, John Boyer, was not only blind, but also deaf; yet, he successfully completed the program and went onto a career as a programmer. Jacquie Whetstone Cummings was the only woman to complete this program and went on to work for Bowling Green University and the City of Toledo. One of the instructors in this program was Helen Mueller Gigley, who as a math major at UC got a unique opportunity to work with people with disabilities, and later completed her PhD in computer science at the University of Massachusetts, Amherst, and worked at the Naval Research Laboratory. Not all the students who went through this program were visually impaired or blind. Jim Henry's eyesight was fine, but he had cerebral palsy, which meant that his body was not particularly coordinated. Despite receiving a bachelor's in math, the only job open to him during this time was that of a sock sorter at the Goodwill. Sterling accepted Jim into the program because he felt that computing should belong to all people, not just a chosen few. Jim successfully completed the program including learning Braille, and had a very successful career at UC developing and writing applications used in the medical field.

In the 1970s UC computing prowess continued to grow. Under the leadership of Bob Caster, the Southwest Ohio Region Computer Center (SWORCC) was created between UC and Miami University. SWORCC not only served UC and Miami, but developed systems for the EPA to monitor our drinking water and assure it was safe. During this time, UC switched from IBM computer systems to the seventh ever made Amdahl computer. It was a huge leap of faith that paid off in terms of computing power and cost savings lasting into the 1990s. It was also in the 1970s when computer science began to emerge from the math department, but it wasn't until the early 1980s that it fully emerged as a separate department.

In the late 1970s and into the 1980s, PCs began to appear in different parts of the university. I took my first PC programming class using a TRS-80 in 1980, under the guidance of Jeff Gordon, who was a pioneer on using PCs in education. Going from writing computer code using punched cards in my first programming class five years earlier to writing code that I could instantly test and debug was a revolutionary step. Computers and their uses became my passion. Although PCs freed ordinary people from the constraints of the mainframe, they did not deliver the full experience until the Apple Macintosh came onto the scene in 1984, having been launched by one of the most memorable Super Bowl commercials ever. The Mac introduced the mouse, a Graphical User Interface, and different font styles. Just as computing was evolving, UC's IT organization went from SWORCC to the UC Computer Center (UCCC) when Jerry York took over the reins from Bob Caster. During this time, something called the Internet began to emerge from being something that a few academics and universities knew about to a tool that we would all depend upon. In 1987, Joe Landwehr, director of Planning and Technology, filed an application for the domain name of www.uc.edu ahead of the University of California and the University of Colorado.

The 1990s saw more changes as PCs were networked together, the Internet began to mature, and the mission of the once-dominant mainframes began to change. During this time, Robyn Render, a graduate from UC's former Evening College, took over the reins of UCCC, which morphed into the Center for IT Services (CITS) and eventually today's IT@UC. She was the first African American to assume the leadership of UC's IT department. In 1999, she left UC to work for the University of North Carolina system, eventually becoming their chief information officer and one of the first African American females to assume such a high position at a large academic institution. This was the year that I started teaching at UC in the Department of Math, Physics, and Computing Technology in the former College of Applied Science, which eventually became the School of Information Technology in the College of Education, Criminal Justice, and Human Services. My career had gone full circle from being a student of computing to being a professor of computing.

From punching cards to write code to punching smart phones to communicate, UC Bearcats have been at the forefront of computing technology since the beginning and will continue to be involved well into the future.

My University of Cincinnati Journey

by Clark Beck

When I arrived on the University of Cincinnati campus the very first time, my nervous system was very nervous. My mom and I had driven from Purdue University, where I had been informed that "your people cannot be engineers," and, "if you enroll here you will not graduate."

What a devastating message to give to an aspiring farm boy who had been taught that he should always listen to and respect the words of educated individuals! Just being told that I couldn't do it only made me want to do it more. After all, my high school teachers had told me that I should go into a career that involved math, science, or some other computational area. Should I believe them or this guy who must know more about engineering than my high school teachers?

I didn't have much fight in me at that time, as those words kept ringing in my ears. But I had to keep fighting, even though I didn't know where the road ahead would lead. The oldest child, the first in the family to go to college, such great expectations of me, especially from my mother. The thought of the embarrassment if I failed. I had heard of a school in Cincinnati that had a co-op program that would help finance the degree after the first year if one could pay for the first year. I decided on the spot that we should drive to Cincinnati that very day to find that school.

It makes no sense now, but I didn't even think about it then. I had no money and did not know how much that first year would cost or where I would get the funds, did not know the location of the school, had no idea of where I would live, and wasn't sure what engineering course I wanted to take. I am not sure what madness kept me going on a road so unfamiliar and unknown. Now that I think about it, I have no idea what caused me to do what seems today to have been insanity.

I had no appointment at the University of Cincinnati and had spoken to no one before arriving unannounced and asking to see the dean of engineering. Dean Howard Justice was called out of a meeting to speak to me. After listening to a short explanation of why I was there, he took my envelope and opened it to look at my transcript.

It is strange that I have no memory what our conversation was like or what he said, except "You can come if you want to but you will catch hell from both sides of the desk." I think I heard only the first part of his statement (accepted!) even though the second part was a warning I did not understand until later.

Now, after all these years have passed, I feel that my personality caused some of my hardship in those early days at UC. I was an independent young man who had been a loner working in the field all day, knowing that I had to fix whatever broke by whatever means available to me. I never expected or asked for help when I needed it in my younger days, and certainly felt I could not now at UC. Asking for help was a sign of weakness to me. I could not ask for help from people I didn't know, especially when I felt that I was not wanted or welcome in the group. It was almost impossible to make friends under those circumstances. How could I when I recalled the prediction at Purdue and the warning from a friendly Dean Justice at UC?

My situation was exacerbated by not being able to live on campus. I didn't even apply for housing because of my lack of funds. Or even near campus. When I heard "no room" I gave up. I feel certain that being close to campus and class-mates would have made a great improvement in my UC years (socially, academically, and mentally).

However, the reality was that, after a day at UC, I rode across town to a poor part of Walnut Hills near Peebles Corner. My first landlady was an elderly widow who owned two identical side-by-side houses in an area that is now underneath I-71. I rented a sparse single room with no cooking facility and no refrigerator and a bath shared with two other familial groups. It was an old house cut up into one- or two-room units. Someone must have had the kitchen and someone else the living room. My room was a small former sitting room with one outside window facing the wall of the next house, a small gas fireplace for heat, a bed, a small desk, and a single chair. My clothes hung in a small portable wardrobe.

I have seen similar room arrangements in TV movies depicting people living, as I was, below the poverty line. They usually had a cheap TV, a luxury I did not have. For my first year, that was home-not-so-sweet home. It was not easy to study on weekends while the couple living in front of me argued. I tried to ignore all the noise, but that was impossible. I cannot forget the night that the younger of the two male lovers on the third floor knocked on my door and asked if he could spend the night since his partner had locked him out. It was my mistake to admit him. That was a sleepless night.

I suppose I would have had more pleasant living quarters if I had accepted the offer from my funeral director brother-in-law. In exchange for a room, I would be the person "on call" to pick up and transfer to the funeral home any calls received during the night. I felt that working a night shift would have made study impossible and make the Purdue prediction a reality. I never second-guessed that decision. I needed all the time I had to study. But the most inefficient study arrangement is alone. Not having a study partner to point out where you made the mistake in the three pages of equations means that you will probably miss it every time you recheck the solution. How frustrating that can be! Especially when you see the solution and note the simple error you made.

The first year in Cincinnati was definitely the worst. Living in a strange city, among strangers in a very lonely environment, was a great strain on me. Even my physical system was stretched to its limit. The sun seemed not to shine the winter of 1952–53.

In the whole of Cincinnati there were only two places I could visit—the home of my half sister and her husband and two teenage daughters; and that of my good friend Jim Hargreaves, to whom I owe a great debt. Jim helped to keep me connected to reality and gave me hope for the future. My sister's house was not a place of refuge: I sensed problems with a man more interested in money than people. I visited seldom, only when invited to have dinner and to help the girls with homework. I still feel that the man in that house did not think that I would graduate, but would be another failure like others he knew.

It is no wonder that the specter of failure was always in the back of my mind. Dogged determination, the need to prove the naysayers wrong, the never-ending desire to fulfill my mother's dream for me, the need to be successful in spite of the odds, just trying to get by today and trying not to think about tomorrow because tomorrow appeared to be no better than today, just plodding ahead with the intent to beat whatever was thrown at me. These things and some other unknown internal force kept pushing me forward into the unknown future.

There were times when the thought of "no future" did cross my murky mind. It was at the times when all seemed hopeless, when it seemed the future held immediate and impossible failure. That thought came at times when the weather was at its worst, when the skies held no sunshine. It was much like the day in Chicago when—as a high school senior—the Naval Training Center gave me the news that I had failed to pass the physical exam and I would not be accepted into the ROTC program.

You see, ROTC was my way to success, out of the lowly place I was in and a chance to wear that beautiful marine dress uniform that my cousin wore when he came home for Christmas during my sophomore year in high school. Although this happened years before I had the UC challenges, it was just another incident in my childhood that contributed to the negative visions about my future, my probability of success, of being a worthy human in this world.

What made that Navy announcement so devastating was the fact that I knew that I had not failed to pass the physical. Consider—I was born and raised on a farm, the oldest son who did his share of hard work, an amateur boxer (until my mom found out), playing baseball, playing football, being on the track team (long-jump state finalist as a junior and mile relay-team state-finalist as a senior)—at six feet and 185 pounds, how could I not pass the Navy ROTC physical exam?

I had already passed the academic exam before I was invited to Chicago for the physical. There were three of us from Marion High School who passed the academic exam and were invited to Chicago for the physical. When we met at the end of the exam, I was elated that I had passed—until the loudspeaker bellowed out for me to report back to station "X." I could not imagine why, but I returned to a place that I had been earlier that day. I was informed in a casual manner that I was overweight and not accepted. But how could that be? I saw many young men more "overweight" than I who were celebrating their acceptance.

My health problems began during that first winter in Cincinnati. All the clothes I had in Cincinnati were those from Richmond, Virginia, where I had lived the previous four years. Those clothes were no match for the winter in Ohio. Looking back, I realize I could have gone to some social welfare agency to ask for a suitable coat. But that was not the Beck way and the thought never crossed my mind. I was driven and all I could see was a path ahead of me—one foot in front of the other approaching a goal that was too far ahead to see. I recall having that feeling several times as I worked on the Beck farm and neighboring farms while in grade school.

I do not recall those as good times. However, I felt I was doing what was best for the family. Living on a neighboring farm from Monday through Saturday where the work meant one less mouth to feed at home and the $5.00 for the week's work did help. Those "earning opportunities" were created when the male son joined the armed forces or left home for a job in the city. I spent two summers like this before finishing grade school. Neither of the farmers had children at home and no children lived close enough for social contact. The pleasant times those summers were Thursday evenings the first year when the local community showed a free outdoor movie. The second year the couple went to the city for a moving picture show every Saturday night and took me with them. They also took an elderly gentleman who played cards at the local bar. He always brought them a special beer-cooked hamburger that they always gave to me after dropping him off at home. I got to spend Saturday night through Monday morning at home. These experiences only strengthened my "loner" characteristic since I was in the field all day.

There was an earning opportunity created for me during my first year at UC. Jim belonged to a Presbyterian church located in the poorer section of town. It participated in a church basketball league with a few other churches in the area. They could not afford uniforms and I think they could not afford the very small salary I was given as the coach. We practiced in the church basement and played games in a local YMCA once a week. I do not remember how many games we played or what our team record was. I do recall that the nights were colder than the days and my teeth chattered as I walked from the church to the bus stop, transferring to the cross-town bus after a cold wait and the cold walk from that bus to home. The warm house was a blessed relief. The other thing I recall is the nervous and scary walks, especially through the neighborhood from church to the first bus. I always felt that I was in danger after dark in that area, and silently prayed for a short and safe walk and wait for the bus. Even when the wait for the bus was not short, my prayers were answered.

Again with my friend Jim's help, I was introduced to a small family-run Greek restaurant a few blocks from where I lived. I bought a card, which had punch circles around the perimeter. Each punch hole was good for a breakfast. The cost of the card was within my limited budget. With cards purchased each week I had a breakfast consisting of coffee, two slices of buttered toast, and jelly. After breakfast, I went off to catch the trolley with a warm but not-too-full stomach. Most days I had enough money to buy a sandwich or a box lunch from the food truck. Some days I was fortunate to have the offer of unwanted fruit from a classmate's box lunch. Some of them must have suspected my situation because only one offer was made on a given day, sparing me the embarrassment of "collecting." I never asked. It was always offered. The lunch meal made a small dinner adequate to get through the night. My evening meals often consisted of a half can of whatever I had from my dear Mom's care package that came each month and contained cans of food that did not have to be cooked (fortunately). The pears, peaches, hominy, corn, beans, pineapple, and peas never tasted so good as they did that winter. I have often asked myself why heavy cans shipped in boxes that required considerable postage were the mode of help rather than a letter with cash? Perhaps it was because she knew that sending cash in the mail was not safe and I had no bank account that could be used to cash a money order or check. Often the postage approached the cost of the food.

Along this entire journey my mother was my greatest supporter. I owe her more than I can say and I pray that she understood this even though I was not an expressive son. I also pray that she did not know just how difficult the first year was. She always appreciated education. Although a good student, she never had a chance to attend college. She was living in a time and environment that did not permit young women to go to a larger city alone, for any reason. I can only imagine how heartbroken she was to be denied a chance to excel as she would have in college. In spite of the lack of formal education beyond high school, she was an influential person in the community. She was respected by both political parties and worked to elect chosen candidates.

I would not return to my single room for a second year since the landlady asked that I pay rent year-round even while I was in Dayton for my co-op job. I was fortunate that Jim knew a widow who was a retired Cincinnati public school math teacher who lived in a relatively large and well-kept house in a much better part of Walnut Hills. She agreed to a reasonable rent and I moved in. She was kind enough to share her Sunday dinner when I did not go with Jim to his church. It was so much better living as a normal person once more! If the first winter in Cincinnati was the worst for finance, hunger, and cold, the second year was academic horror. At the end of the term I had three condition removals. That meant I was too low to receive a D but above an F. My choices were to do nothing and get an F or take a conditional removal exam to get a passing or failing grade. My decision was easy to make. I would take the conditional exam for two of the three courses. The third course, strength of materials, was far too important to mechanical engineering to settle for a barely passing grade. So, I took the F grade and repeated the course and got a passing grade. That voluntary F was the only one on my transcript, as I recall. I guess I was just not able to grasp it or know what was happening because the three condition removals came as a surprise. There was no other time when I came so close to disaster.

In the third year my co-op job was paying my expenses—not the life of a king, but more like a normal poor person. I knew the importance of conserving money for tomorrow's emergency and did so. I was also blessed by friends of the family and my mother's connections to find a couple in their seventies who offered reasonably priced room and board. I had found a car pool to and from work at Wright-Patterson Air Force Base. I had no social life and found a weekend job working at a gas station owned by the well-known and respected Lloyd Lewis Sr. I was now living a dream!

Thanksgiving of this year did change my social life. I was invited to attend a party on the night before Thanksgiving to provide a number of males to match the females. The girls were all college students home for Thanksgiving. I was to be the escort for a student at some other Ohio college. After all, this was a safe one-night adventure and I did need to meet college students who were not male engineering students. During the evening, my partner was attracted to another young man it seems she knew from an earlier time. But there was another young woman who always seemed to be near me with much conversation. She had graduated from the University of Dayton and had her first teaching job in Cleveland. She was back home for the holiday. I walked her home and accepted an invitation to Thanksgiving dinner the next day. My social life was looking up.

Recalling all the things that have happened to me in this life makes me wonder why and how I am still alive. There is no doubt that some power greater than me stepped in several times to lift me from the canyon of destruction, out of the murky sea, away from men of terror and away from thoughts of self-destruction. I do know that during the second year of grad school, more than once I was saved from probably fatal crashes as I drove home from a late class after 10:30 P.M. The rumble of the tires on the side of the road woke me before going down the embankment. The need for sleep and the drowsiness caused by complications from a deteriorating kidney condition were an undesirable combination. I have found many more reasons to believe that I have been and am a blessed individual.

After I finished my bachelor's in engineering and started a job, I ended up going back to UC graduate school under rather unusual circumstances. I was working at Wright-Patterson and was called to the colonel's office with no clue why. After some small talk, he instructed me to "fill out those papers." A brief scan let me know that it was an application to be approved to attend graduate school at the government's expense. Although it was my desire to attend grad school I had discussed it with no one.

The colonel did not tell me why this honor had fallen on me and I didn't ask. After a few days rushing around to complete the forms and deciding that I would apply to UC, I think I knew the reason why. This opportunity was a consolation prize or payment for a wrong done to me a few months earlier. I had been denied a promotion at Wright-Patterson because my supervisor, a major, had decided to promote another civilian. I felt that I should have been chosen, but was not. The colonel was my boss's boss, who had to approve the promotion. He also reviewed the other applicants' resumés. It was never said but I feel I know the answer. I am still indebted to the colonel who had been promoted to a position at another Air Force base when I returned from UC with the MS degree in aerospace engineering. The major was also missing. It was not long until I received a promotion.

Now that it is over, I often wonder how I was able to complete those graduate courses. I did not know it then, but my kidneys were progressing to total failure mode. My doctor in Yellow Springs never mentioned the word "kidney" although he had to have seen the progression over the years that he treated me. He only prescribed stronger blood pressure pills. The combination of the stronger pills and the increasing level of uremic poison in my body sometimes made me wonder which end was up. I am sure I was saved from death when, feeling ill, I took a cab from Dayton to Yellow Springs and found my doctor missing. I was so sick that a new young doctor saw me immediately and just as quickly put me in the back seat of a couple going to Miami Valley Hospital. By this time, I could not sit up without passing out. I felt like I was leaving this planet. The hospital had a room ready for me, where I stayed for three days while they lowered the amount of poison in my body to a level safe enough to perform dialysis. I distinctly remember someone saying, "He looks like he's dead." I thought I was hearing visitors talk about my roommate, but I now know I was alone in that unit. I must have been close enough to touch the other side.

It is appropriate that on this day I should write this part of my UC story. It was October 29, 1972, that I received a nonliving, nonrelated kidney transplant. It was at University of Cincinnati hospital that the gift of life was given to me. It is amazing when I realize that the kidney I received in 1972 has been in my body for almost forty years, almost half of my life—the better half. After receiving it I have seen my two children graduate from high school and college, get married, and give me three grandchildren, allowing me the opportunity to be involved in an interesting life with teenagers. I have also done some of the most beneficial and gratifying work and community service. After a rewarding engineering career in the field of elevated temperature reentry from space for the Air Force Research Laboratory I was able to have a second career in higher education as professor at Central State University and assistant dean at Wright State University's Engineering School. I am most proud that the Wright STEPP (Science, Technology, and Engineering Precollege Program) that I designed and implemented at Wright State in 1987 has provided training and scholarships for hundreds of inner-city high school students. I also take pride in knowing that the industrial arts courses that I taught and improved from 1957 until 1972 have resulted in an accredited manufacturing engineering major at Central State University.

It is no accident that I am still active in sports and have competed in twelve Dayton Senior Olympics competitions and nine U.S. Transplant Games against men thirteen years younger than I.

Knowing that each day is a gift and that more is expected from those who have been given more, I gladly serve Life Connection, the Red Cross, the Optimist Club, Good Samaritan Hospital, the University of Cincinnati Foundation, the Antioch University Midwest board of trustees, and a number of other community service organizations.

As I write this it is evident that I have learned from relating thoughts and feelings long pushed out of memory. I have learned that life is not always fair. I have learned that situations are not always what they seem to be, you can't always know what other people feel, and there are things you will never understand. I have learned that if you want a friend you must be a friend, and you may be misunderstood as you misunderstand. But I also learned never to give up on myself and that I owe more to UC than UC owes to me.

UC Engineering

A Cauldron for Personal Transformation

by Donald L. Vieth

I was a self-conscious, tall, skinny kid who by all accounts was an incredibly poor student. The only A I ever received while attending grade school was in conduct. In grade school, I experienced both physical bullying from older students and psychological bullying from intolerant nuns. On completing my grade school education, my eighth-grade teacher let me know that she did not believe I would ever amount to anything. By this time, I was feeling highly discouraged about my academic future. However, there was a mitigating circumstance—I was growing up with parents who believed in and strongly encouraged their children to be confident, independent, and self-sustaining. It was a philosophy that was drummed into my psyche and would eventually dominate my approach to life. It was communicated to me and my sister that, by the time we got out of high school, we were expected to be capable of being independent and taking care of ourselves.

My father was the first member of the Vieth family to attend college. He graduated with a degree in mechanical engineering in 1930 just in time to confront the personal deprivations and professional humiliations of the Great Depression. He married my mother just after Christmas in 1936 and they struggled financially. Eventually my father found a good-paying job as an engineer with Emery Industries in Ivorydale. By late 1942 the family moved from northern Kentucky to College Hill. My family was close and we spent a significant amount of time visiting with relatives on the weekends. I saw the wide variations of living standards within the diverse Vieth family. As I grew up, it was clear that, compared to my cousins in Newport and Covington, I was living a very good life.

In the summer of 1954, having completed grade school with the stinging prognosis of my eighth-grade teacher, I was contemplating with some dread the academic rigors of high school. I made a conscious decision that I would have to put forward whatever effort at studying necessary to get into college so I could be an engineer like my father. As I began high school, I struggled with nontechnical subjects, but discovered that I was good at the abstract aspects of math and the fascinating details of science. My general science teacher was marvelous and introduced me to geology and I became hooked on this subject. I did well academically my first year and progressed steadily. By the start of my senior year I was consistently making the honor roll, and the last year consistently won first honors.

Numerous occurrences in the fall of 1957 would affect my future plans. One Friday evening in early September, at the beginning of my senior year, my father wanted to talk to me about college. He wanted to tell me that he had been able to set aside $1,500 for my college education, my "grub-stake" so to speak. And then he asked me what I thought I wanted to study in college.

I told him, "Dad, I really want to study geology."

His response was emphatic, "Like hell you are! You are going to be an engineer! It is my job to teach you how to feed a family! Once you learn how to do that, you can be any damn thing you want to be!"

Having listened to his stories about the Great Depression and their impact on the family, I quickly grasped his basic priorities. Effectively, the fundamental path forward for my life was established; only the details remained to be worked out. Imbedded in a number of similar conversations were additional points that would focus the nature of my transformation during my education as an engineer. My father knew that the science courses, especially chemistry, were the ones in which I excelled. He was emphatic that a chemical engineer generally earned a better salary than a chemist, because he was capable of creating the industrial processes and facilities that would make money for a company. He also noted that, generally, only about 10 percent of the engineers really understood the science that was the basis for the engineering discipline they were practicing. His subliminal message was, follow a path that would provide a good financial return on your education and, if you want to be at the top of your discipline, learn the underlying science.

Another event in the fall of 1957 that would affect the course of my educational journey and professional career was a Soviet satellite. On October 4, the launch of *Sputnik* 1 shocked the American government and the effect was enormously significant for engineering and science. It was the birth of the short-lived Golden Age of Science. The government greatly increased funding for education, especially on science education, and for advanced research.

As I resigned myself to ditching geology and embracing engineering, I tried to figure out which engineering discipline involved lots of geology. All the schools that dealt with geology-related aspects such as mining engineering or materials processing were in the western United States. After a while it became obvious that $1,500 would not get me very far if I went west. Since I was supposed to be independent and capable, I had to find a more economical way to get educated. At this time, 1958, the University of Cincinnati was still a municipal university. Costs could be minimized; a year's tuition for Engineering College was $500 plus the cost of books and supplies, if I lived at home. Not only that, the engineering college would find me a job as part of the Cooperative Engineering Program.

In the spring of 1958, I attended a meeting, sponsored by the Cincinnati Engineering Society, for graduating high school students to learn about various engineering disciplines. At UC, the closest discipline to geology was metallurgical engineering although the department was focused on physical metallurgy versus process metallurgy for extracting metals from ores. At that meeting, I talked with several engineers and was attracted to Dr. Bill Koster, who was vice president of Metcut Research in Oakley. After we talked, he arranged to give me and a classmate a tour of his facility on the following Saturday to see and learn more about metallurgy as a science and metallurgical engineering as a profession. I was really impressed with what I saw, especially the microscopy capability and the things that it could reveal about science of metals. They had a very broad industrial research and technology development program in metal science and engineering. My imagination was stimulated and energized. The visit demonstrated that metallurgical engineering could offer new avenues for learning and career development. Furthermore, it revealed that lots of science would be involved. The new hook had been set.

My grades for my senior year had placed me at the level of first honors. I applied to and was accepted by the Engineering College at UC. Most attractive to me was the co-op program where I would learn the practical aspects of the engineering profession through the work program while learning the scientific and technical underpinnings of the specific engineering disciplines through classroom teaching. Because of the requirement for work experience, the time required to graduate was five years. I viewed the extra year in college as a benefit. And, importantly, the co-op program gave me the opportunity to complete my undergraduate education within the resources that I had in hand.

The year 1958 marked a major shift in the philosophy of educating engineers at UC. Engineers apparently were getting a poor reputation as being too narrow, and on the recommendation of the Engineering Joint Council on Professional Development, their education at the university level had to be reoriented and broadened. The Engineering College would now have courses in world history, American history, contemporary problems, world literature, and American literature. It was the first year that students did not have to go to class for a half day on Saturday, leaving them time for non-engineering pursuits.

The actual co-op program would begin in summer 1959 as a work section of seven weeks coupled with a classroom section of seven weeks. So, the "co-oping" process was committed to six sections each year, or forty-two weeks. That allowed ten weeks of free time between classroom and work sections, time to work and make additional money if the co-op employer wanted additional help.

The Class of 1963 that began their education in September 1958 had 400 students. I arrived armed with the major tool of the engineering profession, a complicated slide rule with a carrying case that could be clipped to one's belt. From my perspective, the class with which I was matriculating was a very tough and competitive group. After a week or so, a fact became clear: most of my classmates appeared to be smarter than me. It was clearly communicated and well understood that there would be significant attrition with regard to the number of engineering students during the first year. We were admonished to look to our left and to our right and understand that the students in those seats would not likely be there at graduation. The first year we all took the same courses except for mathematics. There was a separation of the students that were really proficient in math as compared with the rest of us, the nominal students. The nominal student started with introduction to college mathematics and analytical geometry; the advanced students, because of the evolving status of computers, were presented with the opportunity to take Boolean algebra and other advanced math. After this minor difference, we were all back in the same math curriculum. Students fairly quickly organized themselves into small groups that would work collectively to understand the material and establish some proficiency in the various subjects. The concept was to "collaborate and graduate."

The schedule was rigorous, involving twenty-three credit hours each classroom section. Classroom lectures, which accounted for seventeen credit hours, were from 8 A.M. to noon, five days a week. Within that twenty hours, three hours were open in the morning. The twelve hours of afternoon activities, which accounted for six credit hours, involved laboratory courses from 2 P.M. to 5 P.M. four days a week. Friday afternoons were usually free. The learning regime was far more time-intensive and intellectually demanding than anything we had experienced in high school. Students were given a good two hours for lunch, relaxation, ROTC, or academic interest. For me, it was lunch time and food was generally a box lunch, bought from a street vendor behind the chemistry building, consisting as a rule of two sandwiches, a piece of fruit, and some type of sweet pastry. I usually took lunch in a vacant classroom with a group of classmates.

The major focus of the first year was to acclimate and survive the new academic framework, and meet the new and evolving demands to give all the students a common foundation of math, physics, and chemistry as a basis for building solid engineering understanding. The pressure to succeed was more than a step up from high school. Many of my classmates decided they did not like the subject material or the practices demanded of an engineer; others could not keep pace with the learning requirements and failed. They went elsewhere to complete their college education or pursue life on a different level.

At UC, the Engineering College was an empire unto itself. The college was difficult to get into and it was tough to get through. If you made it through, you knew that you were a reasonably competent engineer. The Office of the Dean was responsible for the quality of the college. Cornelius Wandmacher was a great dean who had an imposing physical and intellectual presence. He was well respected and ran a tight ship. Dr. Robert Delcamp was the assistant dean and the individual who took care of student issues. He was an easygoing individual who could find rational solutions to most student issues. These two together provided a very strong and coherent leadership for a top-rated engineering college.

The faculties of the five engineering departments had strongly differing demeanors. The two professors with which students in my program had to contend were Dr. William Licht, head of Chemical Engineering, and Dr. Roy McDuffie, head of the Metallurgical Engineering. The bulk of the initial academic control for the Chems and Mets fell to Dr. Licht, who had a lofty attitude, not wanting to hear about student problems. Over our five years in school, he made many students rather unhappy. The students made their feelings known at the end of the senior year when they bricked up his office door one night. Dr. McDuffie had a far more relaxed "Mr. Chips" persona. He knew the subject material very well, but had a number of idiosyncrasies that made his lectures challenging. He had a great sense of humor and was always willing to listen to the concerns of the student. McDuffie had the ultimate respect of the Met Engineering students.

During the first year, the students were introduced to their co-op job coordinator, the individual that would find, support, and follow the employment of each student. There was a coordinator for each of the five major engineering groups. The coordinator for the Chemical and Metallurgical engineers was Ralph A. Van Wye, a crusty, iron-fisted, pseudo-tyrannical controlling character that wanted to know everything about what was going on in your life. Registration day for each of the classroom sections was a short effort timewise for the other engineering disciplines; however, for the Chems and Mets is could take up to two hours in a long line before reaching R. A. Van Wye. He had lots of forms to gather information, which had to be completed and provided to him; we all believed they were quite irrelevant. When you finally reached Van Wye, you were thoroughly interrogated about your co-op job as well as progress on your life's plan. One of his major concerns was whether the student had married, which he believed should never happen before graduation. After a few registration days, it became clear to the students what R. A. stood for.

On the other hand, the perspective we developed after we graduated was that Van Wye had a very good grasp of what was going on and really was concerned about the success of each of the students in Chem and Met engineering. He kept thorough records and had a file card for all but six graduates. He published and distributed to all graduating students a document entitled "The Flow Sheet" that served as a running update of what was happening with all the graduates, supported by BUBs (Beat Up Bucks) contributed by the graduates who were receiving the publication. "The Flow Sheet" was an excellent vehicle to keep classmates in touch and provide knowledge of what was really going on at the engineering college.

Finding a co-op job, for me, actually began in the spring of 1958. I previously met Dr. William Koster, a graduate of UC Metallurgical Engineering Program and had a long and interesting visit with him at Metcut Research. To a high school senior, it was a very cool place with lots of interesting equipment and operations, a great place to work and learn about the underpinning science of metals. I was hooked on the place.

In my early interactions with R. A. Van Wye, I noted that Metcut is where I would like to work. Van Wye made it happen. I began at Metcut in June 1959. It was a good situation with pay at $1.50 per hour. Every time I returned for the next work section my pay would increase by $0.05 per hour. By the time I graduated in 1963, I would be making $2.00 per hour. I may have been the lowest paid co-op student in the class. Many of my classmates that worked for Armco Steel were making $3.50 per hour or more, but Metcut offered a great job and it provided an opportunity to learn. The work always changed from day to day, no drudgery of doing the same thing over and over.

Metcut gave me lots of overtime since I was reliable and competent at many different tasks. It had a very nice machine shop, a good metallography laboratory, an extensive laboratory for testing mechanical properties (including tensile, fatigue, and creep properties) of metals, heat treating operations, specialized instrumentation services, specialized test rigs building and testing, along with facilities for drafting and design efforts, and preparation of artwork for reports. I got to do everything. It was an open shop—no union to control work rules and who got to do what.

The interesting aspect of working on the floor of the plant was being immersed in the dynamic character of a workforce that included diverse and capable individuals with a variety of levels of education, nature and level of technical skills, understanding of the world, and personal priorities. There was the upper management and owners of the company, the project engineers who had jobs to get done, the machinists who had to make product, the technicians who had to prepare for and conduct testing operations, the preparation of reports, and the presentation of results. One had to pay attention to who the customer was and what were important areas that required extra attention.

I was fortunate to have really smart project engineers as supervisors who covered a wide variety of capabilities. Possibly the most interesting work was in the metallography laboratory working on failure analysis. This is where I picked up some fascinating insights about clients. Since I had to do most of the sample preparation, I often got to sit in on the meetings with the clients with a metal failure problem. I was able to listen to the stories regarding the occurrence of the failure to be investigated. Examination of the failed components as received and the detailed scientific examination often revealed that the failure probably did not occur as claimed. I learned the level of inaccurate information that was provided, sometimes downright lies. This was a firsthand fair warning of the nature of communications in the future; be skeptical about what you hear, cautious about what you believe.

There was a difficult point in the spring of 1961. At that point, the company was doing a lot of subcontracting work on a defense-related project for General Electric, the X-211 nuclear-powered ramjet engine. In the winter of 1961, just after President John F. Kennedy took office, he cancelled the project. Metcut's staff was cut in half, from seventy to thirty-five. I had an uneasy feeling watching the people I was working with slowly disappear. When I returned to school in the spring, my boss indicated that they would probably not have work for me. On return to UC I checked in with my favorite co-op job coordinator, R. A. Van Wye. He found me a potential new job working at the Buckeye Foundry, a very dirty, gray, iron foundry on Beekman Street. I was fortunate that Metcut's workload picked up during the seven weeks I was in school, so I got called back. It was an interesting emotional event to be cut loose from a good job, and the introduction to the worry and uncertainty that such an event entailed.

More interesting was the social situation within the hourly workforce and some of the perspectives held by the project engineers. In the shop and the testing areas, the co-ops received some hazing. It was kind of a rite-of-passage, a mild test to determine what kind of grit you had. If you handled it with a degree of humor, it got you in good social standing with the guys. One of the venues where personalities came out was at the half-hour lunch break when individuals from the various departments gathered around the table on the loading dock for lunch. I was encouraged to join in, no doubt because I would become the focus of a variety of good-natured harassment. I was still on the skinny side (six feet, five inches tall, 155 pounds) and geeky (college student). My lunch usually consisted of four good-size sandwiches and I became known as "Seven Sandwich Don." The conversation was interesting, and often educational; it varied between two basic subjects, Fords versus Chevys and sexual exploits of the staff. Periodically they would talk about fishing. I was frequently the subject of speculation regarding the Ford Falcon I was driving, my six-foot, five-inch frame, and imagined issues of sexual encounters with my girlfriend in the back seat.

In my income tax statements for 1959 through 1962, my earnings from my co-op job averaged $2,000 per year. Frankly, as a college student, from a financial perspective I was in fat city. When I finished college, I still had $1,000 of my initial $1,500 grub-stake and had made my father a $500 loan. The greatest aspect of the Co-op Engineering Program was that I was able to pay for my own college education and was debt free when I left the University of Cincinnati.

At the beginning of the second year, there was a new level of intensity in the seven-week classroom session. For those who survived the shock of freshman year's level of expectation, in a short period of time it became clear that a great deal of complex technical material would be crammed into every seven-week classroom section. These sections developed the tactic of a "campaign" approach to learning. We usually had four to five different technical subjects to master along with one of the new humanities courses. There also were frequent tests to measure the proficiency we were achieving in the subject matter. Engineering students became very proficient in taking tests. By the end of the intense seven weeks, most of the students were highly stressed with feelings of significant burnout. During the next four years, mostly due to the intensity of the classroom work and the "campaign" mentality, nearly all the students would get rubbed the wrong way by someone in authority in the engineering college. The end result by the senior year was a collective sense of frustration and hostility. But there was value in the experience. We all learned how to successfully handle some serious expectations; a preparation for the outside world.

One side effect was the breeding of an attitude or sense of intellectual and academic superiority within the engineering students over the students in the other colleges at UC. The pressure also promoted a situation where the major part of our time was spent within the shelter of the engineering quadrangle, aka the Chemistry Building, Baldwin Hall, and Swift Hall—our version of Fort Apache.

In an effort to broaden the nontechnical, cultural, and social perspective of engineering students, General Electric established a program to encourage engineers in the class of 1963 to read a broader scope of literature. This occurred at the beginning of my second year. GE donated a large number of new paperback copies of classic books. At the end of next three classroom sections, the students that signed up got to pick three books to read while they were on work section. On return for the next classroom section, the student was obligated to attend three Sunday night sessions to discuss the books they selected. So, during the three work sections of my sophomore year, I read nine books. I can only remember three, Edward Gibbon's *Decline and Fall of the Roman Empire*, Thucydides's *History of the*

Peloponnesian War, and Lawrence Ferlinghetti's *Coney Island of the Mind*. After this, along with the history courses taught to engineers by Dr. Gene Lewis, I was really hooked on reading history.

Beginning in my third year, I became confident that I would succeed in graduating. I began to look around at other things in which to be involved. I joined the student chapter of the American Institute of Chemical Engineers to learn more about the professional aspects of engineering practice at different companies. The student chapter would have engineers and management come and present seminars on the business of chemical engineering. I also joined the Professional Fraternity for Chemical Science, Alpha Chi Sigma. With these student groups that stretched across several classes, my relationships with upper-class engineers expanded. This group tended to be fairly party-oriented. I also joined the American Society for Metals and ended up as the student chapter chair. I got into the Engineering College politics as the Met Engineering Department's representative to the Engineering Tribunal.

One of the social aspects of this learning campaign manifested itself in the "Section Change Party" held on the last Friday of the seven-week classroom section. Chem and Met engineers got together in the basement of one of the Clifton Avenue bars to drink beer, play cards, exchange war stories regarding the last "campaign," and begin to decompress. The primary faculty member involved with these parties was Dr. Bob Price. In my last two years, I got the job of choosing the bar and arranging the details for the Section Change Party.

In this time period, the University of Cincinnati had a large Evening College to facilitate the education of people who worked during the day. One of the benefits UC offered a full-time student was the opportunity to take one course in Evening Collage free of cost. At the start of my senior year, the Metallurgical Engineering Program was offering a three credit-hour course in Advance Physical Metallurgy in Evening College. The course was to be taught by the head of the Metallurgical Engineering Department, Dr. Roy McDuffie. Following my desire to really understand the science underlying the engineering I was studying, I checked to determine if I could take the course and get graduate credit for it. The answer was yes, so I signed up for it. I did not know it at the time, but it would determine the course of my professional career.

By our junior year Chems and Mets separated completely. At this point the class consisted of forty-five Chems and sixteen Mets. The 1963 Met engineering class was split into two sections consistent with the work sections and classroom sections that alternated about every eight weeks or so. My section had nine students with seven in the other section. The room on the first floor of the southwest corner of the Chemistry Building became the place where we convened for lunch, collaboration, and card games at noon and at other free times. I did very well in the various subjects related to metallurgy, and found it very interesting and intellectually stimulating. The areas of process metallurgy and production of metals was fascinating; the art and science of making steel was incredible in terms of how it all came together and how the industry was changing.

With the turn of the calendar year to January 1963, the employment interviewing process for Engineering College started in earnest. The Engineering College provided a template for a resumé and would produce the resumé for the students (in the days before desktop publishing!). I interviewed with a number of companies to get a sense of the nature of the work that would be available. Since I was interested in advancing my knowledge of the science of metals and getting an advanced degree, I wanted to make sure that the work was interesting and on a cutting edge in the development of science of metallurgy and its application in practice. I wanted to make sure that the companies were close to a university that had a graduate-level program in metallurgy, and that they valued competent engineers who put in the extra effort.

Metcut, my co-op employer, was interested in offering me professional employment. As a co-op employee, I had been very adaptable and ready to take on any assignment. But I never had any comments regarding the quantity or quality of the work that I performed. Accepting employment with Metcut meant staying in Cincinnati area. They were interested in my getting an advanced degree and would give me time off and pay my way through graduate school. I really understood their business and the value of the opportunity. The work was technically interesting but not necessarily challenging. It was not close to the cutting edge in metal science; the overhanging questions were, "Where were they willing to go in the future? Would I be challenged?"

I interviewed with many companies. Many of them were defense contractors such as Ling-Temco-Vaught, McDonnell Aircraft, and General Electric; plus a variety of other companies like International Harvester and International Nickel. It was an interesting experience learning how to market myself, and also to learn about the companies, the benefits of working for them, the value they placed on knowledgeable and competent people, and how close they were to a good graduate school. Learning the science of metallurgy was still dominant in my mind.

During this period, Dr. McDuffie received a vacancy announcement from the National Bureau of Standard's Metallurgy Division for a Metallurgist/Metallurgical Engineer, at a GS-7 pay grade, to participate in a research program in electronprobe microanalysis. This was a brand-new field that would be incredibly important in a broad range of activities in production and research in understanding the nature and performance of metals. Dr. McDuffie, knowing of my interest and experience in research, sought me out and gave me the inquiry from the National Bureau of Standards. He had a very high regard for the bureau because of its excellent research in corrosion and electro-metallurgy. This was a very interesting job because of the opportunity to get in on a ground floor of an emerging technology, the nature of the Bureau's program for support for graduate studies, and an entrance-level pay above the nominal government entry pay level of GS-5. This was the job I accepted to start my professional career. On graduating in June of 1963, my next location would be in the Washington, DC, suburbs, in one of the top laboratories in the world.

My immersion in the "cauldron," the University of Cincinnati College of Engineering, was for four years and nine months, from September 1958 through May 1963. My experiences were critically important in my development as a person and setting the framework and course of my professional career. For the grade-school kid who struggled with academics, who could read only at a marginal level, who could not spell, who did not grasp readily the concepts of English grammar, who struggled with arithmetic, I was among the 254 students in the Class of 1963 who graduated. I was in the top 10 percent of the class, was tapped for the Engineering Honorary Fraternity, Tau Beta Pi, and the Metallurgical Engineering Honorary Fraternity, Alpha Sigma Mu.

By graduation I was no longer an intimidated person. I could hold my own in an intellectually challenging venue at the university level. I could stand in front of a large group of people and present my thoughts and viewpoints in a detailed, confident, and coherent manner.

The College of Engineering taught me how to think, to deal effectively with unreasonable pressures and expectations, to systematically analyze the issue being considered, to focus on understanding the full nature of the issue to be resolved, to cherish learning and understanding history, and the value in reading diverse literature.

The college provided a means of paying for my own education, made it possible for me to graduate debt free, provided me the basis for being a competent and confident professional engineer, made me an attractive and desirable individual in the marketplace for engineers, taught me to respect the value of all the employees in the workplace, caused me to become intolerant of technical incompetence but to suffer fools graciously, and fostered an intense curiosity and inquisitiveness about science and engineering.

Before *Star Trek*, UC's College of Engineering provided the intellectual motivation to go where no one has gone before.

Jazz in the Workshop

The Story of the "Queen City Suite"

by Steven Lawrence Gilbert

The sound was great every Monday evening in the Student Union music lounge at the University of Cincinnati. Seventy-five Cincinnatians—some professional musicians, others former professionals, all students of music—gathered to play original compositions, work out their own arrangements, polish their own sound. Some envisioned a new "school" emerging, the unique "no coast" style Larry Gilbert called the School of Queen City Jazz.

It may have been unique in the United States, a union/non-union collaboration with a university, and there it was; the University of Cincinnati Jazz Workshop. Its members attended voluntarily, with no fees, no dogmatic agenda, just a desire to jump into the wondrous sandbox of jazz and play. They played and they heard their work played. They exchanged seats in the twenty-one-piece band—musical chairs—so that everyone got to play. This type of sonic exploratorium was part of the underpinning that made the College-Conservatory of Music a destination for great teachers and talented students and a world-class honor for those who graduated.

CCM in the 1950s was a place for some guys returning from war to rehumanize themselves, heal, regain balance, and reclaim their humanity. These GIs paused their dreams to selflessly serve something bigger than themselves, and stop Luciferian power plagues set in motion by hate and fear. And when those victorious GIs returned with all the scars and endless echoes of horror etched in their souls, their better angels brought them back to a place of calm; to a place where the whisper of their highest calling was again heard, their passionate exploration rekindled. And so, little by little, men young in age, wise well beyond death, directed their thirty-something energies into life, love, families, and the wonders and magic of jazz. They were going to go deep into a place of sonic expression and storytelling. They were going to create some magic. They were also going to cash in their GI Bill to get it done.

On Monday evening, April 4, 1960, at 8:15 P.M. in UC's Wilson Memorial Hall, the workshop's second free "Accent on Jazz" concert got under way. The CCM Jazz Workshop had rehearsed, revised, and stretched boundaries all year long, culminating in this spring showcase concert. Opening with "UC Groove," a dynamic piece written for the occasion by Ron McCrobey, this number let the audience know up front that the band was tight, in the groove, and the evening was going to be fantastic. That was an understatement.

Since its beginning in autumn 1958, the CCM Workshop welcomed all musicians—professional or student. The rehearsals were open. The first concert, in April 1959, brought out 1,300 fans. Leading up to that event, the Big Band's music was borrowed from libraries of other well-known and published groups. Within three years the workshop had its own library, which consisted entirely of the arrangements or compositions of its members.

One of the workshop's best-known members was Clayton "Corky" Mooar, its director. Mooar, who had played trumpet and French horn with the Cliff Lash Band during the early WLW and WLW-T years, said, "I am always amazed that the fellows never seem to get tired. After working all day, three hours [of music] would seem to be enough, but there is always someone who wants to run through something once more and the fellows are always willing."

A member of the board of directors of the Cincinnati Musicians' Association (which cooperated with UC in the workshop), Mooar believed the workshop had far-reaching results in the stimulation of live music in Cincinnati. At least, he said, we've lost some great players to steady gigs. Mooar also was convinced that, in the campus setting and removed from commercialism, dedicated players, composers, and arrangers felt free to explore and express themselves in the jazz idiom to an extent that would be nearly impossible under other conditions.

The first, if not inaugural, workshop Big Band had character all its own. Their three years, 1958–1960, showed what can be accomplished musically with one good band playing the works of several members. The workshop represented the sole musical activity many members engaged in. Many of these players, once professional musicians, had become obligated, family-oriented businessmen. Musical mentors nonetheless, these jazz cats set the CCM stage for future players and students to follow.

Hale Clark, bass trombonist with the Baltimore Symphony Orchestra, joined the workshop six months prior to the 1960 concert. He noted, "The only way to get the 'jazz conception' is to play with such a group as this workshop." Cincinnati Symphony first trombonist Tony Chipburn added, except for the twenty-one-piece workshop band, "there just aren't any bands around with four or five trombones."

It's a big band! And of those twenty-one players, the following were local and national treasures: Trombonists Tony Chipurn and Hale Clark. Trumpets Jack Bauer and Larry Gilbert. Sax men Bill Walters, Ron McCrobey, and Stan Myerson. Flautist Mike Andres. Bassist Tony Helbling. Drummer Fred Lucht. Pianist Lee Stolar. Director, trumpet, and French horn player Clayton "Corky" Mooar.

At that year's concert, the second ever, the jazz workshop also introduced a first—a "themed" journey. "Queen City Suite" was Larry Gilbert's interpretation of the way Cincinnati "looked" in terms of jazz. It's a collection of sights, scenes, and sweet memories of the Queen City that helped keep him sane while fighting Japanese in the jungles of New Guinea.

This Norwood High graduate went from working a Bach trumpet in Coney Island's Moonlite Gardens to working a Browning automatic rifle in that equatorial nightmare. When sent to the rear for R'n' R, he played that horn with some of the most "amazing cats" from the NBC radio orchestra. The players were sluggin' it out and then serving up smiles in the Big Band of the 32nd "Red Arrow" Division. The best damn band in the Pacific War. Totally crazy.

"Larry's Victory mail would usually end with a warning to Don [his youngest brother] to keep practicing piano, and to me," said his younger brother Bob. "Well, Larry wanted me to find and send the hottest new big band charts for the fellas to play."

Bob went on reminiscing, "After the war, when we all got home, we'd sit out on the porch with a beer, and if the Reds weren't on the radio, we'd reminisce about Cincy. [Larry] was so witty, so poetic, and scribbled some hilarious, ribald ditties. He was so talented, he had his union card at thirteen! He said, 'Music is the language of the Universe; it speaks with every emotion we know, an' probably more.' And he explored that universe until the day he died. Man, did he love Cincinnati."

From the Gilbert porch on Lysle Lane, those "views" were transferred onto tablature and crossed the CCM threshold into the Student Union of UC. Corky's fellas read the charts, studied their parts, lit a few cigarettes, and started making that piece sing. "Queen City Suite" is in six parts: "The River," "Fifth and Vine," "Mount Adams," "Ault Park," "Coney Island," and "Going Home."

Jack Bauer, first trumpeter, had quite a hand in "Queen City Suite" performance. Bauer had traveled with Henry Busse, Art Mooney, and Les Elgart, and was no stranger to complex music and technique. So, along with Gilbert's horn chops, the brass were striving to feel it, to really get it.

"The band had been in a stage of development until several weeks before [the concert], when the brass section suddenly emerged with a big, brilliant sound!" Said Jack, "I think we can take this one on the road."

Stan Myerson, saxophone, who once played with Del Courtney on the West Coast, said, "The music in the workshop library is the most difficult and intricate I've ever played." Myerson believed that "Queen City Suite" and some of the band's other original compositions are as good as any ever played. And he, with the rest of the CCM Jazz Workshop, backed Larry Gilbert when he said, "I'd like to see Queen City Jazz become as well-known as West Coast or East Coast jazz."

"The Queen City Suite" was a brilliant performance indeed. The second workshop concert in Wilson Memorial Hall was a success; and somehow an audio copy found its way into Erich Kunzel's audio parlor. He would seem to agree: CCM Jazz Workshop was hot. Kunzel called Gilbert five years later and asked if the Cincinnati Symphony Orchestra might take a crack at it.

They did, Friday after Thanksgiving, 1966. With Sergio Mendes and Brazil '66 in the wings, Kunzel counted it down, and Wow! Pow! Now! It was great!

So, fifty years later, wouldn't it be incredible to hear that again with a tight CCM Big Band? And maybe invite the Cincinnati Symphony Orchestra too?

I'll take center-section seats for every performance.

Reflections

by John Bryant

I arrived on the University of Cincinnati campus in the summer of 1957 following my discharge from the US Army. Originally my plan was to enroll at Kent State University for the beginning of the fall semester. I had stopped off at Kent State as I was making my way by train from Boston, where I was discharged, to Cincinnati, my hometown. I met with the basketball coach and played in a pick-up game so that he could assess my skills.

Once in Cincinnati, I decided to enroll in a summer course at UC so as to prepare myself for the beginning of classes at Kent State. Meanwhile I participated in some pick-up games at my old high school gym. My former coach, John Huheey, was impressed by my physical growth and skill acquisition since I had left high school in 1954. He contacted Ed Jucker, the freshman basketball coach at UC, and suggested that he take a look at me.

"Juck" and I met, and I participated in a pick-up game in the men's gym on the campus. Juck was not present at the pick-up game, but based on the reports from those who were, I was offered a partial scholarship to the University of Cincinnati. I accepted the offer.

I enrolled in the College of Business Administration for the fall semester in 1957 and became a member of the freshman basketball team. My freshman English professor was Herman Newman. Professor Newman took an interest in me because I was a returning veteran, an excellent student, and a member of the basketball team.

Midway through the semester, Professor Newman and I sat down at his request to have a discussion. In the course of the discussion, he suggested that I consider transferring from the College of Business Administration to the College of Teacher Education. He told me frankly that because I was an African American, the College of Business Administration would be unable to place me in any meaningful co-op job. He went on to say that I would be able to make a much greater impact for the good of society in the education arena than in the business arena.

Following our talk, I transferred into the College of Education. I was a member of the University of Cincinnati varsity basketball team for the 1958–59 and 1959–60 seasons and completed my Bachelor of Science in Education degree. Although I had one more year of athletic eligibility, by accelerating my academic program and completing my degree requirements, I had to forfeit my final year of athletic eligibility.

I had excellent grades and a modicum of name recognition by virtue of my competing as a varsity basketball player on the University of Cincinnati basketball teams that had played in the Final Four NCAA basketball tournament in 1957–58 and 1959–60. That notwithstanding, I was unable to get an interview with any of the twenty-four public school districts located in Hamilton County.

I went back to counsel with Herman Newman. He stated that this was an unthinkable situation. I had not used up all of my GI Bill allotment, so I began taking graduate-level courses in the College of Arts & Sciences. Meanwhile Professor Newman began to work on my behalf to reverse the unfairness of the situation.

Carl Hubbard, the placement director for the College of Education, was in Jewish Hospital where he was confined with what would prove to be a terminal illness. Professor Newman went to visit him and managed to bring along to that meeting Forrest Orbaugh, personnel director for the Cincinnati Public Schools.

Newman and his wife, the well-known television personality Ruth Lyons, had an adopted teenage daughter named Candy. It was Candy's job to call me and inform me of the progress of those discussions. One day, Candy called to inform me that her dad wanted me to go to the Cincinnati Board of Education to meet with Forrest Orbaugh.

Following that meeting, I was tendered a contract offer from Cincinnati Public and assigned to Withrow High School for the fall term, where I became one of the first four teachers to integrate the teaching faculty at my old high school. In 1965, I became the first African American to be hired as a head basketball coach in Cincinnati Public. The same year Willard Stargell became the first African American hired as a head football coach in the Cincinnati Public School System.

I continued to take graduate courses at the University of Cincinnati, alternating between the College of Arts & Sciences and the College of Education. I completed my master's of education in the summer of 1967. Dr. Charles Weilbaker conducted the culminating seminar that completed my work for the master's degree. He very strongly encouraged me to apply for the doctoral program.

By this time, I had exhausted all of my GI Bill benefits and had accumulated enough credit hours that I was at the point where I would need to begin full-time residency, as required in the doctoral program.

I returned to teach and coach at Withrow High School for the 1967–68 season. At the conclusion of the season, I began my required residency at the University of Cincinnati. The spring quarter had barely begun when I received a call from George Smith, UC athletic director. Smith had been the head basketball coach when I was a member of the 1958–59 and 1959–60 teams. He was now calling to offer me a position as an assistant basketball coach.

We worked out an arrangement whereby I would complete my year's residency requirement utilizing the spring quarter, the summer quarter, and the fall quarter and become a member of the UC basketball coaching staff. Thus, I became the first African American to hold that position at the University of Cincinnati.

The announcement was scheduled to be made at the end of the basketball season banquet to be held at the Netherland Hilton Hotel in downtown Cincinnati on April 4, 1968. In the midst of dinner being served, the Rev. L. V. Booth went to the microphone at the podium and announced that Dr. Martin Luther King Jr. had been shot in Memphis, Tennessee.

As I reflect back on the stretch from the beginning of my arrival at the University of Cincinnati in 1957 to the completion of my doctorate in 1971, I recall the momentous events of that time: the Montgomery Bus Boycott, the killing of Medgar Evers, the March on Washington, the bombing of the church in Birmingham, the killing of John F. Kennedy, the killing of Freedom Riders James Chaney, Andrew Goodman, and Michael Schwerner, the killing of Viola Liuzzo, the killing of the Rev. James Reeb, the killing of Malcolm X, the killing of Martin Luther King Jr., the shooting of James Meredith, the killing of Robert Kennedy, the horrors of Vietnam, the wounding and killing of students at Kent State University, the wounding and killing of students at Jackson State. It was a turbulent time.

In the mid-1960s the University of Cincinnati was in the process of transitioning from a municipal university to a state university. That transitioning process led to the establishment of a two-year college on the main campus of the university. This institution attracted many nontraditional students.

Dr. Harry Grove retired as president of Central State, located in Wilberforce. He joined the law faculty at the university in the fall of 1968. He was hired as a full professor based on his already demonstrated academic accomplishments. Not only did he become the first African American faculty member in the University of Cincinnati College of Law, he was the first African American to hold the rank of full professor at the University of Cincinnati.

During this time period from 1965 to 1970 the university hired Dr. Vera Edwards in the College of Education, Dr. Bruce Welch in the College of Education, Dr. Lawrence Hawkins as the head of Urban Initiatives, Dr. Thomas Jenkins as head of the Department of Community Planning, Mr. Paul Henry in the Department of Community Planning, Mr. Ron Temple as dean of the University College, Mr. Talmadge Warren in the Admissions Office, Mr. Herschel Hardy in Student Personnel Services, Mr. Rob Ridenour in the Upward Bound Program, Ms. Myrtis Powell as secretary to the dean in the College of Arts & Sciences, and Ms. Dorothy Hardy in the Student Personnel Services Office.

Some of these hires were attributable to the Great Society initiatives of President Lyndon Baines Johnson. Others were attributable to the works of a secretive group called the Committee of 28. This group consisted of fourteen corporate leaders, all of whom were white males, and fourteen males deemed to be leaders within the African American community. Among this latter group were Joseph B. Hall of the Cincinnati Chapter of the Urban League and Dr. Bruce Green of the Cincinnati Chapter of the NAACP.

Both Ralph Ziegler and Lawrence Hawkins confided in me that there was indeed such a committee, that they were members of it, and that they participated in meetings held at Hueston Woods, a retreat center located outside the city of Cincinnati. According to Ralph Ziegler and Lawrence Hawkins no minutes of the meetings were kept.

Representatives of the corporate sector came from Procter & Gamble, the Kroger Company, General Electric, and the Milling Machine. The corporate leaders agreed to begin to hire African Americans into management-level positions within their respective organizations.

The University of Cincinnati was not a member of the Committee of 28; however, the president of the university was invited to one or more of the meetings and he, Dr. Walter Langsam, committed to the hiring of African Americans in faculty, coaching, administrative, and staffing positions.

I was totally unaware of this backdrop when I received the offer of employment as a member of the basketball coaching staff. I suspect that, with the exception of Lawrence Hawkins, the others were as unknowing as I was regarding the negotiating that took place at Hueston Woods. Again, I rely on the testimony of Lawrence Hawkins and Ralph Ziegler: the corporate leaders did not want it to appear that they were succumbing to pressure brought by the African American community.

In March 1963, after four little girls had been killed in Birmingham while attending church service, citizens marched in Cincinnati. There was talk of further marches in downtown Cincinnati as well as economic boycotts of major corporations. I became immediately aware of the push on campus by African American students for the employment of more African American faculty and coaches as well as curricular changes. This push for curricular changes led to the establishment of the African American studies program, which became part of the College of Arts & Sciences.

In subsequent conversations with Judge Nathaniel R. Jones, he confirmed that he was made aware of the existence of the Committee of 28 while serving with the National Advisory Commission on Civil Disorders, known as the Kerner Commission. The commission had been established by President Johnson to determine the root causes of the civil unrest that was sweeping across cities such as Detroit, Cincinnati, and Chicago.

Meanwhile, students and faculty members were petitioning to have a greater voice in the overall governance of colleges and universities. This was clearly the case at the University of Cincinnati. I was in the dual position of being a graduate student writing my dissertation and being a member of the faculty and basketball coaching staff. This status afforded me an opportunity to participate in very intense and contentious discussions in 1970 as to whether or not the university should remain open or close in the wake of the shooting of students at Kent State University in Ohio and Jackson State University in Mississippi.

Many students and many faculty members contended that no meaningful, learning-based, preset course syllabi could take place in such a stressful environment. Others, most representing the administration and the trustees of the university, held a very different position. These persons believed that the university should remain open and that the Ohio National Guard should be brought in to enforce that.

What seemed evident to me as I completed my dissertation and received my doctorate was that the role of colleges and universities in the larger society was being changed in very profound ways. Many felt it was imperative to implement affirmative actions to remedy past collective societal behaviors that negatively impacted the life opportunities of many sectors of the society based on gender, ethnicity, and economic class.

The Provost Doesn't Call There Anymore

by Jon Hughes

Every weekday about 3:30 P.M. he walked into the College Inn, 307 Ludlow Avenue, sat down on his stool, second from the far end of the bar, pulled out his pack of Winston cigarettes from the pocket of his blue work shirt, set it neatly on the bar, put matches on top (never a lighter), wiped moisture off an ice-cold bottle of Bud delivered without a word by Aggie, bartender extraordinaire and part owner, and took a long drink.

The unofficial office hours for Dallas Wiebe, professor of English and comparative literature, scholar, poet, short story writer, novelist, and teacher, were now open for business.

The College Inn, next to the fire station near the corner of Clifton and Ludlow avenues, was from about 1972 to the mid-1980s what we in the writing profession called a writer's bar. If you were a local writer, or visiting writer giving a reading at UC, the College Inn was a destination.

The mid-afternoon was when the regulars sat at the bar. It was too late for lunch drinkers and too early for singles looking for each other. Locals just getting off work, or looking for it, retired folks wanting to get out, and writers and their friends and colleagues gathered. The Departments of Math and Classics were regularly represented with Sociology occasionally making a guest appearance during March Madness.

One beautiful spring afternoon, Nobel Laureate Saul Bellow was sitting by the open front door nursing a beer.

Aggie moved toward the ringing phone at the opposite end of the dark-stained wood bar, past Elmer and Jo, past Smitty, past Graham, past the black-and-white campus images of photographer Walt Burton, picked up the phone, listened, then covered the receiver with her hand.

As was the custom in those days, she would ask if the person requested by the caller was "in." "Dallas," she asked the length of the bar. "You here? It's the provost."

Now those were the days.

So, why am I telling you this story?

What happened in that bar ultimately changed the lives of thousands of students, changed the structure of the largest department (at that time) in the McMicken College of Arts & Sciences, and was the foundation for several majors and one new department.

How it happened is almost like a recurring joke: Two professors are sitting in a bar, drinking beer and smoking. One says to the other: "I have an idea. What do you think of this?" The other replies: "Not bad. Let's do it this way."

This started a conversation about a writing certificate program. Then it became a proposal to their department. Some forty years later, that offbeat, out-of-the-box idea evolved into the University of Cincinnati Department of English Writing Program, one of best writing programs in the nation.

Let's back up and put this into perspective. The first half of the 1970s was interesting and unique for many reasons. Nationally, the generation-splitting Vietnam War was coming to a close and a president was about to resign in disgrace. The status of celebrity was granted to those who actually did something extraordinary. To those who appreciated literature, writers were rock stars.

And those literary rock stars often visited UC.

The early to mid-1970s were a heady time in the Department of English. The Elliston endowment brought some of the best writers to campus for readings and residences. In 1972 visiting writers included John Ashbery, Saul Bellow, Wendell Berry, and Galway Kinnell. In the mid-1970s visiting writers included Robert Bly, Gwendolyn Brooks, Louise Gluck, David Ignatow, Denise Levertov, Norman Mailer, Allen Ginsburg, James Merrill, Charles Simic, Gary Snyder, James Tate, Philip Levine, Jorge Luis Borges, and Diane Wakoski.

The English Department, the campus center of literary research and criticism, had two full-time members who taught literature and/or criticism who were also creative writers attracting national attention for their work: Austin Wright, a professor of literature and criticism, published *Camden's Eyes* in 1969 and *First persons: a novel* in 1973, both to critical acclaim; Dallas Wiebe, professor of literature, published the infamous, banned in Farmington, NY, *Skyblue the Badass* in 1969 and co-founded the *Cincinnati Poetry Review* in 1975.

There were no full-time writers in the department. It was not until 1972 that the director of Freshman English (now Composition) had an advanced degree in composition. Prior to then Freshman English was directed by a literary scholar.

The few creative writing courses that existed were taught on the rare occasion when a qualified faculty member was able to get a release from a literature course.

I became a regular at the College Inn about 1973. My walk home from Mc-Micken Hall to the Roanoke Apartments on Ludlow took me right by the front door and most often inside.

Weekday afternoons, any time after 3 P.M., there was Bud and passionate conversations. Story ideas were born. Many died a merciful death. Still others evolved into published poems, short stories, and novels. It was an exciting time for me, an experienced newspaper reporter turned academician, eager to learn and practice what Tom Wolfe called "The New Journalism."

Tobacco smoke hung in the neon-lit, windowless shotgun tavern. The thumping, clicking, ringing pinball machine never stopped eating dimes.

Aggie managed the bar slipping a fresh beer on deck before the last was consumed. Norb, her husband and co-owner, occasionally emerged from the back room, his activities always a mystery.

I met Dallas sometime my first year teaching at UC. I was working at a newspaper in Michigan in 1972 and saw an ad in *Editor & Publisher*, the industry trade publication, for a student media adviser and assistant professor of English. I interviewed on campus in August and moved to Cincinnati with my family about two weeks later. I don't think there was a short list, just me. I lucked out.

Dallas was a curmudgeon to those individuals he found dull and bigoted. His intolerances were legendary: ignorance, sentimentality, injustice, and no sense of irony, which he often found amusing. (He was critical of his home state: "Before you enter Kansas there should be signs: 'No Irony Allowed.'"). After he refused to be one of the Jolly Boys, a secret society of male professors in the McMicken College of Arts & Sciences who selectively invited others to belong, Dallas formed the Melancholy Boys, composed of all the men and women in the world who were not Jolly Boys. This idea gave him great pleasure.

One of my predecessors, Linda Faaborg, began to develop the journalism curriculum before she moved on to an administrative position. She is responsible for making the position tenure-track and in many ways for beginning the process that ultimately resulted in the Writing Program, the BA degree in journalism, and the Department of Journalism.

My first two years as advisor to the *News Record* and the launching of *Clifton* magazine (one of the major reasons I came to UC) were interesting, exciting, sometimes frustrating, and greatly influenced my life-long support of the student media. I also developed friendships that endure to today. I was twenty-seven years old when I took the job, not much older than the students I taught.

By 1974 I made a request to become a full-time, tenure-track faculty member of the Department of English and Comparative Literature. Dallas supported that request as did, I assume, a majority of the faculty, making me the first full-time professor specifically hired to teach writing. With that second stroke of good luck, the door was opened for hires in creative writing in addition to journalism.

The groundwork for change was set. Journalism was drawing a large number of students and creative writing was beginning to do the same. Since the late 1960s a unique creative dissertation was an option for PhD students.

Afternoon conversations at the College Inn led to hours of research—What universities have writing programs? What do they include/exclude? Undergraduate or graduate emphasis?—followed by months of forming a proposal and selling it to colleagues. Poet Jim Bertolino was hired and helped form the final proposal.

The literature faculty stepped up and supported a proposal for writing certificates in creative writing (poetry, fiction), journalism, and something we knew nothing about. A colleague suggested that the third area of professional writing (business and technical writing) be included in the proposal because it would develop over the years. And it did. The three writing certificates grew quickly and expanded into MA concentrations in creative writing, editing and publishing (not sustainable), and professional writing in the 1990s. The creative PhD dissertation began to attract many outstanding candidates.

The College Inn became Arlin's after Aggie and Norb retired and sold the bar. The new name was a combination of the owner's names: Art and Linn. Next it became a jazz bar and then was bought by a local businessman.

I was last in the bar ten years ago. The characters I wanted to see were no longer there. The black-painted drywall covering the windows was removed sometime after the bar was purchased from Aggie and Norb. There were no literary conversations. No smoke.

And, the provost doesn't call there anymore.

For the *Record*

by Judy McCarty Kuhn

We were the new generation. Some called us "Baby Boomers," but we weren't babies anymore. We were, instead, pioneers on the New Frontier. We had nodded agreement when John Kennedy declared, in his inaugural address, "Let us begin anew."

It was the mid-1960s. New buildings were sprouting up all over the University of Cincinnati. The Student Union was under renovation, and by September 1965, we would work in new offices and eat at new venues. Before graduation, a new high-rise women's dorm would open, a new parking garage would house our cars, and the College-Conservatory of Music would move to a new building crowned by a new organ.

For those of us interested in the issues of the day, "new" took on a special meaning. We were the news reporters for the *News Record*.

Like most things new, we had a spirit of hope and humor.

We were a motley crew of volunteer editors and writers. UC had no journalism program then, but some staff members did successfully pursue media careers. Most of us became engineers, nurses, teachers, designers, architects, musicians, accountants, lawyers, sociologists, pharmacists, or physicians. We experienced the assassination of a president, the live-on-TV killing of his alleged murderer, the passing of the 1964 Civil Rights Act and the Gulf of Tonkin Resolution, and intensified racial tension in America. We watched the first campus protests against Vietnam and the counterdemonstrations in favor of the government. We listened as President Lyndon Johnson ordered an increase in US troops in South Vietnam from 75,000 to 125,000.

Despite national events and controversies, we worked diligently to provide campus news. "Our overall goal is to bring an interesting, worthwhile newspaper to the students and faculty members each week which will encourage them to attend an upcoming convocation, participate in some worthwhile venture, or voice an opinion on an important issue," stated 1965–66 editor Sharon Hausman.

We coped with the draft, the war, student government, and national controversy by finding humor in the worst of situations. Cartoonists Keith Kleespies and Jim Ellis were irony experts. Photographers John Rabius and Frank Farmer caught campus antics on film. Writers spent weeks polishing April Fool articles. A few years later, in 1969, the staff cancelled the April Fool edition, saying, "We couldn't help but notice that there's not too much in the world which is very funny." How quickly times changed. Where had all the humor gone?

Even though the paper was published weekly on Thursdays, we rarely had a day off. Staff members covered stories, photographed events, designed pages, proofed galleys, and attended post-mortem meetings. The editor-in-chief accomplished those tasks and more. "The editor was not just a figurehead," said Hausman. "We were at the office or the print shop late every evening, and often took work home to review. Sometimes I was the only available reporter to cover a speech or event. The editor never said 'no.'"

This wasn't the computer era. The new generation worked with typewriters and letterpress printing. There was no UC Webpage, YouTube, Facebook, Twitter, texting, or email. If you wanted UC news, you looked in the *News Record*.

Our goal was to create more work for ourselves: we wanted to print the *News Record* twice weekly. "Worthwhile news" was timely news. Because of our weekly publication and slow letterpress process, some events went unreported for ten days. The paper did have one significant asset—our weekly issues were mailed to every student. The newspapers in our mailboxes glued the "townies" and the "dormies" together. But even the mailing had a downside—it added delivery time to the process.

Reading the *News Record* was often similar to time travel. When John Kennedy was assassinated on Friday, November 22, 1963, Thursday's paper arrived in my mailbox on Saturday. How strange to read about the upcoming Miami–UC football game and all the festivities. The game had been cancelled; Camelot was gone; and I lived in another world.

Most of us didn't apply to work on the paper; we were simply drafted. In the late summer of 1964, Hausman, associate editor at the time, phoned me. Sharon knew I had taken journalism classes in high school and been a section editor of my yearbook.

"Do you want to be the social editor of the *News Record*? Our social editor transferred to Miami, and we need a replacement." That phone call began my three-year *News Record* career leading to the editor-in-chief's office.

Larry Shuman, editor-in-chief in 1964–65, also fell into his *News Record* career. "I got involved in the paper because a fraternity brother of mine was the sports editor. I always kidded him about the sports reporting, and he challenged me to do something about it; so I became a sports reporter. Somehow, I jumped from sports reporter to editor-in-chief."

Despite my "back-door" invitation to join the paper, the three *News Record* rooms in the basement of the Student Union became my second home in 1964–65. The main room housed my desk, the theater staff, feature department, sports desk, and news staff. The news department took up an entire wall.

News editor Diane Lundin had more pages to fill than any of us, but her staff always finished at least an hour before us. She had a knack for delegating responsibility. Members of the news staff knew exactly what to do, worked quickly, and left immediately. It was a revolving door on that side of the room.

The room to the right was the business office. The business staff had a dart game. Frequently, the sports guys would barge in and take over the business office, claiming they needed more space. Usually, they simply wanted to toss a few darts. To the left was the office of the editor-in-chief and associate editor. Most of us were rarely in the "hallowed hall" except for staff meetings.

Dirty coffee cups, empty Coke bottles, old plates with dried food sat on desks, tables, and file cabinets. There were so many fruit flies that a biology major could have experimented all year. One little window sat high in the wall and looked onto a window well. The noise was unbearable. The university was remodeling and building an addition to the Student Union. Besides our talking and typing, we heard the buzzing of saws and pounding of hammers. Big plastic sheets hung around the workmen as they demolished and plastered. The sheets were moved constantly, and we faced frequent detours. One day one stairway would be blocked; another day, another.

At least we were in the Union, close to the food venues and the action. Our friends on the *Cincinnatian* yearbook staff worked in the stadium press box.

We typed our copy on gridded yellow sheets of paper. The color became a staff joke—was that the origin of "yellow journalism"? If I used a pica typewriter, double spaced, and stayed between the margins, the grid would tell me the number of column inches. It wasn't scientific, but it worked fairly well—until somebody used an elite typewriter.

Editor Larry Shuman was studying engineering, but he claimed to be a psychology major. Nobody believed an engineer could have the time or the interest to run the *News Record*. Thin and wearing dark-rimmed glasses, Larry reminded me of Jimmy Olsen. Frequently, Larry jokingly wrote "The Daily Planet" in the nameplate section as he sketched out the front page.

Our advisor, Mr. George Stevens, wore many hats. He taught two journalism classes and advised the Publications Board, the *Cincinnatian*, the literary magazine *Profile*, the Student Directory, the faculty-ranking guide *Insight*, humor magazine *Draught*, and the honorary journalism society Pi Delta Epsilon as well as the *News Record*.

The elder *News Record* staff members were our mentors. Mike Hesse, news reporter, was our writing instructor. Eleanor Hicks answered our international questions. Randall Maxey gave us a conscience and taught us to be inclusive.

When we entered the office, our diverse staff merged into a special clan with a common identity. "I" and "we" became synonyms. We spoke newspaper jargon, but we also created our own. When Sharon Hausman conversed with Mike Friedman and Dana Braun of the news desk, outsiders were completely lost. A friend once asked me, "Are they speaking English?" We blended our regional vocabularies. An East Coast staffer asked me to bring him a "soda" from the Grill. I came back with a chocolate one. "No," he said. "I wanted a Coke—what you call a soft drink!" Before long, I asked for sodas too. And the Cincinnati "please" soon became part of the *News Record* vocabulary.

One staff meeting, about three months into the year, Larry gave me a dirty look and said, "When are *you* going to the press?" I had no idea that editors had more to do. So I agreed to "go to the press," whatever that meant.

It meant more work. Sharon drove me "to the press" one Monday after the paper went to bed. We delivered some copy and all the page layouts. All photos, drawings, and some copy had been sent in on Friday afternoon. The "press" was the Western Hills Publishing Company, printers of two local newspapers, wedding invitations, flyers, business catalogs, and the *News Record*. The "press" used old-fashioned, letterpress technology.

The thermometer read 20 degrees the first week I went to press. Because the machines were hot, there was no additional heat in the area. Besides being freezing cold two feet away from the machines, the room was dirty, crowded, and busy. Big Linotype machines sat against the walls. The pressmen keyed on what appeared to be typewriters at the bottom of huge metal contraptions that soared over their heads. Every minute or so, lead slugs of type would pop out of the bottom of the machines. Then rows of type would be set in a form, covered with a roll of ink, and printed into a galley sheet. It was our job to proof the galleys. Because of the cold, we wore gloves while we worked. It was difficult to write on the newsprint with gloves on. When we found an error, the pressmen would retype the line, run another galley, and we'd reedit.

That was the Monday work. "That wasn't so bad," I thought. "I can do this at least twice a month."

"What time are you out of class on Tuesdays?" Sharon asked on our way back to the university. "Tomorrow, we review the actual pages."

So we went back the next afternoon. When we arrived, there were copies of each page ready for inspection. There were bare spots where we'd miscalculated story length. Headlines were too short or too long. We improvised, adding here, dropping there to make things fit. Sharon had a knack for spontaneous revision.

It seemed to take hours for the copy to be printed out when corrections were made. Soon we all learned to read upside down and backward. We could check corrections before they were printed, when they were only on the metal slugs. Most of us still have that skill. Never underestimate a former *News Record* staffer when he is sitting across from you at a desk. We can read anything you might try to hide.

While I was writing about parties and fashions and Larry and Sharon were managing every aspect of the paper, our nation was embroiled in the beginnings of the Vietnam conflict. On August 2, 1964, about the time Sharon was tapping me for social editor, the destroyer USS *Maddox* engaged three North Vietnamese navy torpedo boats in the Gulf of Tonkin. The United States claimed a second incident occurred on August 4, 1964.

Soon after, Congress passed the Gulf of Tonkin Resolution, which granted President Johnson the authority to assist any Southeast Asian country jeopardized by "Communist aggression." Only two senators dissented.

That October, the freedom of expression issue emerged at "the other UC"— Berkeley, California. "Freedom Summer" veterans set up a table at Berkeley to encourage students to work for civil rights within the community. It was against UCB policy to use campus grounds for noncampus activities. The result was the famous Mario Savio–police car incident, arrests, and a subsequent sit-in at Berkeley.

Of course, we were completely unaware of the future significance of the events in Washington or California. The *News Record* was more interested in the '64 Olympics and UC's George Wilson, member of the gold medal basketball team. George had been our sports columnist the previous year.

Larry might have "kidded" his way to the editorship, but he certainly understood the role of the student press. He believed that the faculty wanted a more liberal policy, the administration desired a more conservative stand, and the student body didn't care as long as we were attacking something. And we were always satisfying the student body.

Our reporters thrived on the irony and word play in the presidential election of 1964. Johnson, who had acted on the Gulf of Tonkin situation, ran on a peace campaign. Barry Goldwater's slogan was "In your heart, you know he's right"—not only a statement of Goldwater's "correctness," but also a pun on his conservatism. The *News Record* covered a Cincinnati Johnson speech and noted LBJ's retort: "Some people say we are wild spenders, but in their hearts they know they're wrong."

After LBJ's inauguration, the Vietnam conflict escalated, and UC witnessed its first antiwar protest. "Students Against the War in Vietnam," a small group of students, professors, and outside demonstrators, paraded near the Student Union. "Students for a Strong Stand in Vietnam" marched near the war protesters. After the police arrived, the protest moved to Siddall. The event lasted for two days.

The protest news added more copy to our small, weekly paper. We dreamt of a semi-weekly or a daily. We didn't need space just for news; our mailbox was stuffed with letters to the editor. One week we had so many argumentative letters that the headline read, "Our Rabid Readers Rage On." Most writers complained that demonstrators blocked pathways to class and denied students the right to an education.

To alleviate the chaos, the *News Record* advocated the establishment of a "Free Speech Alley," similar to one at Louisiana State University. "The Alley [at LSU] is open once a week and students can speak on any topic they choose," the editorial stated. "The forum...now attracts several hundred students for each session."

The Free Speech Alley was intended for more than debate on Vietnam. Columnist Randall Maxey and the Council on Inter-race Relations had been discussing racial stereotyping and insensitivity. The 1965 Voting Rights Bill, introduced in March, was a major national issue. The spoken "Alley" would educate the campus and help bridge the racial divide at UC. And, the Alley would be timelier than the *News Record.*

After reading the complaint letters, the activists switched tactics; instead of parades, "frequent flyers" were thrust in our faces as we walked to class. Within one week, "literature proposing the immediate removal of U.S. forces from Vietnam was distributed along with a petition supporting an even stronger stand in that area. . . . Finally, the ridiculous reached the sublime when someone circulated a petition to end all petitions."

The coup de grace occurred with the "Students for Constitutional Freedom" attempted to show an antiwar film called *Vietnam, 1963.* After running for only a few minutes, federal customs agents from Cleveland, backed up by the FBI and the Cincinnati police, seized the film. Produced in Vietnam, it had allegedly arrived in the United States illegally.

As it turned out, the film was returned and shown on campus the next week. This time, the projector was not working correctly. A member of the ACLU wrote the *News Record,* suggesting that the "technical difficulties" were only related to controversial films!

We made little headway with the Free Speech Alley but found editorial success with "The Secretarial Screen." Lack of student access to administrators was a common complaint, especially for Larry. "Secretaries appear to overprotect college administrators from the student body, while practicing the time-tested bureaucratic device known as 'rerouting.'"

President Walter Langsam responded to the complaints by stressing "secretaries should not screen students who wish to see professors and other staff members." After the editorial and the president's remark, the situation improved.

Currently a dean—senior associate dean at the University of Pittsburgh— Larry recently remarked, "I am now a dean, but do make sure that students aren't screened out—that editorial has always stuck with me."

Larry and our mentors graduated in 1965, and the1965–66 staff was born. Sharon Hausman was editor-in-chief; News Editor Diane Lundin was now associate editor; Barb Shale was business manager; and I was copy and technical editor. For the first time since World War II, women ran the *News Record.*

When school began in September 1965, the $6 million Student Union was completed. A bowling alley sat near our old offices, which were now meeting rooms. Our new offices were on the top floor, just up an escalator. Our suite of three huge rooms, numbers 411, 413, and 415, had windows overlooking the university campus. Just down the hall was the faculty club, a formal restaurant, and the President's Dining Room.

All sorts of dignitaries could be seen coming off the escalator and turning toward the new venues. Whenever a guest speaker arrived at the university, President Langsam would host a lunch or dinner at the Student Union. On one occasion, I covered a president's luncheon for Toughy the Tiger and his trainer, a UC graduate. Toughy, who arrived at the luncheon in a cage and was on his way to the Cincinnati Zoo, had posed for Humble Oil advertisements.

Around the corner from our area were the offices of the other student publications (the yearbook was no longer housed in the press box), a darkroom, and the student government offices. The plan was to encourage communication between publications and student leaders.

In the new Union, we had our own mailboxes, new desks, lots of phones, and even new typewriters. Some might say it was idyllic. Photographers loved it, but the rest of us complained. We were too far from the cheap food venues. And the "sterile" nature of the office was just wrong. The old one had an authentic "pressroom" feel. One afternoon, the news staff grabbed a janitor and found the Union storage area. They retrieved an old desk from the former office and plopped it down in 413.

And then there was the issue of the escalator. Sharon thought it cost about the same amount as a printing press. "They should have spent the money on our own press," she'd say. "We could have published at least twice a week." When the escalator was down, she'd tell us that the press was out of order.

The protesters, who now called themselves "Students for a Democratic Society" (SDS), and their mentors—young instructors in the English Department— soon found our new offices. SDS members and their teacher-advisors recognized the power of the press and became active letter-writers. Rolfe Wiegand, a leader in the group, joined our staff and penned the "Crackerbarrel" column.

Campus polarization came to a head one afternoon when Max Rafferty spoke on campus. Rafferty, the director of education for the State of California, was the author of a syndicated newspaper column. Rafferty opposed "group adaptation" and "life adjustment" education. In a 1961 speech, he had responded to the free speech movement in California by stating that current students were "growing up to become . . . side-burned, duck-tailed, unwashed, leather-jacketed slobs."

I covered the program, which was sponsored by Young Americans for Freedom, a conservative organization. I was excited—it was to be my first news byline. Rafferty was a famous figure, and I expected a crowd. Instead, the auditorium was practically empty.

A rather small, quiet group had attended the Rafferty speech, but less than 100 yards away a verbal battle was held on the library steps. A poet and one "letter-writing English Instructor" seemed to be in charge as students passed by, stopped, and listened to various topics including Vietnam, Santo Domingo, draft card burning, and Chicago politics. Some listeners were sitting in open windows three stories up in the library. The demonstration was obviously planned by SDS to dissuade attendance at the Rafferty speech.

The discussion appeared to be over when the poet took off to the men's room, and the professor to his class. The crowd continued to hang around. Someone called in an erroneous report of a fight in the area, and the police arrived. One officer jokingly told our reporter, "Mattresses should be placed in the drop beneath the overpass to the library due to the perches that some of the students had assumed."

I did get my byline, but the library-perch-mattress distraction was the real story. Yet that story lacked a "perching" picture. The photo deadline had passed.

The week after "Max and Mattresses," another demonstration, this time filled with rowdy outsiders, resulted in pro-government bystanders burning SDS leaflets. Although the *News Record* staff tried to be unbiased, our headline on November 18 indicated our feelings: "UC Students Exposed to More Anti-Vietnam Propaganda." Sharon responded with another editorial about the Free Speech Alley. This time, the editorial suggested that regular sessions of the Alley be limited to UC students and faculty. More letters rolled in. We ran out of space.

In the first issue published by the 1965–66 staff, Sharon's editorial stated, "We hope to serve as a stimulus to public opinion and welcome the views of our readers" ("A 'New' Year"). My copy and technical staff read all articles before they shipped off to the press. Reading numerous letters to the editor made us realize just how stimulating we were. We could have easily filled an entire edition with letters alone. We crusaded for a vocal Free Speech Alley, and we achieved a written one in the pages of the *News Record*.

The protest movement quieted down in the winter of 1966, but the campus hadn't forgotten Vietnam. Dabney Hall ran "Operation First Aid," a supply drive for the displaced in South Vietnam. The AFROTC Kitty Hawk Drill Team sent a doctor bag and instruments to a desperate physician in Loc Dien. UC's chapter of World University Service aided the college students of Saigon. At the Vietnam WUS-House in Saigon, students studied by kerosene lanterns. Fundraising on American campuses provided electrical wiring, a health clinic, mimeograph equipment, and a library.

Al Huneke, owner of the Western Hills Publishing Company, donated to the WUS cause. When I thanked him, he asked me, "Are you going to be the editor next year? We're moving to offset." Encouraged by Mr. Huneke, editor Sharon Hausman, and the promise of offset printing, I applied for editor-in-chief.

I began my editorship in May 1966. We had two major goals: to focus on concerns of the student body, and to expand to semi-weekly in 1967–68. The move to offset printing would change our world and open up new possibilities.

The first topic of the new staff was an all-campus concern—the draft. When we think of the Vietnam War draft, the lottery system comes to mind. But the lottery did not exist in 1966. Everyone seems to believe that all college men were granted deferments. That's not completely true. If enrolled in a full-time college program, the 1-SC deferment was a "mandatory statutory deferment to which each student is entitled once," according to Dean of Men William Nester.

At the end of the first school year, cases were reevaluated. The next step was a 2-S deferment. This deferment was based on class standing. At the end of his freshman year, a man had to rank in the top half of his class; at the end of his sophomore year, he had to rank in the top two-thirds; at the end of his junior year, in the top three-fourths.

In 1966, 1.7 million college men had 2-S deferments.

One afternoon, staff members huddled around a desk in the *News Record* office reading a copy of an exchange newspaper from the University of Michigan. Five Michigan freshmen had collected over $150 in nickels and dimes to purchase a full-page ad in the *Michigan Daily*. In large letters, the ad asked girls to withhold knowledge on exams. This, the freshmen claimed, would elevate the class standing of guys in the draft pool.

Jim Ellis, a *News Record* cartoonist, followed up with a humorous "ad" of his own on the editorial page. In clever script, it read:

!Girls!
Do YOUR part

to save our generation.

As you know

UNCLE SAM

has designs upon college students in the

LOWER half!

So it is up to you girls.

HELP SAVE OUR YOUNG MEN

—Do your part now—

!FLUNK!

Not long after, the Selective Service announced that class ranks had to include men only. Guys couldn't count on the girls trying to be stupid.

News Editor Lauralee Sawyer asked the dean of men to explain the draft system in an article, and the staff interviewed UC Registrar Garland Parker regarding the class rank issue. The registrar said, "A student may determine his class ranking by finding out the all-men's average for the past quarter. If his average falls below this, consider taking the Selective Service Draft Test." To be eligible for 2-S, an undergraduate had to score 70 percent on the test.

The *News Record* printed a news release from the University of Richmond *Collegian* in our May 19 issue. The *Collegian* had received a free copy of *Barron's How to Prepare for the Student Draft Deferment Test*. Although the test was supposed to be on the level of an average high school senior, the Richmond paper sarcastically stated, "The vocabulary section alone would cause consternation to a PhD in English."

When the 1966–67 year began in late September, we increased our staff and planned for the semi-weekly move. Not only did we expand our personnel; we also enlarged the *News Record*'s size. In 1964, we published sixteen pages a week. When Sharon was editor, we expanded to twenty-four and more. By 1967, we ran as many as thirty-six. The entire staff—both editorial and business—greeted new members and worked to fill up the additional space.

Dave Altman, associate editor, had an amazing ability to find columnists with diverse talents and ideas. He recruited Clinton Hewan, a young man from Jamaica. Clinton observed and reported campus prejudices from a "de Tocqueville" outsider position. Like Randall Maxey before him, Clinton helped bridge the racial divide. Clinton also spoke out for campus women. When the first coed ran for student body president, Clinton endorsed her in his column, saying she was a "fresh new start."

Another new writer was Dave Bowring, who had recently served in the air force. His column provided an opposing view to "Crackerbarrel." The culture shock of watching demonstrators (one week, they wore gas masks), meeting anti-war writers in the *News Record* office, and trying to buy lunch at the hippie-filled Union Rhine Room affected the former air force man. In one column, "Our Zoo," Dave described the various "animals" and their scents in the Rhine Room. "These creatures may be observed in animated circumstances about twice a month in the vicinity of the Union, wildly waving their therapy placards and orating in pleading guttural tones." We received numerous letters that week.

After viewing one too many protests, Councilman Mark Painter (later a judge for thirty years, including on the Ohio Court of Appeals and United Nations Appeals Tribunal) proposed a resolution asking for Student Council's approval of the United States' position in Vietnam. The council constitution gave the assembly power to enact and enforce "legislation within the scope of its expressed and implied powers." Amendment G granted power to "express the opinion of the student body on issues presented to it."

For over two years, the *News Record* staff and "Ponderer" columnist Mike Patton had advocated the revision of council's constitution, particularly questioning the legality of Amendment G. "Crackerbarrel" Rolfe wrote, "How can anyone decide and announce what another man thinks?"

An All Student Governments Assembly was held Saturday, October 29 to discuss the issue. To add to all the confusion, Student Court issued an injunction. They were concerned that "Amendment G" had been unconstitutionally added to the document. At least for the time being, council could not speak for the entire student body.

Over 250 leaders were invited to the Saturday morning Assembly. It happened to be the same day as the UC-Tulsa football game. The game was especially exciting: ABC telecast it regionally with eleven million viewers over twelve states. The game began at 2:15 Saturday. Because of all the hoopla, fewer than forty student leaders remained through the entire assembly. They voted 25–7 in favor of council's right to express opinion on issues "of our time for the entire student body." One voter mentioned, "If we attempted to separate the two [national and student issues] we'd spend all our time in Student Court."

The Student Council met a few days later. Twenty-five members needed to be present for a quorum. There were exactly twenty-six members present. One of those was the council president. He only voted in the case of ties. To appease the court, council reworded the proposal: "RESOLVED: Members of the Student Council of the University of Cincinnati do hereby express their support of the effort by American and allied forces to assist the people of South Vietnam to defend their country against armed aggression and to create a climate favorable to liberty and free choice."

The vote was taken. Thirteen members voted in favor of the proposition, eight against. Four abstained. It passed.

"Crackerbarrel" called the wordplay a "semantical quickie trick." Keith Kleespies drew a cartoon showing an anxious messenger approaching a startled Ho Chi Minh. The messenger cried, "Ho Chi! I have terrible news! The University of Cincinnati Student Council has.. . . ." Almost fifty years later, Judge Mark Painter said, "As in the Iraq War, knowing what we later knew, I would have offered a very different resolution."

During the winter of 1967, more national events bombarded our pages. In February, we learned that the Central Intelligence Agency had been funding the National Student Association (NSA) and using its employees as spies. President Johnson claimed he knew nothing about the funding and immediately ordered the CIA to stop secret aid to student associations. We also heard complaints from SDS regarding FBI surveillance of its activities. We questioned racial inequity in the draft system and FBI investigation of African American student leaders. In April, approximately 100,000 people demonstrated in New York and heard Martin Luther King Jr. speak against the war.

Local stories sat next to the national ones, often dwarfed by the issues of the 1960s. Campus articles, however, were always our top priority. After two coeds reported assaults, the *News Record* and Student Council led a campaign to improve campus security. The campaign led to the installation of high-intensity lighting in parking areas, K-9 Corps coverage of campus, and a 90 percent increase in patrolman-hours.

In 1967, the Free Speech Alley, Sharon Hausman's two-year-old dream, was finally approved. The rules and location, however, were still under discussion. The Alley did not begin until the fall of 1968.

The "Local Story of the Year" broke in January when the Ohio Board of Regents supported a plan proposing state affiliation for the university. President

Langsam stated, "UC students would be benefited because of lower fees . . . the benefit to the University would come from the acquisition of a broader financial base without the loss of local ties and support."

Keith Kleespies followed the story with a cartoon. An elephant named "UC" towered over Ohio's governor and an Ohio resident. The citizen said, "Well, Governor, now that we've bought it, what are we going to do with it?"

There were many hurdles ahead before reaching state affiliation, but the Ohio State Senate was already considering the appropriate bill. In 1968, UC entered a transitional period to become a "municipally sponsored, state-affiliated" institution. In 1977, UC became one of Ohio's state universities.

At my final Publications Board meeting in April 1967, the semi-weekly fate of the *News Record* was determined. Dave Altman, the new editor, and I teamed up to show our progress in staff growth, efficiency, quality, and newspaper size. There was just one glitch in the plan—could we afford to mail the *News Record* twice a week? We fought for the mailing. I had believed since my freshman year that the mailing glued the university together. The board wanted to save the mailing costs. Newspaper holders could be set in prime campus locations.

The board approved the semi-weekly schedule. Our primary goal of the year was realized; we would have timely news. But we lost the mailing. The issue of May 25, 1967, was the last mailed issue of the University of Cincinnati *News Record*. It was a bittersweet day.

The move to a semi-weekly was not only the accomplishment of the1966–67 *News Record*; staffs led by Larry Shuman and Sharon Hausman set the foundation for our success. For three years, dedicated volunteers in news, sports, theater, social, opinion, graphics, photography, advertising, and business worked toward a common goal. We weren't just an organization—we were a team. Sometimes things were tense; sometimes frustrating; often humorous; but constantly exhilarating.

During my years on the *News Record*, the university administration didn't always agree with our views, but was forever cooperative. John DeCamp, the public relations officer, was the lifeline to news we would never have been able to discover ourselves. When he retired in 1967, we saluted him in an editorial. Only once in all three years did Mr. Stevens censor us—and it was over just one word. *Mary Poppins* had premiered in the summer of 1964. We wanted to use that "very special *Mary Poppins* word" in a headline. Mr. Stevens had not seen the film, did not know the word, and refused to allow us to use it. We weren't too angry—after all, it would not have fit in five columns of 36-point type.

But it was our word—the newest word for the new generation. It describes, better than any other, our *News Record* camaraderie and our semi-weekly accomplishment. Mr. Stevens would probably agree.

"Supercalifragilisticexpialidocious."

Where It All Began

A Very Short Play with Some Music, Wherein the University of Cincinnati is Revealed to Be the Most Unlikely Place for the Nation's First Musical Theater Program

by Jack Rouse with Helen Laird

"The art of making art is putting it together"
    —Stephen Sondheim, *Sunday in the Park with George*

Setting: A cozy living room in a neat house on a quiet street in Haddonfeld, New Jersey. It is a crisp afternoon in November 2015. Helen Laird and Jack Rouse chat while one of their former students, Madeline Carvalho Lanicani, fixes lunch. Madeline and Jack have driven down from New York to visit Helen and reminisce about their co-creation at the University of Cincinnati that changed the profile of music conservatories and music curriculums all over the country.

The Overture from Leonard Bernstein's Candide *is heard playing softly in the background.*

JACK (*referring to the music*)
…still one of the best pieces of musical theater ever written…

HELEN
…Or is it an opera?

MADELINE
Or does it really matter?
There is a pause while they drink their coffee. Music from Candide *swells and then fades into the background.*

JACK

So, do you think it was one of those aha moments…

MADELINE

…or Divine guidance…

HELEN

Maybe we just didn't know any better…

JACK

or maybe we were damn lucky…

MADELINE (*from the kitchen*)

Perhaps a bit of all three… (*the old friends laugh a bit*)

JACK

Did you think it was really going to work? There at the University of Cincinnati of all places!?!

HELEN

Well, how could we know unless we tried. What about you? Did you believe?

JACK

Guess I never thought we had an option. It was only my second teaching gig… and I was being hired to head a musical theater program? What's that all about? With everyone depending on me I sure didn't want to fail.

HELEN

And some thought it was a bit of a stretch from my days on opera stages in Europe. (*She sings a few bars of one of her favorite arias. Madeline joins in. More memories, more laughter.*)

JACK

…for you to challenge academia with a totally new program.

HELEN

We knew it was going to work because we knew the problem was not unsolvable.

MADELINE

What problem was that?

HELEN

Teaching singers how to act. It had to be done. Someone was going to do it, why not us. *"Something's Coming" from* West Side Story *is heard quietly in the background.*

Who are these people? And what are they talking about? Well, about fifty years ago Helen and Jack were responsible for establishing the first musical theater program in the United States at the College-Conservatory of Music at the University of Cincinnati. Madeline was a voice/opera major at the conservatory and consequently was there at the beginning. With musical theater programs being ubiquitous today, it's hard to imagine a time when they didn't exist. Well it's true, and it all began in 1969 at the University of Cincinnati's widely acclaimed College-Conservatory of Music.

JACK

CCM wasn't much different than any other conservatory or major music school in the middle of the last century...

HELEN *(interrupting)*

...but, Jack, remember that CCM had only came into existence in the 1960s.

JACK

...That's right, I always tend to forget that CCM is relatively new...

HELEN

...but with deep roots stretching back to the 1860s and 1870s in the form of the Cincinnati Conservatory of Music and the College of Music of Cincinnati...

JACK

...hence CCM—College-Conservatory of Music.

HELEN

(Emphatically) At the University of Cincinnati! It took three remarkable institu-

tions to foster the culture that allowed us to create what we did, Jack.

CCM was formed in 1955 when the College of Music and the Conservatory of Music merged. Subsequently CCM joined UC in 1962 as the fourteenth college.

JACK

Who would have thought that here on the banks of the Ohio River, not in New York or LA…not at Julliard or Curtis or Eastman, but here in Cincinnati…that musical theater training got its pedigree.

An internationally recognized soprano who had performed in opera houses and concert halls throughout Europe and the United States, Helen Laird had arrived in Cincinnati in 1964 to join the CCM faculty. Jack Rouse followed four years later, a newly minted PhD from the University of Michigan who was teaching at the University of Wisconsin when recruited to CCM. Helen and Jack had never met prior to their arrival in Cincinnati.

The famous Overture from Gypsy *blasts forth and then fades into the background.*

HELEN

We certainly shared the same vision…

JACK

…although we'd never met before…

HELEN

…A happy coincidence.

JACK

(*Chuckling*) Do you think the fact that both of us were from Rocky Mountain states caused us to think the same way?

HELEN

Who knows? (*She sings*)…"Those hills are alive…"

JACK

Me growing up in Montana, you in Idaho…coming together in Cincinnati. Serendipity?

HELEN

There's something about those endless vistas that make you dream big dreams and keep on climbing…

JACK

…and charging ahead and getting things done. Through all these years, I've never asked you this, Helen. Did you come to CCM, wake from a dream one morning and say, "Let's start a musical theater program?"

The music in the background changes now. They listen as the vocalist on the recording sings from The Man of La Mancha: *"To dream the impossible dream. To fight the unbeatable foe…" The music fades into the background as Helen speaks:*

HELEN (*smiling, listening to the lyrics, tongue-in-cheek*)

Well, I guess it was kind of dream, but not impossible. And certainly there were "foes," but not unbeatable ones. But the roots of that "dream" go way back to my years on the operatic stages in Europe.

Until the 1960s most opera performance in Europe and in the United States focused much more on the singing than on acting or interpreting the drama. In many ways opera productions were primarily a musical experience with a little bit of theater thrown in. And at that time it was enough to satisfy audiences. It was in Germany, where Helen was performing, that a movement began to sing opera in the language of the audience rather than in the language in which it had been written. This basic, audience-centric change started to move opera toward becoming a more dramatic experience. For once the audience understood what was being sung; it was imperative they "act" accordingly.

HELEN

Once we started singing in the language of the people, they could understand what we were saying. Of course they understood the spoken lines as well, so, consequently, we better be able to act the parts. And since I've always loved drama, I intrinsically felt opera should be much more than singing.

JACK

Well, today it certainly is.

HELEN

Thank God. But when I started singers were not trained to act. And in America the focus was on the music, learning the language of the composer...

JACK

...and not worrying so much about the acting or the drama...

HELEN

...in many cases not even thinking about it at all!

JACK

So one of the significant building blocks of your idea for musical theater training was shaped in opera?

MADELINE

Interesting. After all I came to CCM as an opera major. Had there been a musical theater program then, with good scholarships of course, I'm certain I would have enrolled.

JACK

But at that time, weren't most academics of the mind that musical theater was somehow second-rate?

HELEN

Some thought that, certainly. But they were dead wrong. Think of it; musical theater is America's contribution to the world of theater, the theatrical equivalent of jazz. It's dramatic and exciting and funny and sad. It's full of great melodies and silly tunes and compelling theater. And it has huge audience appeal.

JACK

A worthy partner to opera.

HELEN

Yes, I always thought that opera and musical theater was in some ways the same animal—using music and the human voice to convey a drama or comedy and give the audience what they wanted and deserved.

Helen's view of opera and musical theater was definitely not one shared by the vast majority of her fellow artists and educators at the time. American opera programs then still taught a traditional non-acting style of performance that was inherited from Europe. This is not surprising since most American conservatories were started by artists with European roots.

MADELINE

…I do remember Helen always stressing the importance of taking care of the audience…

JACK

…Well, without them we certainly have no reason to exist. (*With sarcasm*) Guess that flies in the face of art for art's sake.

They sip their coffee. The opening lyrics from Applause *are heard: "What is it that we're living for, applause, applause…" This fades into the background.*

JACK

So you took a plane to Cincinnati, got hired at CCM and started the musical program…

HELEN

I only wish it has been that easy. But the stars where beginning to come together under those balmy Ohio skies.

JACK

You mean those stellar institutions: the College of Music of Cincinnati, and the Cincinnati Conservatory of Music and the University of Cincinnati.

HELEN

Absolutely, but there was another star as well…

JACK

Of course, the other Jack. Jack Watson. The dean of CCM who hired me.

HELEN

…and me…without Jack Watson's leadership and, even more, his belief in us and the potential of our ideas, I doubt very much that we could have pulled this off.

JACK

I'll never forget him. To this day I draw on lessons learned from him.

HELEN

I think we all do, Jack. He was a true force of nature. *Jack Watson was the dean when the College and the Conservatory came together as CCM under the banner of the University of Cincinnati. A true southern gentleman and an extremely astute leader, Jack had a background in radio, television, vocal performance, and management. As a young performer, he spent time in Hollywood as a studio and voice-over artist. And he had academic credentials as well, having been dean at the music schools at UCLA and Indiana University. Coincidentally he had attended the Conservatory of Music as an undergraduate. While on leave from a teaching position at Indiana University, he met Helen Laird at an opera house in Europe. The two remained in contact and a few years later Jack Watson invited Helen to join the opera faculty of the newly created CCM.*

JACK

With his Hollywood experience as an actor and a singer, I guess it's not surprising that be believed in musical theater and opera.

HELEN

Jack did bring a fresh perspective. Most deans at that time were coming out of academia… Jack had the academic credentials of course, but he also had a performer's heart and an entrepreneurial spirit.

MADELINE

And a dream he shared with you two.
"The Impossible Dream" swells in the background and fades under.

HELEN

(*Smiling*) It's that dream thing again!

JACK

The Hollywood entrepreneur and respectable dean met the can-do kids from the Rockies and the stars were all aligned.

HELEN

And they were aligned at UC as well. We have to remember that previously the university had no real music program. So while the College and the Conservatory were mired in a conservative European tradition of music education, the university was a blank canvas…

JACK

…open to innovation…

HELEN

…with no legacy to protect, no toes to worry about stepping on. We all played a role in creating a new curriculum, but it was UC that provided the incredible blank canvas that allowed us to think in new ways.

"Age of Aquarius" from Hair *is heard briefly in the background.*

JACK

It was the times, too! The social conditions in the late sixties were all about change. The status quo was being questioned everywhere.

HELEN

Was it ever! Everything was being challenged—politics, social structures, education. Tired traditions were crumbling and new paradigms were emerging.

JACK

Young people, our students, were questioning everything and the time was definitely ripe for those who could let go of the past and look forward.

MADELINE

Serendipity? Or the right people in the right place at the right time.

HELEN

Talk about timing; shortly after we arrived, the university recruited a new president who had that same forward-looking point-of-view.

JACK

Yep, Warren Bennis. There's a reason he went on to become the undisputed guru of leadership theory and training.

HELEN

And what a change he made. Remember the ceremony when Warren was appointed president of the University of Cincinnati? It certainly wasn't the normal staid academic proceeding.

JACK

Not at all! I had wonderful meetings with Warren. He wanted the music theater students to be an important part of the ceremony…to set a tone for a new era…

HELEN

So there we were, a newly formed program thrust into the spotlight celebrating the arrival a new president at the University of Cincinnati with song and dance.
The music in the background changes and swells for a few moments. We hear "Light Sings All Over the World" from The Me Nobody Knows.

JACK

One of the great musicals from that time was *The Me Nobody Knows*. And one of the best songs from that work was "Light Sings All Over the World." That's the one Warren wanted us to use.

HELEN

Perfect for the time and perfect for the occasion. When we performed for the Bennis inauguration I think we felt that we had "arrived."

MADELINE

Not so for many musical theater students, at least not yet. In the minds of some, being in musical theater meant you were not a serious musician. The musical theater kids certainly didn't come to CCM *thinking* they were second-class, but some of the faculty made them feel that way in the early years.

JACK

So true.

HELEN

Oh yes (*they laugh*), I remember passing an associate dean in the hall once and having him say to me: "Helen, there are funny sounds coming out of your studio." "Oh, yes," I said, "it's called musical theater." To which he replied: "Well, some of the faculty will think that is the death of the human voice!"

For a moment we hear a lyric from The Music Man: *"Pick a little, talk a little, pick a little, talk a little, cheep cheep cheep, talk a lot, pick a little more."*

MADELINE

(Picking up on the lyric joins in briefly before it fades into the background) "Pick a little, talk a little, pick a little, talk a little…"

JACK

But you and a few other voice teachers "believed," ignored the disparaging chatter and kept charging forward.

HELEN

But not without bumps and bruises, and controversy. In conservatories and music schools it has always been a requirement that upcoming graduates perform. There simply is no more inviolable tradition than…

MADELINE

…the dreaded senior recital…

HELEN

The senior recital that had to be approved by the hidebound recital committee. Well, I had students who were music theater majors and who wanted to sing Rogers and Hammerstein, or Gershwin, or Cole Porter for their recitals…

JACK

...I remember, and that was not allowed??

HELEN

We only got around it because music education students didn't have the repertory restrictions that voice majors had for their recitals. And when some of the CCM faculty and administration actually *came* to those recitals and heard my students sing they began slowly to become converts to the validity of musical theater.

JACK

Going back to what Madeline said ...it wasn't just the students who were made to feel like second-class citizens. I felt it, too, at times for the whole program. I remember the very first musical we did after I arrived was *Sweet Charity...* We couldn't produce it in Corbett so we were relegated to Wilson Auditorium.

The new CCM facility, including Corbett Auditorium, which was named after the philanthropists Patricia and Ralph Corbett, had only recently been completed. It was a state-of-the-art facility. Wilson Auditorium on the other side of the UC campus was an aging facility that served as a lecture hall and a performance space.

HELEN

(*With a bit of a wink*) A scheduling issue?

JACK

That's what they said. Didn't believe it then; not sure I do now. I think many at CCM didn't yet believe that musical theater should be on the Corbett stage where "serious art" was produced.

HELEN

But that all changed?

JACK

The very next year!! Yeah. Truth be told it all worked out great.

HELEN

And in the ensuing years the program continued to grow.

In the interest of historical accuracy, it should be noted that at the time Jack and Helen arrived at CCM, the UC Theater Department, under the direction of Paul Rutledge, was presenting some musicals on campus and others at the Showboat Majestic. That curriculum was theater accredited and years later it was transferred to CCM as part of what is now known as the Division of Theatre Arts, Production & Arts Administration.

JACK

But I must say, Helen that there was a certain bias then that serious voice teachers don't teach musical theater.

HELEN

Well, you know what I said about *that* back in the day?

MADELINE and JACK

I can imagine.

HELEN

Yes. I said we have to wake up. Musical theater was flourishing. At the time dinner theaters were blossoming all over the country. Theme parks were starting to hire hundreds of performers. Our students had to work. But who was going to hire singers who only did opera?

JACK

That was a highly enlightened outlook for the time, my friend.

HELEN

Not necessarily enlightened. We simply had a responsibility to train them for the business that was out there...

JACK

...whether show business or any other business.

HELEN

I was an opera singer, sure. But I was also a good businessperson as well as an educator.

In the academic world, there is a rigorous process that must be followed before any curriculum can be accredited by the various agencies. This evaluation by an external body/bodies determines if applicable standards are met. If and when they are met accredited status is granted by the appropriate agency. This process often takes years and sometimes involves multiple agencies.

JACK

When I was at CCM, we had the musical theater program, yes, but we weren't authorized to give a *degree* by the accreditation agencies …

HELEN

…(*Laughing*) That's right! We were an enigma, neither fish nor fowl. Neither the National Association of Schools of Music nor the National Association of Schools of Theatre knew what to do with us.

MADELINE

So you had a musical theater program, but you couldn't award a degree?

HELEN

You got it. Pam Myers, our first "graduate" received her degree in voice with a musical theater major…but not a degree in it.

JACK

And if memory serves me correctly the accreditation guidelines weren't written and accepted until several years later…

HELEN

Yes, that didn't happen until I had moved on to Temple University where I chaired the writing of those guidelines…

JACK

…based of course on…

We briefly hear the opening lines of "Putting It Together" from Sondheim's Sunday in the Park with George. *"Bit by bit putting it together. Piece by piece only way to make a work of art." The music fades.*

HELEN

…what we had done at CCM. Today, of course, musical theater programs all over the country are accredited by both national organizations.

MADELINE

I'm sure today's music theater students and faculty, much less the general theater-going public, have no notion how many stars had to align to put this all together.

JACK

Establishing a legitimately groundbreaking program did have its challenges, but it was exciting, and also a lot of fun… One of the reasons it worked was that the three of us had tremendous respect for and belief in each other. Without that nothing great ever happens—in show business or in the business of life.

MADELINE

Certainly my time at CCM taught me about more than being an opera singer. Yes, I knocked around show business for a while: concerts, opera, music theater, the Miss Ohio Pageant—(*they all join her laughing*) before I was hired by the Plaza Hotel.

HELEN

…The first woman pastry chef, I believe.

MADELINE

Very proud of that and now, twenty-five years later, still running my own gig, Duane Park Patisserie …

JACK

…one of the most respected patisseries in NYC. That's quite a leap from opera or musical theater.

MADELINE

Not as big as you might think. Show business and baking are a bit the same at their core. Selling yourself. Confidence. Presentation skills. Ability to take the room. Discipline. Creativity. Giving the people what they want. A new show every night.

HELEN

Absolutely. Studying music doesn't necessarily mean one must have a career in music.

MADELINE

It worked out perfectly for me. Educated in a field I loved. Fortunate enough to work in music for a while. Blessed enough to take those "life lessons" from my music training and profitably put them into practice in a seemingly unrelated field, which I love. Besides, I'm still in show business. Every day I produce, direct, and star in my own show at the bakery. And I have an appreciative audience—and I make money.

HELEN

I always knew that for many of my students it was going to be about much more than the music or the theater. Or maybe I should say that the theater would just be the first of their life adventures and achievements.

JACK

I feel exactly the same way. Much more than the professional skills, it's always been about life skills.

Helen and Jack always believed that, too often, professional music education has not sufficiently stressed the need to prepare students for a balanced life, not just a life in the arts. Happily, that has changed. Students who graduated from CCM in musical theater are not all on Broadway or in regional theaters. Many, like Madeline, gravitated to other lines of work, becoming entrepreneurs, business executives, educators, managers, CEOs. They are working and succeeding all over the world. They attribute their success in large part to what they learned at CCM—not just the music lessons, but the life lessons.

As they sit back and relax a bit the overture from what is often regarded as the first truly modern American musical, Oklahoma!, *is heard. It fades into the background.*

HELEN

Do you ever pinch yourself, Jack, and wonder if it is all real? We were both certainly blessed.

JACK

When I think back, two things really stand out as life-changers. First was the dynamic partnership the three of us had. And second, I'm still amazed at the scope of opportunity that was presented to us by the University of Cincinnati. *That*, my friends, was visionary.

HELEN

We saw the reality of needing a musical theater program. They provided the framework within which it could all happen.

MADELINE

Hey, you two, I was there. The energy, the enthusiasm, and the optimism was the soul of the program. That came from you. And damn, it was fun.

HELEN

If that's so, I'm proud. Happy too. Still makes us smile, doesn't it, Jack?

JACK

For sure. It's easy to be happy when you're just so proud of the product.

MADELINE

Product? You mean the program.

JACK

The program, you bet, but the people even more. Lots of successful, fully realized people, folks just like you, Madeline.

Jack Rouse left CCM in 1975 to embark on a private business career, only recently selling the company he founded, Jack Rouse Associates. Helen Laird left CCM in 1978 to become the dean of the music department at Temple University. Both continue to mentor past students and other young people, a pursuit they find equally fulfilling, if not more so, to starting the nation's first musical theater program. Jack Watson, according to the Cincinnati Enquirer, *"the man most responsible for building CCM into an internationally renowned school of music," retired in the early 1970s to Florida where he passed away at the age of ninety-four.*

EPILOGUE

The lights fade on Helen's living room as she, Jack, and Madeline continues to reminisce about where it all began. The Overture from Jersey Boys *is heard. It establishes then fades under and out as the lights come up stage right. Sam and Janet enter and speak to the audience.*

SAM

Hi, I'm Sam. I graduated from CCM in musical theater several years ago. When I first enrolled I had no idea CCM had the first musical theater program in the country. Makes me feel great knowing it. Like I'm part of history.

JANET

Hi, Janet here. I graduated a few years before Sam. From time to time I had heard that CCM was the "first," and I guess I thought that was cool. But…

SAM

…but our focus was singing and dancing and "being a star."
They both laugh as they do a quick time step.

JANET

Well, I took a pass on the star thing, went for a family and a professional career in marketing.

SAM

I've been lucky. Had my share of Broadway gigs and touring shows. Even got to return to Cincinnati a couple of times for the Playhouse in the Park. It was like coming home, back to the city where I learned so much.

JANET

And not just the lessons about music and drama and dance…

SAM

…Not by a long shot…self-confidence, demeanor, achieving goals, accepting rejection…

JANET

…there is always plenty of that rejection thing.

SAM

Really! And discipline, discipline, discipline…

JANET

Yeah!!

They pause, thoughtfully remembering their days at CCM at the University of Cincinnati.

JANET

Not just an education for a life in musical theater…

SAM

…rather an education for a "life."

JANET

Could be that's what Jack and Helen and Jack really wanted.

SAM

Ya think? (*winks*)

*They lock arms and the music from Stephen Sondheim's "Putting It Together" (*Sunday in the Park with George*) is heard. Now, for the first time in this short play the lyrics are live as Sam and Janet sing.*

> *Having just a vision's no solution,*
> *Everything depends on execution:*
> *Putting it together—*
> *That's what counts !*

As they sing the lights come up briefly on Helen's living room as the three old friends continue to reminisce.

Lights fade to black as the music ends.

Introduction to UC and Cincinnati

The 1972 New Faculty Orientation

by Edna S. Kaneshiro

The University of Cincinnati became my academic home starting in the fall of 1972. After my job interview the previous academic year, I immediately fell in love with this place that had great vertical topography and a substantial body of water. I traveled from Bryn Mawr College where I was doing postdoctoral research, arriving at night. Traveling up I-75, I saw lights way up high and asked my host Bruce Umminger about the sources of those lights. He looked at me quizzically, as if it was a strange question, and hesitantly said, "Street lights, house lights." And I exclaimed, "Hills! There are hills!"

Obviously, I had not researched Cincinnati prior to my trip. I had thought: Midwest—flat, flat, flat. I had this prejudgment. While doing my first postdoctoral research fellowship at the University of Chicago, I was told the greatest relief measured along the Chicago River was essentially one foot. When I went farther south to Champagne–Urbana, I was told that the directions to a professor's house were to drive through sprawling farmlands and turn after you pass a certain large tree (instead of a landmark). Flat. Coming from the island of Hawai'i, I grew up with the Pacific Ocean, with the higher-than-13,000-foot, snow-capped Mauna Kea and Mauna Loa volcanoes, and numerous steep waterfall-cut gullies. Hence, vast flatlands did not exactly thrill me. So it was love at first sight for Cincinnati.

I interviewed with the then-head of the Department of Biological Sciences, Alex Fraser. He had come from the University of California–Davis, to build the department, which involved combining the departments of Botany and Zoology and hiring many new faculty members. He was a colorful character who published a book on genetics, raced go-carts, and decorated the hallways with his paintings. Things I remember from the interview: Alex explained that there is a big difference between a departmental head and departmental chair: heads had more authority and responsibilities than chairs. He also told me that he was not thrilled about hiring women because they got married and left. I was a bit taken by surprise as all along my career path, I had received only support, compliments, and inclusion (job interviews were quite different in those days). I responded along the lines that some men got married, some got divorced, some did not get their appointments renewed, and some took jobs elsewhere. I met Margaret Fulford, a "workaholic" botanist whose work on liverworts from around the world early supported the idea of continental drift (plate tectonics). She asked me if I planned on doing research. It stunned me that there was even a question about that.

I was offered the job with the promise that the lower-than-normal salary would be corrected by a significant increase after the first year; I accepted. By the time I arrived the next fall, the department had a new head, Jack Gottschang. Salary adjustments were made to some others who "needed it" more (men).

Warren Bennis was then president of this municipally sponsored, state-affiliated institution (it was not until 1977 that UC became part of the state university system). An elaborate orientation welcomed the new faculty members to the university and city. I think there might have been a reception at the Bennis's home, but I don't recall going to that event. However, I do remember the bus tour of the area with our guide Dan Ransohoff, a charismatic Cincinnati icon who was known for his knowledge of and love for the city, and for always wearing a warm scarf around his neck. First, he explained to the newly hired faculty members and their families that the area used to be a broad, flat peneplain formed by the melting waters (outwash) from the glaciers to the north during the Ice Age. Then the meltwaters cut through the flat plane resulting in the Ohio Valley lined by the hills—and that's why our hills are all at the same elevation. The road-cuts near the university exposed underlying beds of sedimentary rocks, and that's why one can easily find so many fossils here in Cincinnati and why UC attracts so many top-notch invertebrate paleontologists. We stopped for a while at a safe road-cut area (I think it was winding narrow road near a tall radio tower) where we enthusiastically looked for fossils—no trilobites were found but lots of brachiopods.

Throughout the years citizens of Cincinnati loved and preserved their hills. Many are topped by public parks in which pavilions were constructed to serve as shelters for people who loved the outdoors, and might have been caught in the rain while climbing the hills. Driving through Eden Park, Ransohoff pointed out the Romulus and Remus statue given to Cincinnati, sister city of Rome, by Benito Mussolini prior to World War II. I thought of how different it was on the West Coast where public gifts of art from Japan were destroyed or taken away from public view (sad what a scared public can do).

At the Eden Park overlook, we viewed the curves in the Ohio River and could see the Kentucky side where we later visited. Going through downtown we learned that Cincinnati produced a lot of wrought-iron railings, and some stayed in the city but the famous wrought-iron decorations of New Orleans were actually produced in Cincinnati and shipped down-river. During World War II patriotic Cincinnatians gave up their wrought-iron railings to be melted down and used to help the war effort and that is why the city had only a few of them left. At Fountain Square, we viewed the graceful Tyler Davidson Fountain, a tribute to the life that water gives to Cincinnati and where office workers in suits ate their lunches out in the open air. At the Carew Tower, its architectural features strengthened my love of things Art Deco. At the top of the tower we could see great distances all around us. Indeed, the tops of all the hills were amazingly the same height, the old peneplain! We could also see the highest point in Cincinnati, which was a radio tower on the roof of the Sanders Hall dormitory on the UC campus in Clifton. The view also showed how the construction of Interstate 75 split the city, which, according to Ransohoff, disrupted much of the integrity of neighborhoods and that the relocated poor families suffered. He also mentioned the abandoned subway system that was started around World War I as evidenced by tunnels along Central Parkway. There were several stories invented about why it was abandoned. The one I heard that was quite entertaining was that when the subway cars arrived from Europe, they were too large to make it through the tunnels.

In Kentucky, we stopped at the Covington Cathedral of the Basilica, a smaller replica of Notre Dame in Paris. The stained-glass windows, flying buttresses, and gargoyles were delightful. I love gargoyles, which brought back memories of those on older buildings at the University of Chicago. We were then told about the critical role that northern Kentucky and Cincinnati played during the days of slavery; that Harriet Beecher Stowe, author of *Uncle Tom's Cabin* had lived in Cincinnati and that it was right here that many slaves crossed the river to reach the slave-free North. We were then taken to a house, walked around the side to the back, and were allowed to look into the basement that was used to hide escaping slaves before they crossed the Ohio River. The slave traffic was located right under the local sheriff's nose; his home was across the street from the one we visited. The owner of the house that hid the slaves kept a careful eye out making sure the sheriff was not at home and nowhere in sight before he let the slaves make their way across the river. It is amazing what some abolitionists went through to do what they believed was right.

I believe we got back to the Ohio side of the river using the Anderson Ferry, which runs the oldest paddle-wheeler on the Ohio River, owned by the same family since way back in the 1800s. Some Kentuckians took it daily to commute to Cincinnati, as there is no bridge from that area of the river until you get to the bridges near downtown.

We went through Mount Airy Forest, which Ransohoff explained was the largest municipal forest in the entire country, which I thought was fabulous and chalked up another reason for my already love for the city. Also, he explained that it was a planted forest with many different species of trees that can grow in this region. There was even a grove of persimmon trees and those in the "know," including Mrs. Bennis, were waiting for the first frost so they could then pick the delicious fruit. The expansive forest must have made such an impression on me that I have always lived near Mount Airy ever since I moved to Cincinnati. I also had the thought that such a large forest with so many trees would be an area with clean air. In those times, one often could not see downtown Cincinnati while driving from Mount Airy to Clifton because of this dark, thick smog obscuring the view, not anything like the fog that normally hangs over the Ohio River and valleys early in the mornings. I now try to drive through the forest whenever I need to get to the other side of it, particularly in early spring when I can enjoy the redbud trees before the leaves emerge. I first saw redbuds at Syracuse University where I did part of my undergraduate and graduate studies. There was single redbud tree on that campus and here they are everywhere!

As part of the orientation we newcomers were also treated by the Bennises to a lovely dinner at the Krohn Conservatory, where we roamed through the various rooms and botanical displays enjoying the temperate climate indoors. The evening did not end there. After dinner, we were guests at the Playhouse in the Park. I don't recall what play it was, but it was my introduction to that amazing theater-in-the round overlooking the city to which I often returned in later years.

For many years since 1972 I have told friends and visitors that working at UC is ideal. Cincinnati has all that one would ask of a big city (live theater, good symphony orchestra, great parks, big league sports teams, museums, etc.) without the hassle. I also still feel that there are very few places in the world that I would voluntarily move to from here. The UC new faculty orientation in the years around 1972 included similar kinds of events to welcome its growing faculty.

So, now to get to work. Well, I found myself with essentially four walls to my laboratory and $2,000 as start-up funds. I knew that I needed to sit and write for external grants, which I did, and within a fairly short time got federal grants for my research. But, while working on grant proposals, I found that there were all these students knocking on my door asking to do undergraduate research in my laboratory. I could not refuse even if my top priority was writing grant proposals. So, I took in about seven of them to help set up the laboratory and work on research that involved the same methods, techniques, and supplies. A few more joined us in evening seminar sessions in my apartment covering various topics. We also got together for things like going to the symphony, fishing, and "cultural" outings. In those years, our department had a large number of majors including many exceptional students who were among the top students in the college and university. Almost all of them were from local families, who lived at home and had admirable work ethics. I believe every one of those who spent time in my group during my first year here at UC eventually went on to get their doctoral degrees. We should be so proud of them.

The events for welcoming new faculty, the quality of life in Cincinnati, and our jobs at UC working with very talented students must have also given those fellow faculty members who came that same year as I did a very good impression. Some in the same 1972 new faculty class never left UC, an institution that supported and facilitated the development of productive careers and a city that was well suited for raising families.

The university has steadily grown since then with many more buildings and trees than in 1972, continuously making the campus much more beautiful and distinctive.

Working with Warren Bennis

by Bill Mulvihill

"Leadership is the capacity to engage people."
—Warren Bennis

For more than forty-four years I was blessed to have worked on behalf of our beloved Alma Mater. I spent time in Student Affairs, the Office of the President, Alumni Affairs, Bearcat Athletics, and the UC Foundation. I was fortunate to work with many great colleagues, mentors, faculty, staff, students, alumni, and friends through the years. And I was lucky to be part of several seminal moments in the history of our great university, including our becoming a state university, the creation of UCATS, the renovation of Nippert Stadium and the building of Shoemaker Center, the $1 Billion Proudly Cincinnati campaign, and the UC Bicentennial.

And never, not one day, did I ever feel I had a job. I had a calling that lasted the entirety of my professional career at UC.

Each of us is shaped by the everyday challenges and opportunities we experience during our life's journey. If we are lucky, there are one or two individuals who touch us profoundly as a mentor and a role model. By their words, actions, wisdom, and vision they help mold us into the people we are today.

Warren Bennis was such a person to me.

Dr. Bennis was named the twenty-second president of the university in 1971, when the country and the university were still reeling from the tumultuous 1960s. UC was just coming off the closing of the university in the spring of 1970 in response to the turmoil caused by the Kent State shootings. UC was also experiencing a leadership change as President Walter Langsam retired after sixteen years as UC's leader, having overseen the university's explosive growth and the transition to state-affiliated status.

At the same time, universities across the country were feeling pressured to change the way they conducted business. Students and faculty were far more engaged, passionate, and no longer silent about a variety of issues. Being a university president was a more demanding job than ever. Warren Bennis brought a new style of leadership.

I was fortunate to work for Warren very early in my career and learn from a man *Forbes* cited as the "Dean of Leadership Gurus" in 2007. His impact on my life and subsequently the University of Cincinnati was nothing short of remarkable. He taught me the importance of vision, creative collaboration, listening, engaging others, emotional wisdom, leadership, passion, service, and commitment—values that still guide me today.

It was during his tenure as president that the university fully became a state institution, setting the stage for a historic transformation of UC to an internationally recognized public research university.

As we look to celebrating our Bicentennial in 2019, let us reflect on an important period of time in UC's evolution.

The University of Cincinnati began as a private college and a medical school in 1819. A municipal university was chartered in 1870. In 1958, the Cincinnati city charter was amended to include a two-mill levy for the support of the university. The 1950s and 1960s enrollment demands on UC increased enormously. This led to UC's seeking state aid. In 1963 three municipal universities, the University of Akron, the University of Cincinnati, and the University of Toledo, begin receiving state subsidy for the first- and second-year students who were Ohio residents on the same basis as the support for community colleges.

In 1967 the University of Akron and the University of Toledo became state universities. At the same time, because of UC and the city of Cincinnati's strong relationship, UC entered into an agreement with the Ohio Board of Regents that designated UC has a municipally owned, state-affiliated university, receiving additional subsidy support for the graduate school, the law school, medical school, and undergraduate pharmacy and nursing programs. UC received the community college subsidy, the lowest subsidy rate, for other undergraduate freshman and sophomore students, and no subsidy rate for juniors and seniors other than in the colleges previously mentioned. At the time, the feeling was that this agreement was a fair and equitable one.

Just as importantly, UC was designated by the Ohio Board of Regents in its master plan for higher education as a comprehensive university offering a wide range of graduate and professional programs (along with Ohio State University). I was a student during that time and other than reading about the transition, like my fellow students, I was focused on what was happening in the world around us, with the ever-increasing student unrest about the Vietnam War and a host of important social issues.

Almost immediately, it became clear that while this state affiliation was a positive step forward for UC financially, it was inadequate in providing the financial resources necessary to sustain and grow a comprehensive public research university. Enrollment continued to climb, necessitating the need for additional improvements to the university's physical plant, and the addition of new faculty and other services to support the growing student body. During the 1960s, UC doubled the number of faculty and students, trebled the square footage of education space, and more than doubled the number of degree programs.

As early as December, 1971 Dr. Bennis and university leadership recognized the need to revise the state's agreement. From that point on, a journey began ultimately leading to UC's becoming a full state university.

At virtually every meeting of the board of trustees, Dr. Bennis discussed the deteriorating financial situation facing the university. He called it "UC's single most pressing problem." And, "we are being penalized by the present formula." He suggested "a revision of the subsidy formula to provide more realistic funding for the many kinds of programs at UC."

In April 1974 he said, "Since my election to the presidency I've been deeply concerned about UC's financial problems both long and short term." And in October 1974 he elaborated, "Most of our problems originate outside the university; our case for subsidy revision is dependent on Ohio Board of Regents, the Governor, and the General Assembly."

Frustrated with the lack of progress and understanding the various entities that ultimately controlled how we were funded, Dr. Bennis called on his very unique leadership style. He believed if there was a problem in a large organization, you should create a small organization within the larger organization and give it all the authority necessary to solve the problem. To that end, on March 5, 1975, President Bennis appointed a steering committee under the chairmanship of Executive Vice President Ralph Bursiek to coordinate the effort to revise the university's contract with the State of Ohio. The effort became known as the Contract Revision Coordination Project.

On March 10, 1975, it became apparent that all possible steps must be taken immediately to create a special—temporary—organization to capitalize and coordinate the overall effort. Four university staff members were placed on special temporary assignments with Tom Humes being named project director, joined by Dan Pinger, Bob Robbins, and myself. An additional seven members of the alumni and development offices served as the field team identifying and connecting with hundreds of UC alumni and friends throughout the state.

The goal was to obtain passage to an amendment to Ohio House Bill 155, providing $15.5 million in additional funds for UC's in the next biennium, giving UC a position of financial parity in public funding with other state universities while maintaining its municipally owned, state-affiliated status. Among the benefits of this plan were additional support from the City of Cincinnati and Golf Manor via tax levies, and the ability of the mayor of Cincinnati to appoint five trustees to the nine-member university board of trustees.

Things moved quickly as the hundreds of alumni and friends recruited in this effort played a key role in determination to connect with every state representative and senator to seek support for UC. Through these activities I experienced firsthand the value of building productive, enduring relationships, a core value that would guide my personal and professional life.

One of my most memorable experiences was sitting in the living room of Verne Riffe, the Speaker of the Ohio House of Representatives and arguably the most powerful politician in Ohio at that time. Representative Riffe was a personal friend of my father-in-law, Collins Bennie of Portsmouth, Ohio. Their friendship led to the opportunity for me to represent UC at a very young age and explain UC's financial challenges to someone who would play a significant role in our future.

In the course of these efforts to persuade members of the Ohio State Legislature to support our contract revision and gain the additional $15.5 million of subsidy, an alternative was offered by Representative Jim Luken. He suggested that the university should strongly consider becoming a full state university with all the rights, privileges, and subsidy connected to such a designation.

April 1, 1975, it became apparent that the best option was for full state status. This was not a popular decision at the time. President Bennis demonstrated the courage and leadership to move the university to the right place to become a full state university. It could be argued that this was the single most important moment in the university's last 100 years.

We all knew full state status would provide a significant increase in funding for the institution. But none of us fully anticipated the compounded effect of the enhanced state investment for nearly forty years. One has only to look at our remarkable journey from municipal university to a world-class urban research university. This would never have happened without Dr. Bennis's ability to communicate the dire straits of the university's finances and his leadership in moving UC's constituents to the right conclusion.

Under Dr. Bennis's guidance I learned that being a change agent has its challenges. Robert Kennedy once said: "Progress is a nice word but change is its motivator. And change has its enemies." Dr. Bennis paid a price for his courage and leadership. But he never shied away from his responsibilities. Shortly after a referendum passed in 1976 it became obvious that Warren's time as president was coming to an end, partly because state politics were shifting to the right and the incoming Governor James Rhodes would be appointing all trustees.

After leaving UC in 1977, Warren devoted his academic life and personal life to the study of leadership. *Business Week* named Bennis as one of the "10 Most Influential Thought Leaders writing on Contemporary Business Issues." It took some thirty more years for the University of Cincinnati to recognize the leader we had in President Bennis when it awarded him an honorary degree. He never stopped teaching those of us fortunate to have had him touch our lives.

A perfect example of Dr. Bennis's leadership skills is part of an interview he did for the UC Bicentennial. Reflecting on the process and ultimate result of the state affiliation effort, Warren simply said, "*We* made it possible." He saw the significance of shared and creative collaboration in success.

As I reflect on my own career at UC, filled with unbelievable highs, and yes, some deep disappointments, I am forever grateful for the opportunity Dr. Bennis gave me and many other young people to be part of something bigger than ourselves. To learn the importance of working with others for the greater good. To treasure relationships with people from all backgrounds. To treat everyone as I would like to be treated and to never stop learning.

Thanks, Warren.

Introductions

My UC Story 1973–1979

by Julia Montier-Ball

At UC I was introduced to many contemporary people, places, and things that ultimately shaped my personality as an independent and critical thinker.

I did my best in those years to experience the best UC had to offer, from the wonderful art gallery in the Student Union to the impromptu picnics in Burnet Woods. My life on campus was connected to the community, from the shops on Short Vine to the shotgun building with a loft down on Fourth Street that provided the setting for my final thesis project. In writing this essay, I came to realize just how significant growing up in an urban college setting was in creating a rich path for me toward my career goals. One main contributor to this was the Design, Art & Architecture co-op program, which gave me eighteen months of practical experience and prepared me well for the real world of work. In fact, using my extensive co-op experience as a senior, I launched my first freelance job with the UC Human Resources Department and after graduating, my first job out of college was with the Design and Construction Department at University Hospital, where I worked on multiple projects from design through construction administration.

An early influencer of my UC story in the 1970s was my mid-1950s elementary education. A true beneficiary of *Brown v. Board of Education*, I attended a predominantly black parochial school in the heart of Cleveland, Ohio, that was a model for institutional desegregation. This is where my third-, fourth-, and fifth-grade teachers, three genius black women, propelled me to learn multiplication before the other students; they inspired me to write sophisticated essays and poetry; they taught me how to reach for an understanding of life beyond the three Rs—far beyond the riot-torn streets of Cleveland.

You can believe that when I graduated from eighth grade I was certain I was going to college. I knew this because my parents, both accomplished doctors, had talked often about their arduous journeys from the segregated South to the integrated colleges up North. After a few years in the Civilian Conservation Corps camps, my dad attended Lincoln University in Philadelphia, the nation's first degree-granting Historically Black College. Mom went to Howard University, where she and her sister were arrested for not giving up their seats to a white passenger and refusing to sit in the back of a DC bus. They both finished at Howard Medical School, with Mom getting a second MD at Yale. These were huge footprints to follow in. My parents had instilled in me an unyielding determination to not be mediocre or ordinary.

So in my college-prep all-girls experimental high school of 250 students, I was the only black in my graduating class. I pored over college brochures, absorbing all the pictures of campus life. I was very eager to go to a college where I wouldn't have to leave my cultural identity at the door. After experiencing institutional racism firsthand in high school, I dutifully took a picture for the yearbook and graduated, not even bothering to order a class ring. No regrets—I was going to college and had a career to research.

In June of 1973 NASA launched the United States orbital workshop *Skylab 2*. My dad thought a career in science just might translate into a job, so I applied to five colleges, and subsequently was accepted to them all. But I received the acceptance letter from the University of Cincinnati McMicken College of Arts & Sciences to major in mathematics first. I hadn't visited any campuses. But attending an in-state school like UC would save money, and I did have three other siblings who would also need to go to college, so with great excitement I sent in my registration fee. I was all set, except for a physical exam, which revealed I had a chronic illness. I spent the last four weeks of my senior year in the hospital, and although I got out only on the morning of my senior prom, nothing was going to keep me from going to the university. Finally, it was September of 1973, and Dad was driving south from Cleveland to Cincinnati with Mom trying to read the map. Too excited to look at my watch, I just read books until the car stopped moving.

Dad helped me unload my green suitcase containing five pairs of bell-bottom jeans, a "Say It Loud I'm Black and I'm Proud" tee shirt and my beloved Jimi Hendrix album. As my family drove away, I remember seeing my siblings' faces pressed against the car windows, peering enviously at my glorious escape from home. Standing there alone in the parking lot under that looming shadow of the infamous twenty-seven-story Sander Hall dorm, I felt triumphant, wanting to shout, "Let's get it on!"—right after I found my room on the seventh floor.

My six years at UC were chock-full of galvanizing introductions that would become milestones of my development as a student leader at UC. For example, roommates—in six years I was introduced to seventeen total strangers with whom I shared space and my soul music.

My first roommate didn't seem too thrilled that I was black and, because we never spoke, the silence between us was tense. I didn't complain when after a few days she left for class and never came back. Well, the solitude was great for studying, but short-lived, and I was introduced to another roommate. This time, I got lucky. Not only was Kay a black girl from Cleveland, she and I had similar dreams of success after college. That fall quarter, Kay and I had "big fun" learning our way around 'Nati on the bus and buying Reds hats. We would "style" the dances only Cleveland people knew, and you could hear us way down the hall singing along to the top Motown hits blaring from the radio in our corner room. Until one day it stopped abruptly.

Kay's money had run out. I remember feeling how painfully unjust it was that my best friend, who was just as smart and even more deserving than I, couldn't stay and finish her degree. She dropped her classes and returned home. There were no advisors advocating for her and no emergency funds offered. Sadly, we said goodbye, promising to stay in touch, and we did. Six years later, Kay happily stood next to me at my wedding as a bridesmaid. So that introduction resulted in us becoming close lifelong friends. Wonderfully, at age sixty, she went back to college to follow her dream of being a music therapist.

Next, I was introduced to the student organizations that would help me understand why having a college experience was so important. Shortly after Kay left, I realized my freshman year was almost half over and I still wasn't too thrilled about my progress as a math major. Struggling in calculus, I knew I needed to be empowered to persist. Empowerment came as I was introduced to Eric Abercrumbie, who asked me to join the Hanarobi Gospel Choir; it came in the so-called twilight of the civil rights movement as Marjorie Moseley introduced me to the United Black Students' Association; and remarkably, it came when the brothers of the Omega Psi Phi fraternity introduced me to the Court of the Q-Queens. So, with great expectations, I embraced being spiritually uplifted by gospel music; I observed the leadership of the black student movement articulating arguments for equality on campus; I even "got down" and gained cool points after winning the Que dance contest to become "The Bump Queen." It seemed popularity was happening fast.

Over Christmas break my mom introduced me to a friend, an interior designer who was helping to decorate our new house. Susan had a thriving business and had sold us her own beautiful new sectional sofa. I listened more intently than usual as Susan, an entrepreneur, told me about her interior design career. When she described our sofa, the words Baker Knapps & Tubbs rolled off her tongue slowly like warm sweet golden honey right onto my career-hungry plate. At that moment in time, I knew what I wanted to do.

Returning to school before finals, I immediately applied for a transfer from Arts & Sciences, and was accepted into the Interior Design program in the renowned College of Design, Art & Architecture for the spring quarter of 1974. I was so happy to get into DAA—this minority student had found her passion.

Quickly, I purchased my DAA gear: a tackle box, a large wooden drawing board, a roll of tracing paper, a T-square, and lots of B-lead drawing pencils. I got to know the five or six other black students in DAA quite well, but when I approached them in the hall, they were guarded, hesitant to appear as if we were "congregating" for a conspiratorial reason. I recall they advised that, if seen meeting in public, we could be expelled. In class, my white classmates gave me chilly looks, as if to say, "How did she get in?" This was difficult for me to understand, as I was a culturally and creatively competent individual who was paying full tuition—not on welfare or part of a special program for minority students. All I could do was stay focused on doing my work three times better as they did.

Since I had transferred in to DAA, I had to be in school over the summer after freshman year to make up credits, and was moved up to the twenty-third floor of Sander Hall where every time the wind blew, the windows would tremble. But nothing was worse than those fire drills, walking down all those flights of stairs in the narrow stairwell to the landing twenty-three stories down. The one redeeming quality was that Sander was connected to the dining hall, so we never had to go outside like all our friends living in the other dorms.

My graphic representation class met on the third floor of DAA, with no air conditioning in 90-degree weather. It was so stifling hot, my arms stuck to my drawings. It was hard work holding the pencil at just the right angle with sweaty hands. But learning to create a convincing shadow behind a building's roofline was much harder. Although my days in the studio went late into the night, many times until dawn, I had excelled in the skill of architectural drawing with great details, accurate elevations, and engaging interior rooms in perspective, all meticulously rendered by hand. On my first major rendering of an impressive skyscraper I was thrilled to receive an A- because in that class this score made up the largest percentage of the overall grade. It was my best work yet, and since I had done well on all other assignments, I was so sure it was a simple error when I received a C for the class. A bit worried, I questioned the instructor about my grade, and he confirmed my prior good work, even admitting how well I had done on that final drawing. But when I asked if he would adjust my grade accordingly, he flat out refused to fix his error. Stiff with anger, I stood there wondering, was this just his ego not wanting to admit a mistake? Or, was this his way of discouraging me, telling me I didn't belong there because I'm black no matter how good my work is? There was no one to answer me, and that latter question would remain unaddressed for the next five years while the gravity of the circumstances would escalate, and for the racially motivated bias to become more blatantly institutional.

Sophomore year, I moved out of the dorm, having convinced my dad that it would be less expensive to live off campus. A sorority sister and I found an apartment on Burnet Avenue for $95 a month and recruited a third roommate. It was not pretty, but it was not far from campus and we could have a cat. We had no TV, but we enjoyed living in the community. With no dining hall attached, we ate a lot of grits with cheese and hotdogs.

I had studied hard, in anticipation of my first co-op job. However, in another attempt to discourage me, the co-op placement office said they couldn't find me a co-op job even though all of my white classmates had theirs set. So I scoured the Yellow Pages, dialing numbers for well over a week until I found my own unpaid co-op. Neil Gouda was a tall Hungarian architect who owned a one-man firm in Cleveland, only three blocks from my parents' house. When he hired me, he told me, "I can't pay you, but I can teach you a lot." And that he did. He introduced me to OJT (on-the-job training) and had me drawing up remodeling plans complete with heat-loss calculations, lighting layouts, construction details, and written specifications based on building codes. Filled with a new resolve and a new toolkit of skills, the next quarter I returned to school and breezed right through my Systems Technology class, winning the respect of my advisor, who quietly introduced me to the unwritten "quota system"—the real reason for my miraculous acceptance into the college. If you could imagine being invited into an event, and given a ticket with a seat number 100 on it, but you couldn't find your seat because there never was a seat 100 in the huge empty venue, then you can imagine how uninvited I felt. I thought, okay, no number 100 seat just means I'll sit on the stage if that what it takes. I recall thanking Mark for sharing a truth I already knew.

Sophomore year marked two of my greatest accomplishments during my time at UC—entering Greek life and being elected into student government. Doing both at the same time was an amazing challenge, but somehow I managed to it. A good friend introduced me to the idea of rushing the Delta Sigma Theta sorority, so we could enter into a lifelong sisterhood together. While pledging, another good friend, Tyrone Yates, introduced me to his grand plan to run for student body president.

How could I not be a part of this groundbreaking campaign? If he won he would become the first black student government president ever elected in the history of UC. (A far cry from Mr. Charles McMicken's historic version of a black campaign to send all of America's people of color to Africa, reflected in the same last will and testament through which he created the University of Cincinnati.) While working on Tyrone's campaign, I was asked if I'd run for the open seat of residence halls president. This would mean unseating the incumbent and, in her senior year, she was going to be a very tough opponent. Late into the evening, seated in a booth at the McDonald's in the Student Union, we strategized our campaigns: Tyrone was already a well-known figure on campus, but I needed a more grassroots approach. Driven to win, I began mobilizing a whole lot of students for a word-of-mouth, door-to-door, flyers-under-every-dorm-room-door, phone-calling-students-for-their-concerns-on-dorm-life, campaign. The campaign was energizing, the challenge consuming, but I knew I had to make a good run.

Election Day came and I stood in my red-and-white pledge uniform on the Bridge to hear the announcement. Tyrone Yates had just been elected the first black student body president! Everyone was cheering. I strained to hear, had they mentioned my name? Yes, I had just been elected the first black Residence Halls Association president! More cheers erupted with fists in the air, a sign of solidarity, a symbol of black pride. Such a proud moment!

However, it was a beginning to a story that would unfortunately unfold to my detriment. A flurry of invitations came to meet people, listen to people, and stand for the people who had elected me. I was present at the university president's sherries, did *News Record* interviews, attended student government meetings, secretly gathered with sorority sisters, and did all-nighters in the studios of DAA. But threatening my achievements was a wall of negativity that I couldn't have seen coming. First, the white incumbent who had lost the election filed a complaint against me for alleged illegal campaign practices. All the while, my DAA professors thought they would "discourage me out" of DAA by giving me straight Ds as grades. Student court never pursued the allegation, but what was stirring the pot in DAA? When my term was completed I sought the counsel of a very wise black professor who took me aside and introduced me to some insights on institutional racism, which ended in my stepping out of the spotlight. I literally went underground, put on my blinders, and focused my eyes on the prize. Tyrone went on to become an attorney and is now a judge, but when we meet he always remembers "our" election with a hug and a proud smile.

For the next three years I lived in a house on the corner of University Court and Straight Street. I now had twelve roommates living on three floors, including the two guys who lived in the basement with the keg in a refrigerator. I had a nice-sized room with an enclosed porch that became my studio. My room was near the "phone booth." I spent many hours in that dark closet on the phone with my boyfriend, who went to Cleveland State. The girl in the room on the other side of the phone booth, Joan, was from Taiwan. She chose not to live in the high-rise with all the other Asian students so she could improve her English speaking and understanding of American culture. So, I helped her with her English and she introduced me to her culture by explaining why she slept on a pad on the floor and why she had such strong black tea. We shared stories of our families, homes, and close friends. I will never forget the time she came to me for advice about men. What a cultural shift that must have been for her, since Taiwanese women didn't usually discuss those things. I felt honored, like a trusted friend. The kitchen and living room were shared spaces and we all enjoyed carousing around that large dining table. Of course, my fondest memory of that house is the Halloween party we had in my senior year, as that's where I spent my first date with my future husband, Charles, who became my last and final roommate, nearly forty years ago.

I thoroughly enjoyed my next three co-op jobs, which got progressively more interesting in the years from 1977 through 1979. I did a double co-op at Youngstown State University during a time when that institution were renovating spaces and moving entire departments to swing spaces on campus. Here is where I learned the art of programming, an extremely detailed planning process that facilitated these moves involving numerous people, and had to account for placement of every piece of their furniture. The YSU architect, who was also an interior designer, gave me opportunities to do presentations; interview staff, faculty, and department heads; and meet with sales reps from some of the largest carpet and architectural materials manufacturers. As a result, I became quite the expert at specifying furnishings and creating RFPs (requests for proposals). Good thing, too, because my final co-op was with the big-name architectural firm Griswold, Heckel & Kelly, known for their high-end design projects and international clientele. GHK, as it was called, was located on Madison Avenue in Manhattan. New York City was, for a small-town girl like me, much like my Taiwanese roommate coming to America. For those ten weeks, I lived in the Bronx with my aunt and uncle and their eight children.

After about the third week, I stopped looking over my shoulder and rode that Number 4 train into Manhattan daily with no fear. Just the experience of working in New York would have been enough of an education for me, but my French supervisor sent me out on simple errands that ripened into some very cool adventures. With just his business card, I navigated through the stern security of the majestic French Bank to hand-deliver a design proposal within seconds of the deadline. This premier co-op introduced me to GHK's posh design projects, many eventually published in the glossy pages of *Architectural Digest*. Eventually, I began to emulate a New Yorker sense of style, with its cosmic mixing of cultures, knock-off fashion boutiques, pumping disco clubs in the Village, vibrant artists, grinning street vendors selling $10 "Rolex" watches, and open-all-night coffee shops that served grits with breakfast. I could have returned after graduation and worked at GHK, but my roots were grounded in Cincinnati.

So my UC story 1973–1979 was a continuum of powerful introductions that now in 2017 still seem fresh and enlightening. In the twilight of the civil rights movement, it was unfortunate that the types of discrimination felt by me and other diverse students at UC caused social and academic isolation, resulting in high rates of major changes, extended college graduation dates, and ultimately for some, withdrawals. I lost several good friends to these withdrawals. Thanks to the support of many mentors, like Marquita McLean, John Henderson, Paul Henry, Eric Abercrumbie, Mark Karlen, and my Delta Sigma Theta sisters, I could walk in triumph as the only black senior receiving an Interior Design degree in the UC DAA graduating class of 1979.

RAPP

Changing Attitudes—One Mind at a Time

by Marianne Kunnen-Jones

"Live the questions now. Perhaps then, someday far in the future, you will gradually, without even noticing it, live your way into the answer."
—Rainer Maria Rilke, *Letters to a Young Poet*, 1903

Dr. Eric Abercrumbie, an administrator at the University of Cincinnati for over forty years, calls it "revolutionary." He also considers it the most effective program UC has ever implemented to promote racial understanding. What is this radical initiative that Abercrumbie, the founding director of UC's African American Cultural and Resource Center, finds so powerful?

It's something now more than three decades old—the Racial Awareness Program (RAPP). Its approach can be summarized in four simple syllables found on a ceramic planter sitting on a window ledge in the sunshine outside its office. Etched into the sides of the pot are the words, "Each one, teach one." As its motto hints, it's small in scale. The majority of its work doesn't happen in its tiny office in the Steger Student Life Center. It happens in the hearts and minds of each participant. Founded in 1986, RAPP became one of the first sustained programs founded on a US college campus to promote racial understanding among undergraduate students.

"RAPP is a place to talk about the ouch-y issues and discuss them in a safe place—issues of racism, white supremacy, homophobia, all sorts of issues that people have historically been afraid to discuss, even in classrooms," said Abercrumbie.

Cincinnati City Councilmember Tamaya Dennard was a RAPP participant as a UC undergraduate. She credits RAPP with expanding her understanding of racism. "It taught me to think more about systemic racism and not just how racism and prejudice appears on its surface," she said.

RAPP taught her to be an advocate for anyone who is underserved and to understand "the complexities of prejudice beyond African American people," she added. It also sparked her interest in pursuing a career in politics. She at one time served as a political director for a Cincinnati Council member who ran in the Ohio primary for U.S. senator. Then, Dennard herself ran for and was elected to Cincinnati City Council in 2017. "I've helped to both write and introduce legislation that was based on inclusion," she said.

To place RAPP in the context of our nation's racial history, its formation came twenty-two years after the enactment of the Civil Rights Act, eighteen years after the assassination of the Rev. Martin Luther King Jr., and at about the same time that the anti-apartheid movement mounted increasing pressure, both nationally and internationally, for divestment in South Africa. The apartheid system eventually collapsed in 1990.

Closer to home, the context right on UC's campus also ignited RAPP's inception. Just four years prior to RAPP's founding, the university's chapter of Sigma Alpha Epsilon (SAE) had promoted a "Martin Luther King Trash" party with a flyer that encouraged "creativity and a festive party spirit" with racial stereotypes including "painting your face black," "cornrow hair," and "food stamps," among forty others listed. Students, faculty, and staff of color expressed outrage—as did many whites—and SAE's actions resulted in a two-year suspension of the fraternity.

Again in 1985, campus tensions erupted when the white student body president proposed a halt on funding to race-based student organizations that duplicated the purposes and activities of student organizations that did not have racially centered concerns. He argued that some race-based organizations replicated the activities of preexisting organizations and allowed segregated groups to form. Members of the UC community who disagreed with him contended that many students of color preferred their own groups because they felt their needs and perspectives were not served by the existing, predominantly white ones.

Within this turmoil, UC's administration asked Student Affairs to bring students together to discuss tensions and find possible solutions. According to a historical brief written by RAPP co-founder Linda Bates Parker, the concept emerged from months of discussion and research. In October 1986, an advertisement in the student newspaper, the *News Record*, announced the selection of the first cohort of students to participate in a pilot program. The twenty-five students were chosen, the ad said, from among sixty-eight applicants to participate "in a year-long project to heighten racial consciousness and to improve communications on UC's campus."

Bates Parker explained why a college campus was such an appropriate place for this kind of program. She told the *News Record* that a university is a place "most likely for racism to rear its ugly head. Possibly for the first time, students are confronted with what to do about a roommate of a different race, or where to sit in the student union."

Traditional college-age students are also at an important stage in their identity formation, research shows. It's widely considered to be a period of development when shame should not be attached to experimenting with different "selves," questioning beliefs, and testing new ideas. That means a college program like RAPP is well timed to allow students to explore outside their comfort zones. It provides a safe space to ask questions and speak openly. Its main approach remains much the same today as when it was founded: extensive and intensive dialog with twenty-five to thirty students brought together in each yearly cohort.

The kind of candid conversation RAPP sparks can be seen in a 1990 report on the *CBS Evening News*. Racial slurs had been scrawled on a wall of a UC dormitory lounge over the initials KKK. In the report, an African American participant in RAPP admitted, "For a long time, I was one of the people out there saying, 'Oh, racism doesn't exist.' But, you know, it does. And it wasn't until I got to college that I got that." A white female student opined: "I understand that as a white person I'm taking part in the privilege that the system gives me. But I don't think it's right to blame me for something people did a hundred years ago."

By the time this segment aired on CBS, the RAPP model had already spread to at least three other institutions—including University of Dayton, Ohio University, and Ohio State University.

At UC, over a period of nine months, RAPP cohort members are selected from an application process and then meet twice a month for three hours and attend three overnight retreats. Participation remains voluntary. It follows a format outlined in Bruce W. Tuckman's Theory of Group Development—"forming, storming, norming, and performing." It gives rise to tension. "Conflict is central to it. We don't want a room full of bobble-heads nodding in agreement about everything," said Brice

Mickey, RAPP coordinator. But over the many months of discussion, the program often builds a sense of solidarity and a sense of understanding. In the process, it also often leads to a greater sense of engagement in the university and prompts cohort members to ask themselves what they can do with the new perspectives they've gained, how they can use their new understanding to challenge and end racism, and what new roles they might take in the wider community.

The first cohorts at UC were balanced by race, but today RAPP also embraces diverse ethnicities and gender identities. Discussion at one recent session, for example, invited students who identify as female and those who identify as male to split into two groups for discussion. The female-identified group discussed topics such as the amount of body space men tend to take up while women are expected to restrict their body space. They also discussed how they perceived that men dominate conversation without listening to what women say and view women as interrupting the conversation.

"RAPP puts a real face on the issues. Participants look deeper at their own attitudes and actions and see how they can be part of the bigger picture. It makes them more accountable," said Mickey, himself a RAPP participant when he was a student.

For Brandi Chevere-Ralston, RAPP proved to be the "very first opportunity that I had to really examine the different aspects of my identity, as well as truly examining how various dynamics—race, class, gender, sexuality, etcetera—affected who I was and how I thought and related to others. . . . I wish that everyone I know could have experienced RAPP to some degree. . . . It's an amazing, life-changing program," she said.

Joseph "Jojo" Azevedo also found RAPP to be transformative. Azevedo says it helped him to develop a passion to promote social justice and a framework to better understand it. He went on to work with the AmeriCorps program Public Allies and continued to engage social justice organizations, activist groups, and community events that "strive to empower marginalized people. . . . RAPP has had a lasting impact on my life, whether I'm in situations that call for conflict resolution, analyzing daily media, feeling empathy for others, or creating my own content," he said.

RAPP also has established a record of propelling participants to produce ripples of change in equity and inclusion not only at the University of Cincinnati, but also in communities across the nation and around the world.

Rani Varghese, a participant in the eighth year of RAPP, found that her experience "planted deep roots" within her to pursue diversity, inclusion and social justice work. "My 'RAPP' friends joke that I went on to obtain a doctorate in RAPP. In every personal statement I have put together, to obtain my master's in social work (MSW) and later my doctoral degree in social justice education and graduate certificate in women, gender, and sexuality studies, I have written about my RAPP experience," said Varghese, a faculty member at Adelphi University. "RAPP helped me find my voice, and I have used that voice to speak as loud as I can about issues of diversity, inclusion, and social justice and listen as deeply as I can to people's stories." Those individuals include her clients, students, colleagues, and friends.

Other RAPP alumni became activists who organized efforts such as Cincinnati Black Lives Matter or other student and faculty activist groups on the University of Cincinnati campus.

Mickey asserts that the issues and questions raised today are sometimes different from the past and they would not be discussed were it not for RAPP and its impact. Tough topics would remain ignored or unmentionable if RAPP did not lay a foundation for dialog and advocacy, he contends. The program also builds a greater sense of belonging in the UC community and keeps students from dropping out of college, especially those who feel isolated because of their race or gender identity. RAPP also has been an incubator for leadership.

Arunkumar Muthusamy, who participated in the Accelerating Racial Justice program (ARJ)—a shortened, five-day program operated by RAPP—stresses that "knowledge of RAPP is of paramount importance for a leader because the worse thing about being non-inclusive as a group is being ignorant of the fact that you are being non-inclusive."

RAPP has created leaders who push forward into communities and other institutions as well as student-leaders who become involved in other campus organizations before they graduate. The beneficiaries of that leadership development have included student government, peer counseling, gender identity groups, RAPP, and even UC itself. A one-time RAPP participant, alumna Bleuzette Marshall, became one of the university's highest-ranking examples of this, achieving the title of vice president for equity and inclusion. "RAPP is an incubator for inclusive leadership," said Marshall. "It provides a unique opportunity for participants to engage in courageous conversations that explore and address personal biases and societal inequities. Ultimately, it enhances one's cultural competence and equips them as advocates for social justice."

Remaining small in scale can limit impact. All told in a typical academic year, RAPP reaches one cohort group in its annual nine-month program, plus additional people through its abbreviated ARJ, scores of community outreach workshops requested by on-campus and off-campus organizations, and RAPPORT, a monthly program open to RAPP alumni and the public. In total, these offerings reach approximately 1,000 people per year at an institution that enrolls more than 44,000 students and employs more than 10,000. Lack of funds prevents expansion.

Some believe so much in RAPP's power to bring about positive change, they would like to see it become mandatory. But Mickey argues that the program would not work as effectively that way. Studies show that voluntary involvement is more effective because participants remain more open-minded and receptive than "reluctant" participants who can hold the process back.

Despite its "opt-in" approach and its small scope, RAPP as a catalyst for change can be compared to another program founded at UC and emulated at other universities: UC's renowned cooperative education program. Just as co-op gives students an edge in their careers after graduation, Mickey finds that RAPP produces students with a similar advantage, producing more well rounded individuals better prepared for the workplace and the world.

Knowing that RAPP reaches only a sliver of a large community, some may question whether its "each one, teach one" approach truly does act as a revolutionary lever of change. Even as a small-scale program, it serves a vital role, says Damon Williams, author of *Strategic Diversity Leadership*. RAPP may be incremental in impact. But, he concludes, "It can be the lifeblood of change."

Memories of David Blackburn

by Sarah Jessica Parker

I was eight years old when I was allowed to start taking classes at the Cincinnati Ballet School. I would happily have joined my brother Toby, already a student, sooner, but eight years of age was the point of entry.

I remember so well the long and curving hallway just outside these doors that led to the ballet studios. The sounds of the piano and the smell of work. And the thrilling anticipation of what was to come.

Our car pool always got us to class early (thanks Mrs. Friel) and frequently the company or the older classes were still working.

The doors of the studio were thrown open and I never once missed an opportunity to hang my body around a door or lean in across the threshold to watch. There was always a small gaggle of us lingering, watching, imagining ourselves among the more grown up.

Mr. Blackburn, Mr. McClaine, Mr. Truitte, or Mr. Sabline were usually found in the center of the studios, watching, correcting, teaching a combination, or, in Mr. Truitte's case, hitting a drum. It was performance to me and I believe all of us could have observed for hours.

Eventually our class would begin.

As a teacher, even of young students, Mr. Blackburn's expectations were high, his standards fierce. There were moments of amusement and one could always detect a sort of mischief and humor about him but he took our classes seriously and expected us to do so as well. The work was rigorous. And I remember so clearly his circling the studio, examining closely every single student at the barre. I would love to be able to characterize what it felt like as he neared. And how much I longed for a subtle hint of approval. How hard I tried to illustrate to him an understanding of an earlier correction or convey to him that I was listening. And when you were on the receiving end of his praise it was a source of an enormous and private pride.

Long ago I realized it was Mr. Blackburn, in those very early years of my life, who taught me what it means to be a professional.

It was this environment he created, this early example of dedication, hard work, and the joy that can come from commitment that has been the biggest influence in my work as an actor. And the thing that was most striking about this revelation was that Mr. Blackburn was never speaking to just one student. He was sharing all he knew and all he loved and considered the potential in every one of us.

I recall one time we were in the middle of Studio A. We were doing the adagio section of the class, a particularly challenging section for me, always, every single class. Brutal. It was slow and success seemed well beyond my grasp. I was struggling. And Mr. Blackburn said, "Ballet isn't just about the perfect line and technical proficiency. You have to share what you feel. It's a marriage of body and heart. You are telling a story in dance. And you want the audience to feel something."

"Technique is very important but it is what you bring to that foundation that makes you a ballet dancer." Those words, his words, that illustration of being whole, that window into storytelling liberated me that day and has been the destination I have worked toward my entire life.

I will always remember his laughter, his skill at mimicry, his generosity, his cleverness, his sentimentality, and his love for his life's work.

And I will forever be indebted, for he gave me *my* life's work.

I was a student of Mr. Blackburn's two days a week for less than four years.

But he has stayed with me a lifetime.

And I will miss him forever.

A Celebration of the Arts in Cincinnati

by Jim Cummins

"The Power of the Arts Touches Everyone"
the slogan reads. Fancy words, I thought.
I'm Lt. Luken, head of the "Art
Response Team"—and this is my partner, Dot.

Now don't get your undies in a bundle
before I start—we aren't your "philistines,"
okay? Give me a bull on black velvet—
or better yet, Elvis in rhinestone jeans.

And Dot—good grief, she's memorized whole parts
of that Travolta/Newton-John flick, *Grease*!
It's just our job to root out art that's bad—
you know, obscene. They call us "art police."

I'm sure you all remember back some years—
the Mapplethorpe exhibit came to town?
Featured that picture of a bullwhip—ouch!—
and that old man whose [bleep] hung down...and down...

("and down!" Dot says)—well, that's just what we mean!
We can't be having images like these

besmirching our community values.
That garbage upsets Mr. (and Mrs.) Leis!

"Is there a 'Mrs. Leis'?" Dot asks. "I don't think
I've ever laid eyes on…" But that's okay!
We've got no problem—don't bother us at all,
if it turns out our county sheriff's gay.

We're sworn to guard our city and UC
from swill who'd put a crucifix in piss!
Much better God be scourged & flayed alive—
ribbons of flesh dangling from Him—than this.

Our job's to make sure art does not reflect
sex, politics, or adult psychology.
We want art sending signals that it's safe
to bring your wallet and your family

to Skyline, Graeter's, or some pathetic team…
Excuse me, I have to take this—Hello?
You're kidding me—some freak at the CAC
suspended Mr. Lindner's what in Jello?!

We gotta run. We've sworn to keep art safe
for normal citizens, like you and me.
The power of art touches everyone—
but not, on our watch, "inappropriately!"

My Quest for a Just Community

by Mitchel D. Livingston

According to the Cincinnati USA Regional Chamber, I am a Great Living Cincinnatian. It is a grand title, one that my wife, Carol, has a hard time taking seriously. This recognition is an affirmation of a quest that began three decades ago. It was my quest for a Just Community that brought me and my family to Cincinnati, and it was the University of Cincinnati that helped me fulfill that quest.

My quest began in Albany, New York, where I arrived as vice president for student affairs of the SUNY campus there in 1987 after a stint as dean of students at Ohio State University in Columbus. The Albany experience was part of a search for something I had not found at four other universities, mostly midwestern. I was attempting to find a broader perspective, a broader worldview. Maybe cosmopolitan is the word. Maybe something as simple as finding a more diverse community successfully living together in a college setting. Those were the defining characteristics of what I was looking for in the Albany experience, and Carol was very much a part of that decision. We wanted something unique and diverse before we ultimately settled back into a more familiar midwestern setting.

While things had been relatively quiet around matters of diversity on midwestern campuses, diversity issues were boiling over on a weekly basis at Albany. It really disrupted our sense of the kind of community that we thought we had adopted.

Columbus, Ohio, and Ohio State University did not have that edginess around differences. There were tensions, certainly, and people had their issues with bias and prejudice and discrimination, but it was polite, behind the scenes. You didn't talk about it, because if you talked about it you would only make matters worse. Diversity was something that people were uncomfortable addressing, either in productive or unproductive ways. They ignored it. Just plain ignored it. In New York, it was in your face. All the time. If you didn't do something about it, it really went beyond civility. It tore at the fabric of what a university community should be.

The biggest pressure in Albany was around demographics. The campus was fairly equally divided among "minorities" who constituted approximately a third of the total population. There were Asians, African Americans, Hispanics, Jews, all participating in a well-recognized institution that provided wonderful opportunities. But being close to New York City allowed all the politics of the city to spill over onto the campus. Student groups set up tables and organized demonstrations, and brought in proxy speakers to the campus who would essentially just shout at one another. Black–white conflicts, Hispanic–black conflicts, you name it. That was the dynamic that we had. The challenge for me as a vice president for student affairs was: How do you make peace when a community so beautiful on the surface has such a difficult time living together in harmony?

In the middle of asking myself that question, I met a fantastic faculty member, Morris Berger, who taught ethics in the College of Education. He became my mentor over time and we discussed serious issues. What's happening in our society? What's happening on our community? What can we do about it?

About that same time, I came across a book that really captured my imagination, *Campus Life: In Search of Community*, written by Ernest Boyer. At the Carnegie Foundation for the Advancement of Teaching, Boyer conducted a study of 300 executives at public and private, large and small, urban and rural campuses around the country, asking one fundamental question: What is your biggest challenge? The most frequent answer that was given was, "the conspicuous absence of community."

You might have expected other answers, such as the changing demographic of our campuses, financial concerns, decaying infrastructure, or replacing an aging professoriate. But the issue that seemed most perplexing to the executive leadership was the conspicuous absence of community. That was defined in a lot of different ways: among faculty, it meant commitment to their respective disciplines, to their granting agencies, and to the external world. Among students, it was the challenge presented by coming out of a suburban or an urban environment, with all that I bring in my background and experience, and of encountering people who are so dramatically different from me. How can I make that a positive rather than a negative?

Most faculty and students come to campus hopeful and optimistic about diversity. They choose a diverse campus, but often find that they have neither the tools nor the resources nor the infrastructure on campus to guide them in creating a positive experience. How do you get a sense of wholeness out of that? How do you reconcile a situation in which everyone recognizes the value of diversity, but does not have the wherewithal, the resources, the ideals that would realize what they felt in their hearts when they saw conflict with their eyes?

Boyer identified six organizing principles around which a community could rally and organize to address these issues. One of those principles happened to be Just Community, by which he meant justice as fairness. That comes to us from John Rawls, a social philosopher who defined a liberal theory of justice, but the simple version of it is justice as fairness. Boyer recommended that if leadership really wanted to take on these kinds of challenges, it should begin by creating fairness, using Just Community as an organizing principle.

I borrowed that notion. I really liked the idea. Organizations have their scripts. They have their values. The Boy Scouts, the Girl Scouts, fraternities and sororities, the Masons, the Links, they all have language that they aspire to, and that's a good thing. It gives definition. It draws boundaries. It tells the world who you are and what you are all about.

But Boyer's recommendations were prescriptive. When I started a dialog on the Albany campus, the prescriptive approach faced intense opposition. People really did not like being told what to do. And I remember being caught, feeling that I was trying to do a good thing and getting a horrible response. So I thought, why don't we start a dialog about what it is we want for ourselves? Let's stop fussing at one another and define what it is we want out of this experience. What is it that we most value? Why did we come here?

Once we started talking, we found that, interestingly enough, most people came for the same reasons, give or take, and after two years, we had a whole list of ideals that people said were important to them and they only wished that we could organize in a way that made it possible to live up to them. So, we promulgated that language, and had faculty incorporate it into their curricula. There were contests, plaques, lapel pins—all the kinds of things that remind people who we are and what we are all about.

We ended up with two things. In a Socratic-Platonic dialog, we talked with one another and examined the depths of meaning in community. Justice was at the cornerstone of that discussion, that is, Just Community, and echoed some findings in Boyer's work. Our discussions gave us seven ideals. When students and faculty and staff came onto the campus, they would be introduced to these ideals. People were told, it is your responsibility to engrain this into the discourse of your constituencies. We also had a mechanism to get ownership for these ideals. They weren't imposed from outside. They came out of the conversations that we had with one another. The end product was these seven precious ideals that the community owned and created. And that is the genius, if there is genius, behind Just Community.

Morris Berger and I were invited to take our Just Community experience to Israel, to the first international conference of its kind on multicultural societies with aspirations for social justice. We got to talk about our experience with a world community of educators. We saw that our conversations had a richness that went far beyond the lapel pins and lists of ideals.

Carol and I were at this time facing a personal question: What about our parents who were getting older? We really needed to get closer geographically to be there for them. It had to be the right time, so we didn't disrupt our boys' educations. The shift from primary to middle school was a perfect opportunity for us to break after seven years of the Albany experience. And there was an opportunity in Cincinnati. I asked my colleagues: What can you tell me about Cincinnati? What do you know about the city? What do you know about the university?

I received the worst feedback that I have ever been given professionally. They thought UC was located downtown, on the river. They thought it was a tiny school. They thought it was only a music academy. They thought it was a Catholic school. And on and on. They brought up Marge Schott and her ugly language about baseball players. They brought up the Ku Klux Klan cross on Fountain Square. Every negative thing that any community might have, that is what they remembered. When I asked about the university it was comingled with other institutions and it was clear the image of the university was completely obfuscated by negative features.

Coming to Cincinnati to interview with that backdrop of information, I wondered what I was doing, until I met UC's president, Joe Steger. He said, I will make a commitment to you. This is a place that you really want to be. He said, you have been quite articulate about what you have done at Albany. We could use some of that here at the University of Cincinnati as well. You will have an opportunity to build in that regard. We are at a propitious moment in our ten-year master plan and there is a piece of that that looks like who you are and where you are right now. He said I understand the family situation; you're a car drive away from your parents, four hours rather than an airplane ride. You can take care of your family; you can have a good experience with us. Joe said, I understand you have academic interests and I've got a meeting set up for you with the deans to see if they will accept you as a faculty member.

Dean Louis Castenell as an advocate helped me secure tenure as a full professor, which was defining and important to me and a qualitative step up in terms of my quest for community. I was given a chance to build through the master plan in brick and mortar, creating the Main Street concept and what that has meant to the campus.

Most importantly, I received a chance to convey a set of ideals utilizing the Just Community model. At UC, we had two-and-a-half years of conversations, enriched by a series of esteemed guest speakers. In Fifth-Third Arena, we brought Maya Angelou, Elie Weisel, Colin Powell, and others to help facilitate a dialog about the quest for community. As Maya Angelou said in our first session, with almost nine thousand people in attendance, "How grand it is that the University of Cincinnati would aspire to create a just and caring community," and then told her life's story and wove our quest into hers.

I can remember you could hear a pin drop in that vast arena. When Elie Weisel joined us and walked out on the stage, he looked up and said, "My God, I feel like a rock star." Again the place went silent as we heard his story. Colin Powell, in a private moment, said it is with great respect and admiration that, as I am trying to become something other than a warrior, I admire your work because you are trying to aspire to be a just and caring community. All three of them did wonderful things to help us dig deep in our conversation about the principles that we committed to.

Both at Albany and at the University of Cincinnati, there were people who were captured by this because it was a passion that was in their hearts, too, and it was easy for them to join. At the University of Cincinnati, we had a core of people who have championed Just Community along the way. The one who stands out most in my mind is Lou Bilionis, someone who was captured by the way I talked about the justice model. As dean of the College of Law, engaged in a quest for community both as a legal construct and as a social construct, he gave himself fully to that effort. There were others as well, but none more passionate than Lou, as a practitioner of law, an intellectual examiner of the law, and someone who had the opportunity to apply it in a social, cultural sense around race and diversity and gender and to have a college that had that kind of conscience and what it valued both inside and outside the classroom with the Innocence Project and the work they do with women's programs. It was ready-made for the two of us to become partners and to create a different form of community along the way. What we ended up with is a variety of different approaches to community building, the bronze plaques that say this is what is important to us, the orientation for entering freshmen who go through an experience where they make a pledge and commitment to these ideals, and an enormous banner that is almost as large as the challenge that it is supposed to take on. We gave a really good effort to get people's attention directed to these ideals and in the main I think we did a good job. Each year, UC conducts an annual awards program where a faculty member, a staff person, and a student are celebrated for their contributions to Just Community.

Joe Steger was good to his word. I had a chance to dream and to build in brick and mortar and in values, and he gave me the time that I spent generously to promote Just Community not only on campus, but for over eighteen years in the larger community. There were ten different off-campus organizations that I faithfully served as either board chair, vice chair, or in a leadership role. In every instance, I found the opportunity to blend the work of those organizations that I served with the work that I did on the campus. With Bridges for a Just Community, for example, as a part of the orientation process we took busloads of UC students to the Freedom Center to march in those first few days at the beginning of the school year to trigger their conscience about social justice by putting feet in the street and then, perhaps, spending more time in an iconic facility like that.

Over the years, I received recognition and many awards. I do not serve for that reason, but it's nice when people recognize what you do. I must say that recognition as a Great Living Cincinnatian is a whole different league. It is a summation of all of the other things that brought the university and the community together in real and productive ways. I remember saying at the Chamber event that my service was our way of saying, "We love you, Cincinnati." And the Great Living Cincinnati honor is a way of Cincinnati saying, "We love you back." That's what I took out of that and it was the most poignant moment for me in this whole quest for community. Once again I felt like the university was being owned by its community through these various meaningful and oftentimes heart-wrenching experiences.

In my acceptance comments, I noted that there are fifty-four clearly defined neighborhoods that make up Cincinnati and I have had the opportunity to have my hands in all of them. I was able to embrace them and be engaged in them including working with the Boy Scouts, in high schools doing motivational speeches, on the football field with players. If you extend yourself and have a philosophy to commit in that way, it will give back to you exponentially. That's not just my rhetoric, it's my experience with ten different organizations from Bridges for a Just Community to Arts Wave, the Underground Railroad Freedom Center, and many others. I have said to colleagues, if you want to have a full life here, don't just look at what you do at your job. Take that into the community, make yourself available to serve that community and watch the way that it gives back to you.

I have had three real opportunities to leave Cincinnati as vice president of larger institutions, or as president. Those opportunities allowed me to resolve the question: Do I need to be a university president before I am through? When I looked at all that I was able to do here in Cincinnati and the impact that I could make on my campus and larger community I asked myself, why do I need to be someplace else? One more rung up a ladder? It was easy to decide that the Cincinnati community was much more rewarding and more fulfilling. What human being is able to have this much joy, exposure, richness, connection, community that a university provided?

This is not the Cincinnati that was defined for me when I was leaving the State University of New York at Albany. This is a community that has its own way, its own values, its wholesomeness. Yes, it is conservative, but that is the least compelling characteristic of Cincinnati. The most significant one is, if you go after it, it will make opportunities for you to embrace it. And vice versa. As a result of that embrace, we made a decision to stay here. To retire here.

It was President Joseph A. Steger who said to me, "Forget about what all of those people said about this place. Let me tell you, you can dream here and the time is right, both in brick and mortar and your ideals. You will be welcome on this campus and in the larger community. Just know that the latter is not where I spend a lot of my time. If you want to engage with the community, you have my blessing."

I dedicated my acceptance remarks at the Chamber Awards program to Joe as someone who dreamed for the university through his master plan and for the community through his appointment of at least this one vice president. I knew I carried that burden/opportunity everywhere. I became UC no matter where I was. Joe allowed me the opportunity. He was the dreamer, no longer with us. As I accepted the accolade of Great Living Cincinnatian, I looked up to the heavens and I said, "Joe, I hope I did you proud."

For my wife, Carol, this is our community. We made that commitment. For our sons, Jeremy and Joshua, we raised them here and no one may say anything bad about their Cincinnati. We can rest assured that when we are no longer here they will be continuing our work. They know they have no other choice in their own hearts and minds. I once said to them that I don't want to put any pressure on you boys and the response from both of them was, "It's too late."

Of Structures and Spaces and Structural Spaces

DAAP's Genesis of New Architecture at UC and Cincinnati

by Jay Chatterjee

I remember October 11, 1996, as vividly as yesterday. It was a sunny and crisp autumn day, perfect weather for the ceremonies we had planned to introduce our new College of Design, Architecture, Art & Planning building to the Greater Cincinnati community.

The day before the opening, the entire DAAP College pulsated like a beehive. Several large telecommunications trucks were parked outside on Clifton Court. Thick yellow electronic rubber tubes ran along the hallways and corridors of DAAP, with students strewn among them busily working. Groups of students working overnight had produced dozens of pastel-colored cubes and other decorations for the opening ceremony.

Serious planning for our gala ceremony had occupied nearly two years. The day would start with a ribbon-cutting, except that the students had designed the ribbon-cutting with a DAAP twist. Instead of ribbons, there would be a wall of pastel-hued cubes reflecting colors of the building, blocking the fourth-level east entrance. After the opening speeches, invited dignitaries would proceed to "deconstruct" the wall to enter the new building, a lighthearted homage to some of the ideas expressed in the DAAP building's design.

Dr. Terrence L. Frenz, University of Cincinnati's esteemed bandmaster, composed for the opening ceremony a special tribute to the new DAAP building titled "Structure," to be performed by the UC Marching Band. (After years of attending UC sports events as a fan, I was thrilled that the ceremony would have "a touch of Bearcat.") Danute Miskinis, a well-known local impresario whom I had hired as the event coordinator for the opening-day activities, had also built the gala event around the notions of "structure." She had proven to be very knowledgeable in locating and scheduling wonderful performers who would deliver the message with a great deal of humor, grace, and talent.

The initial ceremony took place on the eastern deck at the fourth level, beneath the eastside stairway, affectionately known as the "tongue of the beast" by those who saw the building as a giant prehistoric creature emerging out of the ground, shaking and snorting. As the ceremony kicked off, an exuberant UC president Joseph A. Steger, Ohio Senate president Stanley Aronoff, architect Peter Eisenman, and I marched up the stairway with the UC Marching Band following. The band cut quite a dash with their red and black uniforms and glistening band instruments against the backdrop of the pastel-hued building. We stopped at the plaza level, and the guests settled down in their chairs. The band completed their piece on "Structure."

As the president began his remarks, I recalled the day when Peter Eisenman and I paid him a visit to learn about his hopes and expectations for the building we were just beginning to plan. Eisenman was resplendent in a pair of white trousers, white buckskin shoes with red rubber soles, a light blue bow tie on a white shirt, white suspenders, and off-white jacket for the occasion, a far cry from today's sartorial informality! Many renowned architects had competed for the coveted DAAP project and Eisenman was feeling good about his selection. A ripple of excitement ran through the college, especially among students, upon word that he would design the new building.

Eisenman did not present a single image during his competition presentation. Instead, he talked about who he was as a person and what he believed about architecture. His strategy obviously worked. He got the commission and now we had to work together to make it a reality.

We climbed up those long sets of steps southward to reach McMicken Hall at the top of the hill and continued through the "Academic Ridge" area to reach the Van Wormer Building, a Palladian edifice, where the President's Office was then located. Looking back, the symbolism of that long climb did not escape me. I was filled with all kinds of reflective emotions on the difficulties we had experienced on the way to get to that point.

Our discussions with the president began well, but came to an abrupt pause when he made a startling observation that he did not want any major architectural statement at the corner of Martin Luther King Drive and Clifton Avenue. We were momentarily baffled and nonplussed, since that was exactly what we had intended to accomplish. On further conversation, we realized that the president did not like the way the College of Law was oriented to the campus, that is, turning its back to the university and with its front access directly leading to Clifton Avenue and the city transportation services. This was the very type of spatial arrangement that President Steger believed gave UC its "commuter college" image.

He clearly had a view of a campus more in line with Franco-British traditions of campus delineation. Although he did not quite articulate it that way, it was clear to us that he wanted all future buildings to be grouped around squares and greens with inward orientations. He certainly did not want a repeat of what happened at the southwest corner of the campus at the northwest corner. As far as our building was concerned, he sought two specific assurances. First, it would be located as far away as possible from the Martin Luther King Drive, to comport with the Cincinnati Park Board's preferences for continuation of greenery across MLK Drive. Second, all major entrances would have inward orientations to the campus. True to the president's desire, Eisenman's design kept a very low profile, up away from the corner of Clifton and MLK, with much of the structure built underground. The new entrance was located at the eastern end, with the other and older entrance still remaining at the original southern location. Both entrances were designed to connect with the existing foot traffic patterns.

At the opening day ceremony, President Steger emphasized that it had been difficult to sustain the project through all the ups and downs at various stages of its development. He felt, however, the result clearly showed the importance of this building to the University of Cincinnati, not least for what it said about the future of the university. Senator Aronoff emphasized the importance of the building for the State of Ohio, and Peter Eisenman discussed some of the unique architectural aspects.

Implementation of the DAAP addition was complicated by a couple of factors. Most significantly, this was the first time an out-of-state architect was allowed to participate in partnership with an in-state architect in a publicly funded project. I had negotiated this special arrangement with Carole Olshavsky, the State of Ohio architect at that time. The general unfamiliarity with such an approach among the facilities groups at the state and UC levels, with all the processes involved in such a situation, caused delays with inevitably negative budgetary impacts. On the other hand, the arrangement had proven to be a real game-changer for our architectural strategy at UC, and for other campuses in Ohio. The second factor was the building's unfamiliar structure, which required a unique computer-driven approach to define its structural elements, and a relatively new three-point laser system to locate its walls at proper angles. I do not think this building would be possible without these technological advances.

After the opening remarks, our dignitaries and guests pushed down the wall of cubes blocking the entranceway. As all the cubes came tumbling down, some of the guests spontaneously tossed them around, creating a sense of general excitement. The band marched inside and everyone followed them, gathering in and around the central atrium, and then the band marched up the grand staircase, surrounded the atrium at the fifth level, and began to play.

A throng of curious visitors, onlookers, and students milled around the atrium with a growing sense of anticipation about the highlight of the day, a panel discussion by renowned architects to explore architectural ideas and thoughts as refracted through Eisenman's new creation, looking forward to the millennium ahead. The idea would be not to look backward but forward.

Students lined up long ahead of the event for a spot upstairs along the perimeter of the second-level balcony. The place was packed and rippled with anticipation. The moderator asked Eisenman and the panel whether the building was about the end or about the beginning of a "movement" in architecture. Or, did it serve as a "transition" building between differing architectural movements? Many of the major architects of that time were present and most responded with gusto to the question and with occasional good-natured jabs at Eisenman. Architects such as David Childs, Henry N. Cobb, Michael Graves, Charles Gwathmey, Richard Meier, and Bernard Tschumi among others participated. Needless to say, all seemed to enjoy the national attention the platform of the videotaped and PBS broadcast panel would provide.

The moderator asked if I had deliberately gone out of my way to engage "name" architects to participate in UC projects, and I replied that I looked for architects who had something important to say or add to our architectural knowledge in their capacities as authors and teachers as well as practicing architects. Indeed, Eisenman at the time was less known as an architect than as an architectural intellectual.

Listening to the vibrant and compelling exchanges, I reflected upon the years of effort and preparations that led not only to that day, but also to the promise it held for dreams and aspirations for the following decades of campus transformation yet to be realized.

As the DAAP building progressed beyond the initial stage, I approached President Steger with the proposal that we apply the same DAAP process to the College of Engineering addition, which was the second project scheduled for implementation in the Campus Master Plan. He recommended that I discuss my proposal with Dean Constantine Papadakis.

During my first discussion with Dean Papadakis, he expressed a great deal of skepticism and asserted that he had X amount dollars and needed the maximum amount of space for those dollars, not fancy architecture. This is not an uncommon desire among clients. As planning and design progressed, he completely reversed himself, and later went on to hire Michael Graves for a building at Drexel University when he became president of that institution. He also added, at the last minute, an additional floor atop his Graves-designed building at UC so he could move the Dean's Office out of historic Baldwin Hall. The story was much the same for a dozen subsequent projects.

One of the most enjoyable aspects of working with architects as a group, and especially the architects involved with UC's campus transformation, was to listen to almost constant good-natured bantering among them. Michael Graves, whose Engineering Research Center building started later but finished earlier than the DAAP building, offered at the opening ceremony for his building to let Eisenman use the main hall of the engineering building for an opening ceremony while, he projected, the DAAP building remained under construction for the next decade!

Dean Robert Werner of the College-Conservatory of Music was also concerned initially about his college's major funders, who were generally conservative and not likely to support contemporary architecture. I felt Harry Cobb, with his solid reputation, quiet confidence, and dignified manners would work well with the CCM donors. Indeed, Cobb's style proved truly beneficial to the college.

I remember feeling very touched by Frank Gehry wishing me not "to get in trouble" when several decision-makers expressed doubts about choosing him for the Vontz Center for Molecular Studies. Nevertheless, at the end of the day, much to my satisfaction, the choice of Gehry prevailed. Thanks to that decision we now have the first "curvilinear brick building" in the United States, if not in the world. Initially, Gehry wanted to try titanium, an idea rejected by the leadership at UC's East Campus, who wanted bricks.

An alumni group informed Charles Gwathmey of Gwathmey Siegel Kaufman Architects that he could not touch the front façade and the cupola of the Tangeman University Center building. Gwathmey's design maintained those two elements as mere pastiche, but created a wonderful interior space after gutting everything behind the façade.

At the recommendation of President Steger I was involved on all of these architectural projects. Working with these architects was often a very exciting and enervating experience. They were all idiosyncratic in their own way, with their own follies and foibles, which seem to accompany extraordinary talents. Having chaired almost all of the selection processes across the campus, I had come to know and understand how they approached their work. I also had the privilege to work with all of them, at various stages of their projects, in my other role as the chair of the Design Review Committee of the campus.

When I assumed the deanship of DAAP—one of the largest visual arts and environmental design colleges in the country—in 1982 I clearly understood that my responsibilities would involve such interactions across the campus. Given the widely acknowledged deplorable physical condition of UC campus at the time, it was apparent that one of my responsibilities as dean would be to provide active leadership to develop and guide a compelling vision for the physical structure of the campus, and consequently for the resultant cultural environment of the university. We would need a unified and comprehensive approach to the whole campus structure if we were to expect any degree of success in our efforts. A "one-off" approach at DAAP while ignoring the rest of the campus would ultimately fail. By 1985, it became evident that for this idea to take shape we would need to attract some major talents. We also needed some urban designers and landscape architects with approaches based deeply on the cultural roots of an area.

The University of Cincinnati campus at that time was already covered by near-ly 40 to 50 percent in built-up areas. This development had taken place without any overall guiding principles to pull all existing facilities and structures together in a unified urban design. We did not find ourselves with a "tabula rasa" situation to group all new architectural edifices together in a planned manner. The types of architectural unity represented at Miami University (i.e., Collegiate Georgian), or at Duke University (i.e., Collegiate Gothic), were often cited as examples to pursue. This idea was neither feasible nor desirable. Rather, I felt we needed to come up with a new vision that would speak to tomorrow, based on diverse architectural approaches of the time as well as the region's cultural roots, with landscape archi-tecture and urban design components to tie the structures together. Our approach would need to weave all the future new and diverse architecture together through an Urban Design/Architecture Plan.

I always felt that buildings that were true to their times made better sense than to impose an overall style. We intended to avoid pitfalls seen at places such as the University of North Carolina's central campus. In the old central axis, all the buildings were true to architectural styles of their times. Tying the old campus "ar-chitecture of its time" was the great central mall. The area became a classic exam-ple of the "academic village" approach made famous by Thomas Jefferson at the University of Virginia. Unfortunately, later extensions of the UNC campus forgot its roots, and its architecture was basically frozen in the mode of pseudo-Georgian Colonial style. The orthogonal guiding system of the central mall was lost.

Indeed, the story of the University of Cincinnati through the following two decades would be a fascinating tale of two interwoven "themes," one empha-sizing diverse architectural approaches of the time, and the other cultivating a culture-based urban design and landscape architecture approach, which would weave together all the new architecture. Both themes together would establish an intriguing, complex, yet strongly legible pattern for the campus. To accom-plish these goals, we needed a comprehensive and innovative master plan for the campus, with the clear understanding and strong support of the leadership of the university.

The effect of re-envisioning the UC campus over the next two decades—as it transformed from bricks, mortar, concrete, and pavement to a campus of greens and plazas and pathways and walkways connecting various facilities and struc-tures—was nothing short of magical. A campus previously known for its "commuter-college" image was declared one of the most beautiful campuses in the world by *Forbes* magazine in 2010. Gradually, the campus became home to the work of some of the world's most renowned architects, pulled together by the work of a talented young landscape architect with a deep, culturally rooted approach.

At the beginning of this process, on the request of President Steger, I chaired a committee to select a landscape architect for the "Campus Green" project to convert a massive and highly visible parking lot into a green space. I viewed this project as a prelude to the master planning process, and was able to introduce George Hargreaves, at the time a junior faculty member at Harvard, to the University of Cincinnati. Following Hargreaves's selection, I participated in one of his studios with his students at Harvard focusing on both a "Master Plan" for the whole campus and a "Campus Green" plan within the broader context. With the permission of President Steger, I presented the Harvard students' work to the UC board of trustees, with a specific intent to initiate discussions on a master plan. It had the desired effect.

Hiring George Hargreaves proved to be a game-changer for the introduction of urban design and landscape architecture as a strategy for campus planning. Hargreaves eventually was selected to coordinate the entire campus master planning process. To pull together all of the architectural work into a unified whole, he had designed a system, which he termed "The Braid," stretching from the southwest to the northeast of the west campus and beyond. The Braid followed the natural site conditions of lowland areas of the campus, with purposefully weaving strands emerging here and there embracing new and diverse architecture along its greenway wherever feasible. Hargreaves's work eventually sprinkled our university campus with metaphoric images of ancient Paleo-Indian Mounds to address our need for a culture-based approach.

As I listened to the banter of our architectural panelists at the DAAP building opening ceremony, I was reminded that in assuming the deanship, I faced some major internal issues as well. The college suffered from an acute identity problem and was riddled with strife, longstanding distrust, and feuds among programs and faculty. Many programs were dispersed all over the campus, and some were even housed at off-campus locations. The spatial separation exacerbated the lack of understanding among disciplines, and contributed to a proliferation of administrative structures and duplication of facilities. Also, lacking physical proximity to each other over a long period of time, the faculty had failed to develop any shared experiences and values. In order to be better prepared for DAAP's new building, we simultaneously launched a complete reformulation and restructuring of the college. Ten former departments were consolidated into four schools to promote collaboration; we consolidated both academic and physical facilities; and computer graphics, workshops, and photography were all reformulated at the college level.

The college badly needed more space to accommodate all programs in the same facility. We needed additional spaces for programs, but also for lecture halls, galleries, libraries, and computer and photographic laboratories. Additionally, we needed space for what I had termed a "living room" for the college, an idea borne out of my experiences at the Harvard Graduate School of Design and at the Architectural Association School of Architecture, London. In those schools, such common areas contributed much to the growth of ideas and discussions among faculty and students over the ambience of food. We also needed spaces for our students to just hang out at the college, given the amount of time they are expected to spend physically on campus.

The need for a new addition, and as well as a "redo" of our current facility was, therefore, the first and only item on my agenda when as a newly appointed dean I met with President Steger. During our discussion, he promised funding support for our college as the first priority over the next two successive biennial state budget allocations for the university's spatial needs. We knew that in becoming part of the state system, the University of Cincinnati would receive more than its usual share of funding because of the requirement of meeting the state's minimum spatial standards. University of Cincinnati lagged in this area compared to rest of the system at the time.

President Steger also approved additional funds for space-planning purposes. As a consequence, we launched a year-long planning effort involving program faculty, students, staff, alumni, and others. Peter Eisenman led this effort, separate and distinct from his architectural contract. Our planning effort was unique and unparalleled at that time in the university.

When Eisenman and Robertson Architects (later known as Eisenman Architects) was selected from six nationally prominent architects, they were assigned to partner with Lorenz Williams of Dayton to design our new addition and a renovation of our old building. The Aronoff Center of Art and Design, as the new wing of DAAP came to be known, is arguably one of Eisenman's most significant architectural works, and the one requiring perhaps the most complex and intriguing solution to specific site and programmatic conditions. His friendship with Jacques Derrida, the French philosopher and linguist whose semiotic analysis of language is known as "deconstruction," led Eisenman to explore similar notions as architectural constructs at DAAP. Based upon his lifelong theoretical research related to "grids," he generated a very inventive structure responding to our situation. He called the proposed structure a "torqueing and twisting" curvilinear grid system, designed in response to specific site condition, which fell out and away on the east side.

To Eisenman's credit, though the structure is an addition, most people usually perceive it as an independent building. In reality, the project is far more complex. His clever juxtaposition of new architectural language into the old building, and vice versa, and his creation of a "shifted" palimpsest of the old building's chevron-shaped circulation system to create a new order of movement pattern, made for a unique and an iconic work in architecture. These actions not only allowed him to both acknowledge and even celebrate the old building, but carve out an imprint for his own new addition. Between the new building and the old building, he created a majestic interior space for a "living room" for the college, arguably one of the finest interior spaces since the Guggenheim Museum.

In May 1996, we finally started to move into our new building. On moving day, the college filled with students and faculty, boxes, dollies, workers, trucks, and miles of tape. There were also a lot of curious onlookers, alumni and architects, architectural students from across the world and construction workers. A festive mood prevailed. Indeed, almost everyone walked around for several weeks following the "move-in" day with an excited demeanor and an optimistic smile on their faces. It was as if everyone realized that something important and historic was happening in that moment of time in his or her lives and in the life of the college.

I believe at the end most of our objectives in transforming our urban campus were accomplished. We were able to develop and implement a unique vision for the campus, which enabled us to attract great architectural talents of our time. These architects extended our knowledge and thought processes on architecture as well as designing and constructing great buildings. During their selection processes, I was not concerned with how many buildings they had completed; I was interested in architects whose work started with a particular theory-based approach. It was not an accident that we selected architect-educators like Eisenman (Yale), Graves (Princeton), Cobb (Harvard), Gehry (USC), Thom Mayne (UCLA), and Tschumi (Columbia) among others. All were associated in a teaching capacity with some of our great universities. Later, they came to be known as knowledge-based architects.

The power of the idea generated at UC eventually would start to influence decisions throughout the local community. Cincinnati would go on to select Zaha Hadid (AA School) for the Contemporary Art Center and Cesar Pelli (Yale) for the downtown Aronoff Center for the Arts. (I had the privilege to serve on both of these search committees.) Additionally, architect Daniel Libeskind (Cranbrook) was selected by a Northern Kentucky development group for "Ascent," a residential structure in Covington. At the request of the Chamber of Commerce, I served as a debating foil for Libeskind on his architecture generally and "Ascent" in particular. The event took place at the National Underground Railroad Freedom Center before a packed audience. Considerable excitement accompanied the advent of "new architecture" in Cincinnati. In selecting these architects, we were able to catch the zeitgeist of architectural thought and knowledge at the turn of the millennium.

As opening day reached the evening hours, student volunteers greeted guests arrived in evening clothes, who were ushered to a reception at the third-level entry hall. Student fashion models flitted everywhere in futuristic student-designed garb, cutting dazzling figures with their gold and silver metallic dresses, sparkling and glistening in the interior light. Other students guided guests from the entry to the gallery foyer for food and wine. A jazz quartet played and guests milled around the new spaces until they were led down the grand staircase to the main auditorium for the gala show.

Welcoming our guests, I emphasized the significance of our building to our work at UC. The show included a performance artist who presented a humorous skit of her attempts to move around the new building, unwittingly bumping into columns and walls, and following paths and stairs, which apparently lead to nowhere, and otherwise spoofing the building much to the merriment of the assembled guests. Another group, all painted with silver body paint, two men and a woman, celebrated the building with a montage of cantilevered juxtaposition of their bodies depicting daring structural compositions. (I wondered later if this ensemble presaged the later popularity of the Blue Man Group?) A pianist performed compositions depicting his interpretations on the theme on "structure."

After the show, the students led an upbeat group of guests upstairs to the grand staircase, which never looked so gorgeous and festive. The entire gala was themed with the pastel colors of the building, with student-designed artifacts depicting parts of the new building serving as centerpieces at the dining tables.

I had long realized that the importance and success of this occasion was essential to the future aspirations of the college, and for future planning and development at the university. Therefore, the event was planned just as much as a celebration of the entire university as of the College of DAAP. This new venture celebrates the past, but in the process it especially regenerates the students and faculty, and forecasts an exuberant and exhilarating new future for UC.

POSTSCRIPT

This narrative is presented as I personally experienced, promoted, and advanced the unfolding vision for the university. The ultimate responsibility to support and execute UC's campus transformation lay on the shoulders of President Joseph A. Steger. The program would overlap almost entirely the period of his tenure and would become a major legacy of his presidency. Eventually, it would entail an estimated $2 billion of public investment in campus physical infrastructure over two decades, but I believe the benefits far outweighed the cost. Without Dr. Steger's active leadership and direct involvement, it would not have been possible to accomplish this monumental task.

Dale McGirr, longtime vice president for finance, took over the administrative responsibilities for facilities planning in the early 1990s. His knowledge of finance and his particular ability to structure budgetary processes to respond to specific requirements of the project plans were invaluable to plan implementation.

Equally important to the process was the appointment of Ron Kull as the head of a restructured facilities division, and also to the newly created position of University Architect. Kull joined UC in 1991, after nearly two decades as the city architect for the City of Cincinnati. His knowledge, talent, and expertise in focusing and moving a large bureaucracy to implement our objectives were essential to the success of the transformation process.

UC

An Urbanist University

by Terry Grundy

No one in Cincinnati and at the University of Cincinnati could have foreseen just how grim 2001 would turn out to be—a real *annus horribilis*. When the national tragedy of 9/11 occurred, Cincinnati already was reeling from the civil unrest that had seized the city from April 9 to 13, as residents and visitors to the city expressed their rage at the tragic shooting by Cincinnati police of Timothy Thomas, a young, unarmed African American man. For days, the city was on virtual lockdown as the looting and rioting raged on. One hundred and fifty-eight people were arrested and eight hundred were issued curfew violations. It's estimated that the city suffered nearly $4 million in damage to businesses and perhaps $2 million more in emergency responder costs and damage to public infrastructure. A subsequent boycott of Cincinnati is estimated to have cost the city up to $10 million in lost business.

Painful as the spring events were to residents and civic leaders alike, it's to their credit that most people chose to interpret the riots as a wake-up call. Many reflection and dialog sessions were held, and some generated planning processes that have led to positive and lasting effects. One immediate effort was Mayor Charlie Luken's commission, Cincinnati Community Action Now (CAN), which was charged with doing "deep dive" research into community issues and proposing community solutions to the most challenging problems affecting the city. Later, Better Together Cincinnati, launched by the Greater Cincinnati Foundation and other local philanthropic funders, came together to provide leadership and resources to implement several of the programs proposed by CAN.

UC faculty and staff participated vigorously in these efforts and it would be impossible to name everyone who lent a hand. However, two UC institutes deserve special mention. Working on the principle that "what gets measured gets done," UC's Institute for Policy Research, directed by Dr. Al Tuchfarber at the time, took on the critical role of providing the data needed to track the social, economic, and demographic realities of the City of Cincinnati and surrounding region. Later, as reform of policing procedures took hold, the UC Policing Initiative (now the Institute of Crime Science), directed by Dr. Robin Engel, provided the research underpinnings for the Cincinnati Initiative to Reduce Violence (CIRV).

Today, Cincinnati has a well-deserved national reputation for being a city that practices what social scientists call *collective impact*, that is, an approach in which government, business, philanthropy, nonprofit organizations, and citizens come together to tackle deeply entrenched social problems in innovative and structured ways.

However, in the months immediately following the April 2001 turmoil in Over-the-Rhine and the Central Business District, no one felt at all certain that these wholesome outcomes were possible or even likely. You could detect a palpable atmosphere of shock and gloom wherever you went. The recent unrest and the city's evolving responses were about the only topics of conversation at the meetings of civic organizations.

One night, the venerable Cincinnatus Association had Charlotte Otto as the speaker at its monthly dinner meeting at the University Club. Otto, then global external relations officer for Procter & Gamble, was a key participant in discussions being held by business and government leaders to address an important aspect of the problems confronting us: what to do about an Over-the-Rhine that was increasingly neglected and derelict, and a Central Business District that was lagging badly. Business leaders were well aware that the city had lost 9 percent of its population in the 1990s. The city's tax base was stagnant, with a parade of downtown employers leaving for the suburbs, causing a dramatic softening in the downtown office market.

"We have about eighteen months to get this right," Otto announced to the Cincinnatus members. "If we make all the right moves, there's a chance we can pull out of this slump. If we don't—if we're too timid or succumb to the usual infighting—well, it's 'last one to leave, turn out the lights.'" To say that the association's members found her words both alarming and bracing would be an understatement. Somber-faced UC people in the room, besides myself, included Jay Chatterjee, former dean of the College of DAAP; Al Tuchfarber, professor of political science; Steve Howe, professor of psychology and, at that time, research consultant to the city's Department of Neighborhood Services; and Jane Anderson, adjunct associate professor of political science.

Later, in the University Club's cozy bar, Tuchfarber and I looked at each other gloomily. "She's right, you know," Tuchfarber said. "Yes," I replied, "but the question is whether or not enough people *realize* she's right and will get off their duffs to do what has to be done."

Both of us were deeply dismayed by the possibility that we would soon be seeing the irreversible decline of yet another great old American city, our beloved Cincinnati. It was not just that we loved the city; it was that we both subscribed to the view that cities are places of immense historical and cultural value and, in fact, are the places where most of the innovations that move a society forward occur.

In long conversations that followed, we examined the question from every angle and ultimately agreed on some important key principles:

- Cincinnati's decline had been going on for many years and tracked closely similar declines in almost every historic city in the Upper Midwest and Northeast—all of which had seen steady, and in some cases catastrophic, population losses for at least three decades.
- However, we had seen anecdotal evidence that at least *some* historic American cities had managed to avoid precipitous population and economic declines and others that had declined had begun to show signs of recovery—though we were far from sure how they were accomplishing that.
- Part of the problem seemed to be that Cincinnati, like other older cities at the core of metropolitan regions, had become the place in which the bulk of the region's low-income population was increasingly concentrated—and this put an unsupportable financial burden on the city's finances.

"There's an important public policy dimension to all this," Al summarized, "but at its root it's a demographic problem. We need to find out who left cities like ours and who's coming back to the cities that seem to be recovering." The logical strategy was to recruit Steve Howe, a UC professor of psychology and a terrific urban demographer. Steve was happy to help. "But be careful," he said. "The older cities that didn't lose much population probably are bigger 'gateway' cities like New York and Boston. As for the cities closer to us in size that may have slowed down population loss, let me see what I can dig up."

When Steve got back to us, he shared findings that were partly surprising. Not surprising was the fact that, indeed, essentially every older city in the country—especially in the Midwest and Northeast—had lost population steadily since at least the early 1970s. This was attributed to "white flight" or, more precisely, "middle class out-migration" since even nonwhite middle-class households had left older cities. Some cities, like Detroit, had lost so much population that it wasn't certain they would ever be able to recover.

Consoling was the fact that a handful of cities—including New York and Boston, as Steve had hypothesized—not only had stopped hemorrhaging population, but were showing signs of demographic recovery. "Look," Steve said, "you shouldn't get too excited yet because these are very early trends. We just can't be sure these cities actually have turned the corner—but the signs are encouraging."

"What I think," he went on," is that we're seeing the first stirrings of a repopulating of some older cities. I'm not sure yet but I think that they're beginning to attract a new kind of middle class. They're definitely not luring back the old middle class that abandoned them—no city's been successful at that."

This was very intriguing and we asked Steve to bring us more data, even speculative data, about this supposed "new middle class." He got back to us promptly. "Here's what I'm seeing," he announced. "There seem to be four demographic groups that are beginning to move back into these old cities." Here's how he described those groups at the time:

- *Empty Nesters*, individuals and couples who had reared their families in the suburbs but wanted to come back to the city now that their kids were grown. They were retired or nearly retired, had some money, and wanted to move to an easy-to-maintain place where they could enjoy the kind of cultural and social life that only cities can offer.
- *Young Professionals*, possibly even the grown children of the Empty Nesters mentioned above. They were just launching their careers, probably weren't married yet or responsible for children, and wanted to experience an "edgy" urban lifestyle. They were, in essence, the talented young people that all businesses say they want to attract.

- *The Bohemian Cluster.* As Steve described it, this wasn't a single group but rather a cluster of groups, made up of artists and creative people of various sorts, "counterculture" bohemians, some gay and lesbian folks, etc. They often were the advance guard that moved into a city's faded but promising neighborhoods and began to revitalize them—urban pioneers, as it were.
- *New Americans*, which is to say immigrants to the United States from other countries. As Steve explained it, this last group was responsible for more in-migration to older cities than any of the other groups. The trick, it seemed, was for a city to attract immigrants with some education and job-ready skills.

Steve's insights highlighted in very clear terms what we had to do—launch efforts that would make our city attractive to the people who were beginning *to want* to live in older American cities once again. It wasn't entirely clear that the cities attracting these groups were doing anything in a conscious way to attract people in this emerging new middle class. But it certainly was clear that Cincinnati had to do whatever it could to attract as many people from these four demographic groups as possible.

But there was a problem. For three decades or more Cincinnati had been steadily losing population, steadily failing to attract people who had a choice about where they lived. A larger and larger proportion of the city's shrinking population were people who *didn't* have a choice about where they lived, principally low- and very low-income folks.

Confronted with this reality, civic leaders in Cincinnati had done what you'd hope ethical, compassionate people would do: they had launched more and more programs designed to ameliorate the effects of poverty. From one point of view, it was exactly the right thing to do—but it didn't include strategies to make the city more attractive to other demographic groups. The grim truth is that a city can't long survive if the greatest portions of its population are net consumers of governmental and charitable services rather than net payers. The city had allowed itself to become, over time, the social services agency of last resort for most of the poor people in the region. We had worked ourselves into a conundrum of compassion.

We understood what we had to do, and that was to change the way government, business, and civic leaders *think* about the city, its value, and its prospects for success. We needed to provide a context, a forum if you will, in which city leaders could examine the data and confront the fundamental issue of demographic decline in a positive and constructive way. In effect, we needed to launch a "thought movement" that would reframe the role of an historic city like Cincinnati within its region and explore strategies for repositioning it as a "city of choice." We brainstormed who needed to be a part of the initial group, reached out to them promptly, and drew together as many as were willing to participate. A movement was launched, one that captured the imagination of many people and, in its way, helped to reframe many of the issues confronting Cincinnati.

Naturally, there had to be a first meeting, and a prominent Cincinnati hostess was kind enough to let us hold the first gathering in her magnificent drawing room with its views of the river and the city's skyline. About forty people showed up and the crowd included politicians, foundation leaders, leaders of civic organizations, and a sprinkling of business executives. Semi-regular meetings followed, all well attended and most with a strong showing of UC-connected people. Not long after the launch of the movement, meetings became so spirited and well attended that they had to be moved out of the living rooms of members to public spaces, sometimes in an Over-the-Rhine coffeehouse or bar. People were quick to embrace Urbanist principles and most took it upon themselves to promote those principles in other groups and civic efforts in which they were participating.

The move to public places was necessitated when a group of civic-minded young professionals approached us. They had heard about a shadowy group called "the Urbanists" and wanted to know if they could join in. It goes without saying that all of us "Old Urbanists" were delighted to welcome them to full participation in the cause!

It wouldn't be possible to provide a roll call of the thoughtful and generous people who helped make Cincinnati's homegrown Urbanist movement influential. However, I would be remiss if I didn't mention two philanthropic leaders with strong ties to the University of Cincinnati. Both Otto Budig and Buck Niehoff were early supporters of the Urbanist movement, while also being supercharged supporters of UC through their co-chairing of the Proudly Cincinnati capital campaign and other UC initiatives.

Budig, a 1956 graduate of the College of Business and life member of the UC Alumni Association, went on to give distinguished service to the UC Foundation board of trustees and also to provide unwavering and remarkably generous support to Cincinnati's urban amenities, and especially to its precious arts and cultural organizations. Cincinnati Urbanists will long remember and bless him for his willingness to underwrite the costs of the catering for the group's early meetings. An army marches on its stomach as the old saying goes—and a civic movement does too!

Niehoff, a 1972 graduate of the UC College of Law, went on to provide a series of strategically focused leadership gifts to the university and served as member and then chairman of the UC board of trustees. One of his contributions does double-duty for UC and the Urbanist movement: his establishment of and ongoing support for the Niehoff Urban Studio at the university. The studio is an innovative, interdisciplinary initiative that gives UC students real-world experiences in transforming urban neighborhoods and confronting multifaceted urban problems. Its enlightening public programs are very well attended. One long-time Urbanist described the studio as the "living room" of Cincinnati's Urbanist movement.

From its inception, the Urbanists' principles exerted a strong influence on the thinking of political and philanthropic leaders as they worked through the best possible strategies for revitalizing the city. Cincinnati mayor Roxanne Qualls prior to 2001, and later mayors Charlie Luken and Mark Mallory have been closely aligned with the movement. From time to time, the City Council has had a majority of members who understood and were willing to implement Urbanist principles and strategies. As well, the leaders of several area foundations, when they could, steered their foundations' investment decisions toward-Urbanist oriented initiatives.

No one would claim that Cincinnati's remarkable resurgence in recent years is due exclusively to the contributions of the thought movement called the Urbanists. There are many other stories about Cincinnati's revival that are well worth telling:

- How A. G. Lafley of P&G and Jim Zimmerman of Federated Department Stores launched a planning effort that led to the creation of the Cincinnati Central City Development Corporation (3CDC)—which in turn led directly to the dramatic revitalization going on in Over-the-Rhine and the Central Business District today—and how UC alumni fill so many of the organization's key staff positions;
- How talented graduates of UC's Master of Community Planning program came to fill most of the leadership posts in the nonprofit community development corporations bringing about the revival of neighborhoods in the urban core;

- How UC's investment in Uptown's community development corporations jump-started a robust resurgence in the residential neighborhoods and commercial districts around the West Campus;
- How UC alumni, faculty, and staff fought hard to save the controversial Cincinnati streetcar project—and *almost* got it all the way to UC (more to come on *that* story, I'm sure); and
- How the emergence of the "Urbanist-oriented" philanthropy practiced by the Carol Ann and Ralph V. Haile Jr. US Bank Foundation is changing the way citizens and community leaders think about creative civic engagement, the development of new community leaders, and community revitalization.

While we can't posit that the original Urbanist group is directly responsible for any of these developments, it's clear that many of the original thinkers in the group were intimately involved in all of the projects. Nearly all community leaders who have been in Cincinnati since the *annus horribilis* of 2001 acknowledge that the Urbanists played a vital role in setting the stage for the wholesome transformations that have occurred over the past sixteen years. UC isn't just an *urban* university, it's an *Urbanist* one. UC alumni, faculty, and staff can swell with Bearcat Pride in realizing that the university played a pivotal role in making the Urbanist movement in Cincinnati an influential one.

Confessions of a Famous Jingle Scientist

by James J. Kellaris

Musicians often resort to working a day gig—ideally one that offers steady bread, flexible hours, and dental coverage. One that can support an artistic career habit disorder compulsion, as well as a family, in that order of priority. There is no disgrace in having a day gig. Why be a marginally successful, starving artist when you could be a marginally successful, well-fed one? That was the impetus that drove me to graduate school in business, and ultimately to a faculty position at the University of Cincinnati's Lindner College of Business. I needed a day gig.

When I arrived at UC as a newly minted PhD in the autumn of 1989 to seek my fame and fortune, I was, frankly, primarily interested in fortune. That is the whole point of a day gig. And, to be sure, the fortune thing worked out just fine. The bread placed me on a respectable, solid footing from the get-go, on a trajectory for ever-higher tax brackets. I was the envy of my fellow starving musicians, who changed my *nom de gig* from "monster chops" to simply "the whore" in honor of my crossing over to the dark side of economic stability and weekend musicianship. The day gig hours were flexible. I had the freedom to work whichever sixty hours per week I wished, after which I could pursue music in my abundant spare time. The UC dental plan (which can be summarized as "chew on the other side") was theoretically better than the one offered by the musicians' union. Thank you, AAUP.

With fortune securely in place, the fame part of "fame and fortune" was not even on my radar. Man, was I ever in for a crazy ride, fame-wise. There was no way to anticipate what would unfold over the ensuing years. Like the time that...

Perhaps I am getting ahead of myself here. UC hired me to do basically two things: conduct research and teach classes. Conducting research involves identifying unsolved problems and investigating them to find solutions. In terms of career management, however, research also means carving out a niche—a specialty in which one can gain recognition—and, importantly, developing a record of publications, for the greater glory of Mother UC, not to mention keeping one's day gig.

My research niche was a given before I ever began a PhD, and on its way to being well established by the time of my arrival at UC: the influences of music on consumers, or "people" as they are called outside of marketing academic circles. What else would a musician with a PhD in marketing study? In the immortal words of Aristotle, "Duh."

As my music in marketing research evolved, it became evident that I had somehow become a professional jingle scientist. Music in advertising. Music in retail environments. Music on "musical hold" during telephone calls. Music warping shoppers' time perceptions. Sonic logos, or "sogos" as my former PhD student Dr. "PK" Vijaykumar Krishnan Palghat calls the brief, auditory signatures that identify brands.

My earliest research took a Biology 101 approach to investigating how music influences outcomes of interest in marketing. I dissected music into component parts to ascertain the direct and combined influences of tempo, tonality, timbre, etc. A journalist dubbed this "the sinister science of aesthetic engineering," speculating that marketers could use it to turn shoppers into helpless, compliant zombies. (Oh, if only!) But that was not exactly my intent. I just like to figure out how stuff works.

It did not take long for me to realize that music is far too complex to break down into individual, constituent properties and examine every possible combination thereof. Moreover, music was only half of the equation. Two people can hear the same thing and have different reactions, so those reactions are obviously a joint product of music and the individual.

Frankly, this realization left me a little frustrated and discouraged. I needed to try something different—a new topic, a new approach. But it was difficult to focus on my next move, because I had a persistent tune stuck in my head.

Call me Dr. Earworm. Some years ago—never mind how long precisely—having little or nothing in my wallet, and nothing particular to interest me in the behavioral lab, I thought I would meander about a little to investigate the watery part of the mind.

By far the most fun research I've conducted at UC was my investigations into the earworm phenomenon. An earworm is a song that gets stuck in one's head. I wanted to investigate this topic for two reasons. First, music is used in marketing to get messages across. Getting a message stuck in the head of a prospective customer is "free air play." That seemed highly relevant to my day gig, so I set out to discover the how and why of stuck songs. Secondly, I wanted to investigate the phenomenon because as a musician I have often been infested with earworms.

(A brief digression: Reporters often ask me what songs get stuck in my head. It's complicated. The answer is "Byzantine chant," which may seem very odd, unless you know that my wife of forty years is the choir director at Holy Trinity–Saint Nicholas Greek Orthodox Church. Exposure begets earworms, and earworms are idiosyncratic. Anything can get stuck. End of digression.)

My investigations led me to propose a theory of cognitive itch. According to the theory, catchy songs act like mental mosquito bites. The only way to scratch an itch in your brain is to repeat the offending song silently in your mind. Of course, scratching will only make the itch worse—trapping the hapless victim in a vicious cycle of scratching and itching. Voilà—an earworm is born.

I set out to discover what attributes of music cause a cognitive itch. Evidence showed that stuck songs tend to have three characteristics: repetition, relative simplicity, and incongruity—something odd in the design of the music that violates listeners' expectations, if only slightly. I presented my findings at an American Psychological Association conference.

A reporter from the *Los Angeles Times* wrote a story about my paper. Soon thereafter, the story appeared in the *New York Times* and other major papers literally all over the globe. It got extensive radio (NPR, BBC) and television (CNN, MSNBC, *CBS Sunday Morning*) coverage as well. *Parade* magazine (readership 54.1 million) cited my earworm research on their annual "Best and Worst of Everything" list. And, if you go to WebMD.com and type in the search word "earworm," you will find a report on this "medical problem," which cites this research.

This research evolved to include the listener side of the equation, including characteristics of people who are more likely to experience longer or more frequent earworm episodes, as well as lay theories about why songs get stuck, and strategies to rid oneself of the annoyance. The topic and findings resurface from time to time in the press, perpetuating the fame of Dr. Earworm and his hideous children. The term "earworm" even wiggled its way into the Merriam-Webster's dictionary. As my daughter said in summation, "Dad, you're a little bit famous."

Years ago, I bragged to Dean *du Jour* IV that my research had generated more press coverage for UC than the winning basketball team. His reply was an epic instance of balloon bursting: "Perhaps that is true, but is it what we want to be known for?"

Ouch.

In addition to pushing back the frontiers of mankind's knowledge by conducting path-breaking, cutting-edge research on important, esoteric things that I cannot explain to perfectly intelligent readers in layperson's terms, I was also hired to do something called *knowledge dissemination*, or—in the parlance of normal people—*teaching*. My first teaching assignment was a large lecture hall section of Introduction to Marketing with over 300 students. It met at 7:30 A.M. I had no prior experience teaching a class of that size, but I had seen the gladiator movies where Christians got fed to lions, so I had a pretty good idea of what I was in for. Moreover, having performed as a musician at festivals with audiences of 10,000, the large lecture hall seemed intimate by comparison.

Intro, as the students called it, is an ideal setting for the leaders of tomorrow to doze off in the auditorium seats of today. But that would be no fun for me. So I cultivated a teaching style that might best be described as *edutainment*—a combination of education and entertainment, sort of Harvard Business School meets *Sesame Street*. Principles and pizazz.

One method I used to capture students' attention is the demonstration experiment. Although common in science classes, the technique is seldom applied in the marketing classroom. It became my thing. Demonstration experiments allow students to discover principles in a vivid and memorable way. They also encourage thinking by analogy.

As one example, consider this demonstration of (spoiler alert!) the behavioral principle known as the "contrast effect." Three buckets of water are placed before the class. One contains hot water, one cold water, and one room-temperature water. Volunteers are recruited to immerse their hands in either the hot or cold water, then they are asked to put their hands in the room temperature water to estimate its temperature. Those who were primed with hot water perceive the room temperature water as cool; those primed with cold water perceive the very same room temperature water to be warm.

What does this have to do with marketing? When asked about the underlying principle, students often guess it has something to do with water or temperature or hands or buckets or something else concrete and specific to the context of the experiment. It is baffling to them because it seems to have nothing to do with marketing. This presents a perfect opportunity to introduce a second, related experiment—one designed to foster thinking by analogy.

Consider an experiment in which students are asked to judge how expensive a garment seems on a subjective cheap–expensive scale. Half are first exposed to a more expensive garment, and half to a less expensive garment. When they rate the expensiveness of the target garment, the results follow the same pattern as the "water buckets" experiment. That is, the same garment seems relatively cheaper to those exposed to a more expensive garment, relatively more expensive to those exposed to a cheaper garment. Students discover that the contrast effect that governs judgments of water temperature perceptions governs human perception in general—even price perceptions and perceptions of the ethicality of business practices. A third demonstration experiment involves rating the ethics of a controversial, mid-scale business practice on an ethical–unethical scale. After reading a newspaper account of a homicide or a story about an Eagle Scout, the very same gray-area business practice can seem more or less ethical depending upon the point of reference to which it is implicitly contrasted.

There are other, many other, such demonstration experiments in my edutainment repertoire. A particularly memorable one involved electrifying a kosher dill pickle in the dark with the assistance of Dr. Susan Mantel, who was my PhD student at the time, but is now, by a twist of fate, our associate dean of undergraduate programs. (Dr. Mantel, I would like to take this opportunity to apologize for making you wear a white lab coat during the pickle experiment.) It is a very theatrical effect, with a sci-fi lightning storm visible inside the pickle, which becomes translucent. The students' task was to estimate the duration of the time interval during which the pickle was illuminated. Half of the students were told about the task in advance, half after the event. Not surprisingly, the two groups used different strategies to estimate time. Hence their estimates differed radically.

What does this have to do with marketing? The experience of time is sub-jective. Ideally, marketers would like to be able to shrink subjective time during waiting situations, and augment perceived time during other situations, such as when restaurant patrons are seated at a table, enjoying a meal. Managing time perceptions can increase table turnover without making patrons feel rushed. Boom! Dollars.

Yet another technique I used in the classroom was the "omelet review." Going over answers to a multiple-choice exam can get a little boring, so I multitasked. Not to evoke ethnic stereotypes, but being of Greek descent I naturally have a full complement of diner operational skills. Hence I brought an electric burner, a frying pan, eggs, and other food items into the classroom on exam review day. Without comment I made myself a delicious omelet in front of the class. (Recall that the class met at 7:30 A.M.) As I was going over the exam and enjoying my omelet, the student with the highest grade volunteered correct answers to most of the questions. I asked him if he would like an omelet. With minimal disruption to the flow of the review, I determined his preferred ingredients, made, and served the omelet to the deserving student. Ditto for the second and third highest grades in the class. Toward the end of the review, I asked if anyone else in the class (of 300-plus students) would like an omelet. An eager hand went up. He looked genu-inely hungry. Having memorized only about 100 of the 300-plus students' names, I asked the student for his name, then looked up his exam grade on the list. It was a C. So I reached into the box of ingredients, pulled out a granola bar, and tossed it to him. His look of disappointment was obvious. "See how this works?" I asked. (Postlude: Mr. C got the highest grade on the next exam.)

During the early years of my UC career I learned through trial and hideous error effective ways of communicating with students, both face-to-face and via written feedback on exams and assignments. In the good ol' days before political correctness, I would write helpful comments in the margins of papers such as "what were you using in lieu of brains when you wrote that" and "if you can't solve a problem of this magnitude, what good do you think a business degree will do you in the workplace?"—a phrase I had learned from the legendary Professor Ronald "Tiny" Dornoff (may his memory be eternal). But decades of classroom experience have refined my approach to communicating with students. Perhaps I have mel-lowed with the graying of my beard. Now, mindful of the Golden Rule and prin-ciples of respect and professionalism, I am more likely to tone down a critique by adding gentle words of encouragement, such as "if you can't solve a problem of this magnitude, what good do you think a business degree will do you in the workplace *you pathetic snowflake*?" Mother Lindner does not coddle her young.

Not surprisingly, this innovative approach resulted in multiple teaching awards at the business school: The Michael L. Dean Excellence in Classroom Education & Learning EXCEL Teaching Award, the Ronald J. Dornoff Fellow of Teaching Excellence, Lindner Teaching Fellows, Dean's List of Teaching Excellence, etc. (NB: There is no actual "etc." I just added that to make the list seem longer.)

As gratifying as formal teaching awards are, what really touches my heart the most are students' comments on course evaluations. Here is a small sample of some particularly memorable ones:

> In marketing class Dr. K taught us about the art of ambiguity. All I can say about that is I cannot recommend this professor too highly! Waste no time in signing up for this class!

> Dr. K made a huge impact this semester, every time he bumped into me in the hallway.

> I love the way this professor says he learns from us students. He said this semester was a time of personal growth for him. I would estimate approximately 10 lbs.

> Dr. K instilled a lot of curiosity in me. For example, I wonder what his real job is.

For the record, I love my students and I love my day gig. But my love affair with UC was once in peril.

Throughout history, many good men have fallen prey to the overpowering temptation of concupiscence. David had his Bathsheba. Sampson had his Delilah. Amnon had his Tamar, which is a relatively obscure and unnecessary reference from 2 Samuel.

My temptress was named "outside offer." She was a sultry little tart. No disrespect to little tarts in general.

Courted by a well-endowed, private university in the Sunbelt, opportunity seemed to be knocking like a jackhammer on my door. I was torn. I was conflicted.

I was sorely tempted. But I wanted to do what was best for my family, so it became a matter of prayer. I looked for a sign.

At this critical juncture in life's narrative, Dean *du Jour* IV summoned me to his office and presented a counteroffer that brought me back to my Bearcat senses. In recognition of decades of work in the auditory domain, I was offered the James S. Womack/Gemini Corporation Chair of Signage and Visual Marketing. Let us pause here for a moment to marvel at God's sense of humor. I was looking for a sign; I was offered a signage chair. And yet there are those who believeth not.

Endowed by a generous gift from Sharon and Jim Weinel in 2007, the Womack/Gemini chair presented new challenges and opportunities for professional growth. As any zookeeper will attest, when the apes start showing signs of boredom, tossing them a new toy usually perks them right up. That is how Dr. Earworm morphed into Sign Man, my new superhero identity.

Of course, I didn't know anything about signs or the signage industry, but such an obstacle would not thwart me. The new job title alone made me an instant expert, so I ran with it.

Now in addition to reporters calling me about musical issues, such as why the NCAA theme music is so darn catchy (*New York Times*, April 2, 2017), reporters ask me probing questions like "Why isn't there an apostrophe before the S on the Tim Hortons sign?" (*New York Observer*, April 2, 2015). The answer to this perplexing mystery can be summarized in a single word: Canada. Canadian law requires signs to be bilingual. If the restaurant sign said "Tim Horton's," with an apostrophe, it would be construed as English and thus require a second line reading *de Tim Horton* in French. Given a sign of fixed size (also regulated by law), writing the name of the restaurant twice would shrink the letters, thereby reducing legibility and conspicuousness. I am not making this stuff up, although my professorship licenses me to do so.

The Womack/Gemini chair also opened the door to my testifying as an expert witness in legal cases involving signs. In one case, a deposing attorney leaned in for the kill, his *coup de grâce*, his ultimate gotcha moment: "Is it not true, professor, that according to the mathematic formula in your report the sign in question would have to be *seventeen times the size of a football field* to be legible from the road?" My expert response, which was transcribed faithfully and now a matter of legal record, was "huh?"

A moment of confusion ensued as I reexamined the formula. Then it finally hit me.

"Oh. That last number there—the one at the end of the formula—yeah... that's a footnote, not an exponent. See the footnote down at the bottom of the page, counselor? That tells you the source of the formula. I think you plugged the numbers in and raised them to the footnote[th] power." This revelation made stuff come out of the transcriptionist's nose, so we took a break until she could stop laughing. I can neither confirm nor deny a slight bladder leakage.

The Womack/Gemini chair has afforded me opportunities for which I am profoundly grateful. New research, new people, new adventures—elucidating mysteries of missing apostrophes and making the world a better place for motorists that may or may not have entered an area monitored by an unmanned speed camera from a side street that may or may not have had a proper warning sign with letters that may or may not have been legible within the cone of vision from a given distance at a given speed of travel, depending upon the angle of placement.

Musicians don't get no respect—and that goes double for composers, triple for those day-gigging as business professors. I believe that is because humans are primarily visual processors. In most people, the sense of sight dominates the sense of hearing. Hence visual artists are rock stars, composers are chopped liver. What composers do is invisible, abstract, and therefor largely irrelevant. Visual art, by contrast, is concrete even when it represents abstract ideas. Like, you can hang that stuff over a couch.

This sad circumstance fueled my brief foray into the visual arts. My plan was to apply aesthetic principles of musical composition to the realization of visual objects, so people could literally *see* my artistry. Not having any technical skills whatsoever posed a minor obstacle, but it was easily overcome by declaring myself a conceptual artist.

My transition to conceptual artist was way too easy. Yet, I realized that it would not succeed unless I could make it into a struggle. I needed to harness my suburban, professional class rage and show the world that *this shit is real*. So I did a series of unsanctioned, site-specific, suburban street installations to express the horror of finding black spot on one's roses the day before a garden party and other such first-world tragedies.

But that was just a warm-up act. Having taken my message to the streets, my next stop was the UC campus.

I did a series of UC-theme pieces, among them a number of "false gods" constructed of refuse found behind the Lindner building. Three of these pieces were publicly exhibited. "Tenyar, demon god of captivity" was a stick figure constructed of duct tape over coat hanger wire, trapped in a red and black cage. "Komiti, dark destroyer of time" was a demoniac figure chewing on a broken watch (because subtlety matters). "Caffeini, spirit of wakefulness" was constructed from a crushed Mountain Dew can that no doubt got a student through the first hour of some mind-numbing accounting class.

Conceptual art leans heavily on the description that accompanies it. Hence I did a number of installations around the business school that involved taping a pencil to a wall, for example, with a museum-type wall sticker placed nearby, saying,

> Minimal, yet expressionistic, this micro-monumental oeuvre investigates the metaphor of painterly intervention, with a biomorphic fluency that creates an enigmatic, yet accessible narrative. Not so much statement as gesture, this optical *tour de force* explores the formal qualities of cathartic repression and liberating containment, using an artful mélange of aesthetic vocabularies with a playful sensibility rooted in ironic juxtaposition of incongruous, contrastive elements. The resultant psychological tension is intended to evoke *beaucoup de je ne sais quoi* among viewers both lay and non-naïve. This seductively ludic work revels in non-normative transformations, contextual shifts, and spatial appropriations, drawing on the poetics of existential irony and shit like that.

The housekeeping crew or building manager would take my installations down almost as fast as I could put them up. When I asked why they were removing my art installations, they replied, "Because they don't belong there." I took this as a great artistic victory, as I had clearly succeeded in being misunderstood. And lo, this did come to pass during the reign of Dean *du Jour* V.

I have a secret—a dark secret. One that is becoming less and less secret by the nanosecond, so I might as well confess it right now. Witness: I am a famous composer. Perhaps the most famous composer you've never heard of. It's true.

Although I studied composition in music school as an undergrad, I had nothing to say, musically speaking, at that age. So I was not really a composer. I was a young musician with solid technical training, a smattering of talent, and a very shallow pool of experience to draw upon. Delusional ambitions aside, I was not exactly poised to set the world of classical music ablaze.

I became a composer decades later. It was the day my left hand exploded with musician's cramp (a focal dystonia), to be precise. Faced with the prospect of retiring indefinitely from musical performance, lemons to lemonade, I began composing in earnest, in the copious free time my sixty-hours-per-week day gig afforded me. With technical training, decades of listening and performing, not to mention world travel, Skyline Chili, and other broadening experiences, I became fascinated with the idea of dusting off the pencil and giving composing another go.

The result of my emergence as a composer surprised me. First prize in an international new music composition competition; premieres in New York, San Francisco, Philadelphia, Providence, Kalamazoo-no-less; Regina, Canada; Bolzano, Modena, and Acqui Terme, Italy; Rioja, Spain; Sydney, Melbourne, Brisbane, Australia; commissions; residencies with the Classical Mandolin Society of America, the Federation of Australasia Mandolin Ensembles, l'Accademia Internazionale Italiano; work published and distributed internationally by Trekel Musikverlag, Hamburg; work recorded by the New American Mandolin Ensemble (NAME) in Boston; national and international press.

Heady stuff considering I was just giving composition another go. Success is gratifying, all the more so in a second domain, but I was determined not to let it go to my head. That is until one day in the summer of 2013, when I read this sentence in an Italian newspaper: "This evening's concert at the Museum of Contemporary Art will feature works by composers such as JS Bach and JJ Kellaris."

Lightening does not strike twice, but apparently fame can. Try as I did to fly under the radar at my day gig, there came a turning point. At some point my weekend hobby turned into what might appear to be a second career. At some point the press started referring to me as "a composer and marketing professor at the University of Cincinnati." And, as if to leave no doubt that I had been outed as a closet composer, at a recent board meeting of the Academic Advisory Council for Signage Research and Education, I was introduced as Maestro Kellaris and asked to help "orchestrate" a strategy.

It is said that God works in mysterious ways. Last December I was at a low point on the roller coaster ride of life. Nothing horrifically tragic, just the senior citizen blues. Aches and pains. Arthritis. Bad back. Voice disorder acting up. The heart-break of moles in my otherwise pristine lawn. First-world problems. Wondering if my drab, wretched, miserable life will ever get any better than it was at that moment, or if the inevitable downhill slide had begun to pull me into the cruel, dark abyss. No big deal, really, but I was also in the midst of a bit of an existential crisis. You know—meaning of life and whatnot. Lawn moles notwithstanding I was generally content, but just sort of wondering if I had TOTALLY WASTED DECADES OF MY LIFE.

That is when I heard a knock at the door. Not the jackhammer knock of op-portunity this time; rather, a gentle, friendly, almost timid knock. Home alone, unshaven and in pajamas, with stage III cigar breath, I had every reason to ignore the knock; however, against my better judgment and for reasons I cannot explain, I reluctantly answered the door.

It was some new neighbors calling. They simply wanted to introduce them-selves and present a small Christmas gift—a box of chocolates, which I cynically imagined they were regifting to rid themselves of unwanted calories. Mom, dad, and two charming, perfectly well-behaved children (who are not permitted can-dy?). We made light chitchat. I thanked them for their kind gift, welcomed them to the neighborhood, and…why is she staring at me?

"Are you Dr. Kellaris from UC?" mom asked.

"Guilty," I replied.

"I was in your Intro to Marketing class in 1990!" she beamed.

That would place her somewhere between #318 and #930 out of 20,000 Intro students. I had scant hope of recalling…but wait. What was her name again? She repeated it. Miracle of miracles, indeed I remembered her. She had done so well in the course that she returned as a teaching assistant. Still, when she said she enjoyed the class and learned a lot from it, I took the comment as merely a social courtesy to an old professor. Of course, she enjoyed my class and learned a lot from it—what else could one possibly say?

But then she continued. She recalled specific lessons she had learned, recounted how she had applied marketing principles beneficially in her career, and continues to do so, and thanked me for giving her a solid foundation and great start so many years ago. She recalled *content*. Relevant content. Valuable content. Useful content.

I was in shock and cannot recall the rest of our brief conversation. As the door closed I burst into tears. Not weak, girly-man tears, such as a DAAP faculty member might cry, but rather über-macho LCB burlyman tears, such as one would cry during Germont's aria "Di Provenza il mar, il suol" in *La Traviata,* or when your pickup truck needs a new transmission. Knowing that perhaps I had not wasted decades of my life turned out to be the best Christmas gift ever.

The chocolates weren't so bad, either.

My Search for H. M. Griffin

by Paulette Penzvalto

When I first learned about the University of Cincinnati, I was a little girl studying opera privately in my hometown of Cleveland. I knew that my idol, soprano Kathleen Battle, had studied there and that the Conservatory was renowned for producing topflight performers in both opera and musical theater. As I got older, I grew to view it as sacred ground and when I was invited to audition for their most advanced opera program, the artist diploma, it was one of the most surreal experiences of my life. I had worked hard for years, overcoming a severe learning disability and financial hardship in order to pursue the global opera career, which had primed me for that moment. I was so amazed when I found out that I was accepted and incredibly grateful to have been given the opportunity of a lifetime.

I expressed my gratitude to the school by engaging in volunteering throughout my time there and giving back to the school in any way that I could. I saw an advertisement for positions in the student government and was elected president of the university's Graduate Student Governance Association. I was invited to serve as a member of the president's cabinet and it was in this capacity that I was first introduced to Greg Hand, also known by his friends as simply "Hand," a unique and interesting fellow who directed communications for the university. Hand was a kindred spirit—he shared my aptitude and appetite for researching "missing history." I have a long-held passion for research and have spent much of my personal and professional time at the library reading up on the life and times of composers and the history of their operas. Because I was educated in advanced research technique, I am often called upon to find things that not even Google can find. Hand saw this spark and introduced me to a quest that had eluded him for years, the search for a photograph of the school's first African American graduate, Dr. Henry Malachi Griffin.

Hand became familiar with Dr. Griffin through his research in early university history. He had discovered that when the university planned to build a new campus on the southern end of Burnet Woods in the late 1880s, the heirs of Charles McMicken had filed a lawsuit in order to prevent it from happening, because they had discovered evidence of black students being admitted to UC. This jeopardized the future of the institution because the elder McMicken's will stipulated that funding was contingent upon solely white students being permitted to attend. The lawyer for the heirs asked Cornelius Comegys, chairman of the UC board, to testify to whether it was true that black students were admitted. "Yes," Comegys replied. "A very distinguished one graduated about five years ago." Griffin had indeed begun his career with that act of successful rebellion, and it was noted by the *New York Freeman* that he was the first "colored student" to graduate from UC in 1886. Although Griffin is considered to be a pioneer in university history, Hand discovered that no photographs had been preserved in the university archives, nor had any picture of this illustrious alum been known to have *ever* existed. The sad fact is, it is likely he was excluded from class photographs because of his race.

Dr. Griffin's achievement is perhaps rendered even more remarkable when considering his family history. Historical evidence suggests that his father, Peter, came from extremely humble circumstances and may even have spent the earlier days of his life as a slave. His father eventually married and became a farmer. Henry did not, however, adopt this family tradition, and instead enrolled as a freshman at the University of Cincinnati in 1882. He did possess his father's work ethic, and worked as a coachman in order to support his studies. He resided on Barr Street with a husband and wife, both schoolteachers.

On June 17, 1886, Henry attended his commencement ceremony, and the *Commercial Tribune* reported that "Henry M. Griffin (colored)" had presented the abstract of his thesis on Plautus and he was awarded the degree of bachelor of arts. The *New York Freeman* (June 26, 1886) stated that the graduation of Griffin was "especially noteworthy…for the reason that the will of the late Charles McMicken, who gave the money to found and maintain the University, forbade the admission of colored students. But times change and the trustees have quietly ignored this proviso and freely admitted colored students; although Mr. Griffin is the first to receive a diploma."

I was inspired by Dr. Griffin. He had overcome enormous circumstantial barriers and prevailed, and I keenly felt the injustice of this important student's image being left out of the history books. I promised Hand that I would aid in the search and proceeded to comb the local archives, spending copious amounts of time at the Cincinnati Library examining microfiche from the late 1800s. It was exciting and I couldn't help imagine myself not unlike another titian-haired sleuth, Miss Nancy Drew. Unlike Miss Drew, I soon determined that my research would need bolstering, and called my uncle, an avid genealogical researcher in keeping with his steadfast Mormon tradition. If anyone could find a photographic needle in the proverbial historical haystack, it would be him. I provided him with all of the facts on Dr. Griffin that had guided my search thus far, all carefully curated and transmitted to me by Hand. However, even my uncle, who had access to robust genealogical software and state-of-the-art databases, was at a loss. I was discouraged, but undaunted. The more I learned about this young man's perseverance, the more profoundly I felt the importance of continuing the search.

I learned from Hand that Dr. Griffin had headed west after his graduation and worked as a teacher in Sedalia, Missouri, near Kansas City. He taught at Lincoln School, which, at a time when "separate but equal" was the norm, had remarkable success. A local newspaper wrote: "That the colored child is capable of high mental training is no longer doubted by intelligent observers, and Lincoln School is a standing answer to all who assert the contrary." Dr. Griffin's presence certainly acted as catalyst of this change of attitude and he continued his work as an educator, eventually rising to the role of principal of the Howard School in Warrensburg, Missouri, which was a remarkable institution that had been built by African American citizens assisted by the Freedman's Bureau in order to educate their children on a high level, something which the existing educational system did not allow.

Dr. Griffin continued his labor of love and worked to educate and inspire the young to achieve their goals. He eventually began to realize that he too was being called to follow his dreams even further. He made the decision to head east and traveled to New York City, where he enrolled in Long Island College Hospital Medical School. I was impressed by his courage to make such a remarkable journey, and shortly after my own graduation from UC in 2012, I was invited to

Juilliard and found myself following Dr. Griffin's footsteps to the Big Apple. After spending years in the Midwest, the culture shock of arriving in New York made me think about the spirit of this young man, who blindly took a giant leap outside of his comfort zone in order to pursue a dream that many may have viewed as foolish. It was heartening to learn that the 1905 *Medical Directory of New York, New Jersey, and Connecticut* revealed that H. M. Griffin had graduated from Long Island College Hospital in 1904 and went on to practice medicine in Harlem.

Indeed, for the next twenty years Dr. Griffin was an active member of the National Medical Association, the African American version of the American Medical Association. I enjoyed discovering one small irony—while I had to give up my car out of necessity upon arrival in New York, Dr. Griffin had in fact been an early adopter of the automobile. He owned a DeTamble, manufactured in Anderson, Indiana, and he was often seen navigating the city streets on his way to and from house calls. The *New York Age* reported in 1910:

> Dr. H. M. Griffin, who has his office on 135th street, is the first one of our doctors to use an automobile. Dr. Griffin explains that he does not like the idea of those Southern physicians getting ahead of New York, and therefore he recently purchased a small runabout in which to make his professional calls. The doctor learned to run that car in a week but he is taking little chances. He explains that he is well insured, and there are a score of undertakers in the immediate vicinity and a hospital on the next corner.

Dr. Griffin served the people of New York and continued to practice medicine until a year before his death in 1931.

Now that I was in New York, I had a distinct advantage—it was much more likely that Dr. Griffin would have been photographed later in life, and perhaps even at his medical school graduation. One afternoon, I left Juilliard and visited the archives of the Brooklyn Library, where I pored over several reels of microfiche before suddenly coming across the headline "Long Island College Hospital, Graduating Class of 1904." I drew a sharp breath.

I had found it! Before me, I saw a photograph featuring every member of his graduating class. Excitedly, I sent the scanned images over to my mentor Hand, and we proceeded to delight in the discovery. There was one drawback—while the number of individuals matched the number of names in the graduating directory, the photograph was not indexed and it was impossible to accurately determine which of the men was Dr. Griffin. While this was not ideal, I now had a photograph that had been published in the *Brooklyn Eagle*, and its corresponding article served as incontrovertible evidence that H. M. Griffin had in fact been a part of the 1904 graduating class.

In order to index the photograph, I knew I would have to dig deeper. I explored the archives of Long Island College Hospital, now called SUNY Downstate Medical Center, where he had received his MD. After some Googling, I reached out to the woman listed as historian at his alma mater, Cheryl Marriott, who immediately felt invested in our search. I emailed her the photograph, along with all of the information Hand and I had collected over the years, and she did a cursory search of the archives. As it happened, the archive had recently moved and all of the physical files had been shuffled around, so cross-referencing this photo was challenging and Cheryl's valiant efforts were understandably unsuccessful. She confirmed that we had actually produced more information on Dr. Griffin than the archive had itself, and she encouraged me to travel to the library in order to search through the materials. Working at Juilliard meant that I had few days off and the archives were open only for limited times, so I planned well in advance when I would travel to its location in Brooklyn, choosing a date in early February. Unfortunately, weather and scheduling conflicts meant that a number of difficulties, including a blizzard, intervened and we were unable to meet until June of 2014.

When the day finally arrived, I eagerly prepared all of the materials I had collected and arrived at the archive anxious to meet my new friend Cheryl. She came out to the street and greeted me, and as we entered the archive I instantly understood the magnitude of the job ahead of me. We dug through decades of written work and publications in order to find hard copies of all of the student newspaper yearbooks and archives, hoping to find an indexed version of the graduating class photo. I locked myself into a study room and searched through every possible lead. Again, I came up empty, but after seeing his name in print and connecting with his roots in a substantial way, I felt a much closer connection to the elusive doctor.

I began to realize that every item of knowledge, however small, was a gem and contributed to a larger picture of the person I was researching. I managed to uncover some bits of information previously unknown, including that fact that Griffin was an engaged alumnus of his medical school and even attended an event there two years before passing away. There were several moments when my weary eyes thought they had glimpsed a miracle, only to be disappointed. Perhaps the most disappointing of these moments came when I was searching for an obituary during the time shortly after his death. I came across a photograph of an African American man and read his name: "Dr. Henry M...Minton." After the shock wore off, I realized it was not him. Sadly, there proved to be no photograph, indexed or otherwise, to be found. LICH already had photos from 1886 of two African American graduates they had been unable to identify. Now they had three, as I had just added to their woes. I wrote an email to my mentor, informing him of our progress. "Please inform all interested that while I have not found the photograph, I managed to substantiate the earth-shattering fact that Dr. Griffin attended a party in 1929."

After exhausting the resources at the archives, I returned to the city discouraged, but undeterred. I continued to follow leads at local and national archives until I learned about the Schomberg Institute for Black Culture in Harlem. I arrived there early one day and met with a librarian from Dayton, Ohio, who seemed moved by Dr. Griffin's story. Together, she and I selected books, articles, and journals from the time, following every possible lead, including documentation of his presence as a member of the platform party for an event held by Booker T. Washington in 1912. Seeing a record of this filled me with pride, as the research Hand had conducted indicated that Washington thought very highly of Dr. Griffin and, when he was contacted by a representative of the Urban League investigating segregation in New York Hospitals, Washington suggested she contact Dr. Griffin and another doctor, and described both of them as "high-class men." I carefully combed through the photo archives, cross-referencing by name and occupation, until I was convinced there was nothing to be found. All of the librarians and archivists at both the Schomburg and the LICH archives were extraordinarily helpful and engaged deeply with his story—all of them insisted upon being kept informed as our search progressed.

Inspired by Dr. Griffin's determined rise to the top of his field, I applied to Columbia University for graduate study in history, and was accepted. I chose to further my interest, which now developed into a passion, working with inimitable scholar Professor Stephanie McCurry, widely regarded for her work on the immediate post–Civil War moment, and the history of postwar societies and processes of Reconstruction in the nineteenth and twentieth centuries. I was in heaven, and used the opportunity to expand my research skills and scour a veritable treasure trove of black history. While I was unable to successfully index my elusive photograph, I did have the chance to do more work on missing history, this time on Charlotte Forten, a contemporary of Dr. Griffin who worked in the early days of the Reconstruction to educate the freedmen and women on St. Helena's Island. I felt that it was fitting to use the skills that Dr. Griffin had, in a sense, encouraged me to hone, in order to bring light to the experience of other important civil rights leaders.

My passion for research and discovery, as well as the example of Dr. Griffin's unwavering determination to succeed, caused me to keep striving for excellence. Eventually, they led me toward another dream and I found myself standing before the doors of the technology research giant Google. A combination of grit and determination led to an exciting new journey out West. Rather than focusing merely on what is already lost, I've turned my efforts to helping Google's vital diversity work, helping to ensure that important history is accurately captured and that every voice has a platform from which to speak.

Since my arrival at Google, I have continued my quest for the photograph, calling upon the inner resources of the powerful search engine, in hopes that by the time this essay is published, we will be able to put a face to the name of Dr. Griffin. In the meantime, I am grateful for his legacy. Dr. Griffin transformed the University of Cincinnati from a narrow-minded institution into one that supports students of all backgrounds and abilities. His courage to ask for an equal education paved the way for generations of students to follow. His life has even inspired many, myself included, to reach beyond the circumstances which life has set forth, and to challenge all circumstantial barriers in order to achieve dreams which may, at first glance, seem too remarkable to be true. Indeed, the greatness of our university and of the singers and engineers and doctors who currently garner accolades stretches further back into the annals of our storied history. Dr. Griffin blazed a trail that was followed by many illustrious graduates, including the woman who served as my inspiration, African American soprano Kathleen Battle. Dr. Griffin has proven that small acts of rebellion matter and that no one should ever be permitted to define our limits for us. His University of Cincinnati produces students who are motivated to not only to reach for their own star, but to also reach behind, and pull back the curtain of time, in order to reveal the bright light of those who have paved the way. If I have learned anything about Dr. Griffin, it is that this living legacy would mean more to him than being recognized in a photograph; it is the sum of our collective action, which serves as a small amends to a great man.

Cincinnati Storystorm

by Julialicia Case

Before I came to Cincinnati, I sent my stories to Cincinnati, through cables and ether, accompanied by careful cover letters, for the evaluation of the editors of the *Cincinnati Review*. I had never visited the city, but I imagined steel mills and automotive factories, imagined grit and resilience and practicality, and so I sent them my toughest stories, the ones I expected could make it alone, at night, in a foreign place. *Those are the kinds of stories they like there*, I thought.

I lived in Illinois, in a town dwarfed by soy processing factories, a place where you could drive for hours and never leave the corn. I was newly married, and my life was the quietest and simplest it has ever been. I taught as an adjunct at a nearby college, but I spent my days writing, sending stories to cities I had never seen. I made pumpkin muffins and homemade granola, and ran for hours on a trail that wound through prairie and pine forests. I was born in Illinois, but I had never before lived there, and it was comforting to think of my life as a kind of homecoming, a place where a woman prone to wandering could unpack all of her boxes and plant a garden.

My husband and I are gamers, and we spent our evenings playing online, talking over our headsets with people from Canada, South Korea, Australia. It seemed like a life that could stretch into a lifetime. I could walk the dog every day, could perfect my St. Louis–style ribs recipe and eat brunch on Saturday mornings in tiny diners with plastic plates where women who never cared to impress anyone made eggs that tasted like the ones I made for myself at home. At night, I could cast spells and complete quests, and meet people from all over the world. *It could be enough*, I thought.

Then came the summer I decided to try my first writers' conference. I was excited to be admitted to Sewanee and offered a scholarship, but I trembled the whole long drive to Tennessee, arriving in the parking lot certain my insides were crumbling to pieces. At check-in, a woman with pink hair, a graduate student in the fiction program at the University of Cincinnati, handed me my key, and suddenly I was surrounded by people studying things: people who wrote and edited journals and planned exciting lessons to teach to their students. I was so nervous that, for ten days, I could only eat potatoes and dessert, but I attended almost every reading, and listened in fascination at every lecture.

An alumnus of the Cincinnati fiction PhD program participated in my workshop at the conference. His collection of stories had just been published, and he shared a piece he'd written about a family who kept a minotaur in their backyard. Still, years later, I remember the sadness of the minotaur and his swampland maze, felt all the stories of that week sticking to my skin, burrowing their way into my marrow. One night at the bar, I leaned against a plastic tiger statue while another student from Cincinnati's graduate program read a story about women perfecting their fighting skills under the aurora borealis in Alaska, women who had had enough. As she read, we were motionless, still, caught in the language, the room so quiet the walls seemed to buzz. Even the bartender stopped stacking glasses. *This is what stories are for*, I thought. For the rest of the week, as I wandered the campus and walked back and forth to the dining hall, I heard the question in my head: *Are you doing enough? Are you doing enough with your life?*

I applied to graduate programs in the fall, uncertain if anything would come of it. Cincinnati was the latest deadline, and I almost didn't finish the application. In my mind, the city was too cool for me, seemed to require a toughness and fortitude I wasn't sure I could muster. All around me, people my age were settling in and burrowing down. My husband was tenured; we were people of the prairie now. But I kept thinking of the minotaur, of those women in Alaska. I kept thinking of the city and the university that helped to nurture those stories. When the acceptances came, the faculty at the University of Cincinnati sent kind, frequent emails, and the graduate students added me to Facebook groups before I'd even accepted my offer. "We have to visit," my husband said, and so we drove.

It's funny how certain life choices make themselves, how the biggest, most drastic decision can become as simple as taking a breath. The first day of my campus visit, on my own, before I had spoken to anyone, I walked across Campus Green, marveled at the way the new Nippert Stadium emerged like a secret from behind the Campus Recreation Center. *This is okay,* I thought. *I could come here. This could all be okay.*

To be completely honest, I am afraid of almost everything. My life is a series of resolutions, a constant resolve to push past the anxiety, to let it beat in my chest like a small bird, but to never give into it, to never let it have its way. During my visit, I had coffee at Rohs Street Cafe with the faculty and tacos in Northside with the graduate students. Everyone was generous and welcoming. I even spent time downtown, where Carew Tower and the Great American skyscrapers blocked the sky, and there was no agriculture in sight. Everywhere I heard that voice. Always it said, *This will be okay.* I expected that meant it would always be okay, the other schools I visited, the other people I met, but it soon became clear it was a Cincinnati voice, a language of the city, maybe, telling me, telling all of us, *Things may not be perfect or ideal, but they are something we can handle. We can all handle the things that seem impossible.*

On the first day of fall classes, the professor immediately began to talk about fiction. She stood at the chalkboard and diagrammed the pieces of different types of stories. We started with westerns, their conflicts and resolutions, antagonists and themes. She held the chalk calmly as if the lesson were nothing special. I sat stunned, watching her and listening, seeing how the elements worked, like the underside of the world revealed, its gears and mechanisms suddenly visible. *I almost missed this,* I thought, marveling. *How terrible if I had never been a part of this.* I've completed almost two semesters now, and I feel that amazement, that gratitude, almost every single day here.

From the outside, the doctoral and master's programs in creative writing may not seem like much. We're a small program, unassuming, everyone working hard. Externally, my instructors and classmates look like regular people: denim, laptops, water bottles. It only takes a few minutes, though, a small conversation, before it's clear that their hearts and minds are magic, filled with moonlight and phosphorescence. The stories they tell are beautiful, surprising, and precise visions: a town where people's sorrows turn to stones; a man caring for a stolen baby tiger; an entire city beset by hauntings. Each week, my classmates describe the world in poetry: the heartbreak of parenting, the complexities of sexuality, the mysteries of love. I am awed by the depth and scope of their wisdom and talent, but most of all by the kindness here. Writing is not a faint-hearted pursuit. It requires solitude and diligence, requires immense, repeated rejection. It can be so easy to fall into competition and jealousy, but the writers here are quiet warriors, watching out for each other as we send our work into the world.

Cincinnati may not have the reputation and status of powerhouse cities like New York and Los Angeles, but Cincinnati writers are everywhere. They are publishing books, winning awards, presenting at conferences, and teaching at colleges and universities all around the country, passing on their ideas about craft to their students. The *Cincinnati Review* is one of the nation's most respected journals. Our faculty members win esteemed awards. Every month or so, we all nestle among the books in the Elliston Poetry Room and listen to writers such as Ander Monson, Julie Schumacher, and Carl Phillips read their work and answer our questions. Afterward we go to Arlin's Bar & Restaurant on Ludlow Avenue to buy them drinks, share baskets of fries as we talk about stories, the books we love, the things we've experienced, the strange experience of making words our daily work.

Stories seem so simple, so commonplace, and yet they are so important, such a crucial component of the people we are and the lives that we lead. UC summons storytellers, encourages and shapes their craft, and helps to define and influence the books of our time, the stories that will act as artifacts for generations to come. This semester, I've been helping to read the slush pile for the *Cincinnati Review*, sorting through the submissions people send to the journal, their deepest, most interesting visions. Each year, thousands of writers submit work from everywhere: Brooklyn, San Francisco, India, Malaysia, South Africa. It may be hard to notice it from the outside, while watching a football game or walking to class, but right now at this moment stories from all over the world are arriving at the University of Cincinnati. At this moment, writers all across the globe are thinking of us, considering our city and honoring its role in storytelling.

Returning to school has been a strange experience. A year ago, I thought I understood myself as a prairie person, a woman of freight trains and cottonwood trees. But here I am with my husband, considering the Ohio River from the overlook at Mount Echo Park. Here I am, sitting at my desk late at night, the lights of Brent Spence Bridge gleaming in the distance. My future is open, uncertain, and that is a terrifying sensation, but also an amazing one. Sometimes, while walking across McMicken Commons, I imagine those stories, all of our stories, hovering in the air, floating around us. They hang in the air like a snowstorm, stories like quiet, careful snowflakes. In the middle of snowfall, the world is so calm and watchful. We can't predict the outcome, can't understand in its midst, what the snow will bring. Inside the cozy warmth of our homes, we know, though, that things are changing. We know something important is happening, slowly, silently. In the morning, our world will not be the same.

Serendipity and Stewardship

The Preservation Lab

by Holly Prochaska

S erendipity. Librarians love serendipity. Librarians evoke the word and sing its merits more than most other academics. The joys of strolling through the stacks and seeing all the monographs on a subject clustered together awaiting discovery, banking on proximity. The efficiency of online journal browsing providing instant access to bibliographic citations that interconnect and branch like family trees. Happy accidents that may take a researcher down the rabbit hole or lead to the Holy Grail: an innovative idea.

It was a serendipity of seating choices that led to the formation of the Preservation Lab, the first joint academic/public library book and paper conservation lab in the country. But of course, it was created and shaped by institutional needs as well. Two prominent institutions and stewards of Cincinnati's rich cultural heritage were both seeking a path to preserve the future of their unique collections in an economical and sustainable way. But the reasons, the persuasive arguments, and the collaborative agreements—they all came well after the idea, which started with a simple happenstance of seating.

In July 2010, the preservation librarian at the University of Cincinnati (me) sat down next to a Public Library of Cincinnati and Hamilton County conservation assistant, Veronica Sorcher, who I had met before at book arts workshops and lectures. We were attending a regional meeting to discuss preservation needs and activities in the state. In between the work of the meeting, Veronica and I discussed the various initiatives at our respective institutions, and she mentioned that the public library had submitted a grant to the State

Library of Ohio in hopes of opening its own preservation lab at the Main Library downtown.

My thoughts ricocheted from one idea to another at this news. How exciting it would be to have close colleagues with whom to share knowledge and expertise. Maybe we could pool our resources and jointly purchase large equipment—box makers, guillotines, suction tables. Perhaps we could share the cost of bringing conservation experts to Cincinnati to train both of our preservation staffs.

Then...wait!

Why do we need two labs just two miles away from each other? Wouldn't we be performing the same type of work: book and paper preservation? Why should the public library start a lab from scratch when the University of Cincinnati already had a lab? Couldn't we both make a bigger leap forward if we combined our resources and expertise, and worked together?

What does a library preservation lab do?

Preservation labs preserve and conserve the collections of their parent institutions. In libraries, preservation labs generally have a focus and expertise in books and paper. "Preservation" refers to the decisions and practices that reduce the need for "conservation," and includes activities such as environmental monitoring, disaster recovery preparation, pest management, proper storage and handling, and so on.

"Conservation" refers to the physical treatment and repair of materials to stabilize them physically. In a book and paper lab these materials are commonly single sheets, such as maps, or bound volumes, such as manuscripts. Two other important distinctions within a lab are the workflow paths for special collections items and general circulating materials. Special collection items, which make individual libraries unique, have immense cultural value and often considerable monetary value, and, therefore, are treated by professional conservators or under their direct supervision. General circulating materials, mostly textbooks and trade publications with high circulation rates, are repaired by skilled conservation technicians and student assistants who are generally trained in-house.

The University of Cincinnati Libraries has operated a preservation lab since the early 1980s. The services offered by the lab have fluctuated since its opening, from a fully functioning lab performing both special collection and general collection treatments with a suite of preservation services (environmental monitoring, exhibit prep, commercial bindery prep, consultation, etc.), to a basic lab offering general repair, end-processing, and bindery prep. In early 2010, we were somewhere in the middle: providing general collections repair, with a contract conservator working twelve hours a week tackling the special collection conservation backlog, while slowly expanding into other preservation services. Staff included two conservation techs, a (commercial) bindery technician, a contract conservator, and a half-time preservation librarian.

The Public Library of Cincinnati and Hamilton County had never had a preservation lab. The library took a distributive approach, relying on contract conservation for their special collection conservation, a commercial bindery for repairs that could be made with rebinding, and a room dedicated to basic repairs performed by two conservation assistants. Wanting to expand the repair operation, the public library applied for the grant to fund book and paper conservation tools, equipment, supplies, and training.

In July 2010, not only were the two institutions in adjacent seats, we were in a similar position in terms of wanting to expand preservation services, having focused our limited resources on primarily addressing general collection repairs while falling further behind on the backlog of special collections conservation.

So now we leave the topic of serendipity, with its ease, and move to the second phase of our story: the hard, deliberate work to create a collaborative lab, sustain it, and have it grow and improve. Not surprisingly this stage begins and ends with meetings. Many meetings.

After the Library Services and Technology Act awards were announced and Cincinnati's public library was not among those receiving a grant, I met with its former assistant director, Jason Buydos, to discuss the broad topic of collaborating on preservation. The initial brainstorming sessions ran the gamut of collaboration schemes, from a pay-for-services model (with UC providing services) to a fully integrated preservation lab shared by both institutions, jointly staffed, funded, and administered.

A spoiler in paragraph two has already revealed that the two institutions agreed that the collaborative lab model better met each institution's needs and goals. UC had an established lab facility with tools, equipment, supplies, and general collections repair expertise, but no funding available to hire a full-time conservator. In contrast, the public library, in anticipation of a successful LSTA grant, had set aside capital for personnel (two conservation assistants and a conservator), but lacked the funds to establish and equip the physical lab.

We each had a part of the solution available to us and we were each ready to collaborate and experiment to build the collaborative lab. Encouragement for exploring the innovative service model that could address both institutions' conservation and preservation needs was quickly forthcoming from UC and the public library administration. In order to bolster support from each institution's stakeholders, it was decided the Public Library of Cincinnati and Hamilton County should reapply for the LSTA grant, this time as a collaborative lab. If awarded, it would provide the funds to double the tools, equipment, and supplies necessary to accommodate the addition of the public library staff in the existing UC lab. Moreover, the support from the State Library of Ohio, in the form of an award, would provide a political "vote of confidence" for this new model of collaboration. While our institutions awaited the grant award announcement, public library administration and I forged ahead drafting the Memorandum of Understanding between our organizations, working on plans to renovate the preservation lab to accommodate the larger staff and additional equipment, and coming to agreement on financial and production reporting standards.

Huzzah! In October 2011, the State Library of Ohio awarded the Public Library of Cincinnati and Hamilton County $81,012, with the public library providing the required matching funds. With this financial and political support, both UC and the public library administration were fully committed to making the collaborative lab a reality and were therefore ready to make the Memorandum of Understanding official (i.e., call the lawyers). While UC general counsel and the Hamilton County prosecutor's office reviewed the draft document, the lab staff began integrating into one team.

Immediately after the award announcement, the two public library conservation assistants began working half-time at the UC Preservation Lab located in Langsam Library. The public library staff members were trained by UC staff on all the general circulating repair treatments, ensuring that the lab would have one standard best practice. And we all began to learn from one another the subtle differences between our two institutions: the variances in our collections and materials, the differing priorities for conservation, dissimilarities in catalogs and cataloging standards, and bits of jargon, abbreviations, and acronyms that seemed like a foreign language, or worse—hazing. While this important time of team building was going on, the new equipment was pouring in and the department space was being renovated. Such an exciting time!

On December 29, 2011, the official Memorandum of Understanding between UC Libraries and the Public Library of Cincinnati and Hamilton County was signed (in a parking lot at 4:00 P.M. on the hood of the public library assistant director's car, by a representative from the Hamilton County prosecutor's office), just in time for our official opening on January 3, 2012. With the addition of our lab conservator, who began late that January and brought the final missing piece of special collections care, the collaboration was in full swing with materials flowing in and out of the lab from both UC and the public library.

Now, UC and PLCH have four years of experience with the collaboration. We swiftly moved from serendipity to hard work to model for other collaborations (though we've never left hard work or meetings). The lab has generated broad interest from other institutions hoping to rejuvenate or build new preservation services. Lab staff members have presented about the collaboration at major conferences (American Institute for Conservation, American Libraries Association, Ohio Library Council, Connecting to Collections), hosted visitors, conducted tours, and acted as preservation consultants. We continue to learn and grow, and to try and share our knowledge both through the lab's blog (http://blog.thepreservationlab.org/) and the digital resource page (http://digital.libraries.uc.edu/preservation/). As for me, I personally am even fonder of serendipity, ready to see where it might lead next.

A quick note on timing. The kernel of an idea began in July 2010. Brainstorming started in November 2010. Full support was obtained after the grant award in October 2011, and we officially "cut the ribbon" in January 2012. Anyone in academia, or any large organization, can appreciate the lightning-like speed of making this project a reality. It speaks to the institutional support, strong wills, and amazing support and teamwork from dozens of people at both institutions.

There are many people to recognize for helping to make the collaborative preservation lab a reality, but special thanks must be given to Kimber Fender, the Eva Jane Romaine Coombe Director of the Public Library of Cincinnati and Hamilton County, and Victoria Montavon, dean and university librarian emeritus, University of Cincinnati, for their leadership and support of the initiative from its inception.

The Challenges of Creating the Bearcat Transportation System

by Jerry P. Tsai

On Monday, March 27, 2006, the Bearcat Transportation System officially began service for the students, faculty, and staff at the University of Cincinnati. To the general UC population, the ribbon-cutting probably seemed like the typical pomp and circumstance that the university did for most new initiatives. Unbeknownst to most were the years of trials and tribulations overcome by the members of student government in order to make the BTS a reality.

I served as the undergraduate student body president at UC during the 2006–07 academic year, just after the BTS officially began running. By the time of this publication, hundreds of thousands of rides will have been delivered in the thirteen years since its inception. Quite the accomplishment for a student-led initiative.

This story begins in the winter of 2004, when Justin Shafer and Ben Hines ran for student body president and vice president. This was my freshman year and I had the privilege to be a part of their campaign team. In the months leading up to the official three weeks of student campaigning, we worked diligently to formulate a meaningful campaign message and identify the most important issues our fellow Bearcats wanted addressed by the student government. Though there were numerous topics we could focus on, the two biggest were campus safety and transportation. At the time, student government provided an on-demand transportation service called NightWalk (now called NightRide), but this was not a comprehensive transit system. In the brainstorming sessions for the campaign, we created the idea of a shuttle system for students that would transport them from nearby neighborhoods to campus during the week for class, as well as a nightlife shuttle system for students to enjoy the Cincinnati and northern Kentucky entertainment areas on Thursday, Friday, and Saturday evenings. This was the genesis of the Bearcat Transportation System.

Justin and Ben won their elections that spring and began the process of delivering on their campaign promises. I served on their cabinet as one of their executive vice presidents, and saw firsthand the process involved in taking an *idea* of a transportation system and making it into an *actual* transportation system. Needless to say, there were many hurdles to overcome and hoops to jump through.

Over the next year, Justin, Ben, and the team navigated through the process of figuring out the funding for the BTS, who would run the system if it were actually put into place, what it would take to get the system approved by university officials—and the list goes on and on. Ultimately, the initial start-up funding would come from the students in the form of an increase to the student fee. But this couldn't just happen; it required the entire student body to vote on a referendum to approve or reject an increase in their student fee to implement the Bearcat Transportation System. And this vote would have to occur during the next student government election in spring of 2005.

That spring there would actually be two referendums on the ballot, one for the BTS and a second for a smoking ban on campus except for designated areas. Prior to the referendums, we launched an aggressive informational campaign to ensure the students were aware of all of the details—pamphlets, information sessions, town hall meetings, and more. This also included printing and distributing a map of the routes that the BTS would operate, should it pass, routes that I had the opportunity to help create.

During the winter quarter of 2004–05, Bill Brash and I were working in the student government conference room when Justin came in and asked, "Are you guys busy?" Not wanting to continue whatever homework we were doing, we responded, "Nope, what can we help with?" Justin then asked us to figure out what the nightlife route for the BTS should be if we wanted to have a stop in Mount Adams, Newport on the Levee, and Main Street in downtown Cincinnati. This sounded like a fun project, so we jumped right in!

With today's technology, this would likely be a thirty-minute project, but in 2005 Google Maps didn't exist and we did not have the luxury of GPS or smart phones. This meant that Bill and I had to figure out this route using physical (yes, paper) maps and a basic online mapping system called MapQuest. As you could imagine, this took much longer than thirty minutes. Once Bill and I determined what we thought was the best route, using highlighted paper maps as well as numerous sheets of printed MapQuest directions, we were ready to drive the route.

Together, we jumped into Bill's car to test out what would eventually become the nightlife route for the BTS. What should have been a pretty straightforward forty-five-minute route ended up being a multiple-hour ordeal as Bill and I struggled to navigate the many one-way streets of Mount Adams, resulting in numerous loops around the same streets and exclamations of "How do we get out of this place?" and an intense stretch of crossing the I-471 highway, to name a few of the highlights. Despite this, we eventually figured out what the route and stops should be for the BTS nightlife route. Afterward, Bill used a mapping computer system he had access to as an urban planning major to put together a map of all of the BTS routes, which would end up being used in the promotional materials, brochures, and pamphlets for years to come.

In April of 2005, the students passed the transportation referendum approving an $8 increase to the student fee to be specifically designated toward the creation and operation of a Bearcat Transportation System. (As an aside, the smoking ban was also passed by the student body at this time.) With this passage, we thought the BTS could begin at the start of the following academic year in the fall of 2005. Little did we know that the State of Ohio would push the launch date back almost a full year!

Andrew Burke and Dominic Berardi served as student body president and vice president during the 2005–06 academic year, and I served in their cabinet as well. Though we had officially gotten approval from the student body to proceed with a fee increase to implement the BTS, that year the State Legislature passed a budget that would allow for only a 6 percent fee increase for all state universities. The University of Cincinnati had already budgeted for that full 6 percent increase and therefore the $8 fee increase for the BTS would be an addition, putting UC out of compliance. The Ohio Controlling Board was not okay with this, since it had the responsibility to make sure all state universities did not exceed the 6 percent tuition and fee increase that was passed by the legislature and signed by the governor. At this point, it looked like the BTS was not going to happen for another two years, when the next state budget would be up for a vote.

Andrew, Dominic, and the team realized BTS's grave situation and also knew we could not let all of the work from the last year and a half go to waste. We were determined to figure out a way to keep the BTS alive. Through personal connections to UC College of Law alumnus and State Representative Bill Seitz, we were able to get a letter written to the Ohio Controlling Board in November 2005 that clarified that the $8 fee increase for the BTS was an initiative voted on and approved by the actual students to provide a service that would help the entire student body address transportation insufficiencies. This was not a ploy by the university to bypass the 6 percent cap, but rather a democratic vote to voluntarily increase their fees by the UC student body. Later that month, a small group of student government officers and university administrators including Andrew, Dominic, UC Vice President of Governmental Relations and University Communications Greg Vehr, and I attended the Ohio Controlling Board meeting on November 15, 2006, to explain why the $8 fee increase should be allowed outside of the 6 percent cap.

Though we did not learn the fate of the BTS that day, we did eventually get the approval from the Ohio Controlling Board to proceed with the BTS. About four months later, on Monday, March 27, 2006, the Bearcat Transportation System officially began service for the students, faculty, and staff at the University of Cincinnati.

Because of the hard work, perseverance, and creativity of the many individuals involved in creating the BTS, Bearcats today enjoy a transportation system that increased safety for students traveling to class, connected students with entertainment districts throughout Cincinnati, and expanded the transportation resources available to the UC community. One of those expanded services is the partnership between UC and the Southwest Ohio Regional Transit Authority (SORTA), which operates the Metro bus system in the greater Cincinnati region.

During the 2006–07 academic year, I served as student body president alongside Jeremy Driscoll, the student body vice president, and, in conjunction with the university administration, we were able to form a partnership with SORTA/Metro that provided all UC students, faculty, and staff free rides on the Metro when they presented a valid UC ID. This partnership still exists today, but with a discounted fee per semester. Without the successful implementation of the BTS, the SORTA/Metro partnership would not have occurred so soon.

Additionally, my experience helping to create the Bearcat Transportation System at UC has positively influenced my life after college. In September 2017, Aslyne Rodriguez and I co-founded EmpowerBus LLC, providing workforce-ready citizens with reliable transportation to and from work. My experience with the BTS and SORTA/Metro partnership influenced the creation of this social enterprise designed to help create pathways to employment and family stability. We currently serve the Central Ohio/Columbus region by transporting New Americans (immigrants and refugees) who need a way to get to their jobs at manufacturing and distribution centers.

It is very cool to see my time in student government working on the Bearcat Transportation System turned into something that is so meaningful for the students at UC, but also now extends beyond campus to the citizens of Central Ohio. This is an incredible example of how a UC experience and education can and will continue to positively impact the world. For anyone who has ridden or will ride on the BTS, remember that there were numerous opportunities for it to fail. But due to the grit, determination, and ingenuity of numerous student leaders over numerous years working toward a collective vision of a better university, we have something that improves UC's and Cincinnati's quality of life.

From International Student to Bearcat for Life

by Sid Thatham

For an international student, life at an American university can be really overwhelming. For some of us, it's a pretty big deal to leave family and friends behind for the first time and take our first flight to travel thousands of miles to a new place and live among strangers. But this endeavor has a lot to offer beyond just academics. For many of us, an American degree means better career prospects and job security; we tend to forget that the paramount importance of this experience is to learn—not just about our course material, but about ourselves as well. Most of us fail to consider that there is so much more that we can take with us in addition to our degree when we leave our university. My home for the past three years, the place you all know as the University of Cincinnati, has taught me all of that. The people and the life I've enjoyed at UC has surely transformed me for the better and will continue to do so.

My full name is Srinivasa Thatham Sampath Kumar. I am a graduate student from India. At UC, I go by Sid Thatham. It saves the time and effort required to pronounce my name right. Right off the bat, life at UC has given me a sense of individuality. While some of my fellow students from India at UC and friends at other universities in the United States had a tough time settling down, I felt at home from the outset, thanks to the amazingly friendly people on campus and a wide variety of resources available for us.

UC embodies the practice of experiential learning and a climate of inclusiveness and civility. There has been so much going on here since day one that I have hardly had time to get bored or feel homesick. I've had a plethora of chances to participate in both academic learning and co-curricular learning with equal passion. These opportunities have not only helped me learn about myself, but about the needs of others and my responsibilities toward their needs as well.

I was elected as the president of the Indian Student Association for the year 2013–14 and became an international ambassador for UC during the same time. This helped familiarize myself with international students' greatest needs. I wanted to represent a possibility that all international students have what it takes to make a difference. This was the drive behind co-founding UC AirportRide, a student-run shuttle service to the Cincinnati–Northern Kentucky Airport, free of charge for all UC students, with two friends of mine on the undergraduate student government. With students already paying a lot for books and other things apart from their tuition, any money not spent is money saved, right? One of the numerous messages I got from the new students at UC says: "Thanks a lot, Sid. You've been of great help to current and new students. You have no idea how valuable you are to UC, leave aside the Indian Student Association. Personally, my transition to UC has been very smooth when compared to my friends at other universities. Cheers!"

With a campus as diverse and vibrant as ours, the greatest influence on most of the college students here is the UC community. Our university has given me and my fellow students opportunities to work together with groups that are often segregated, and has encouraged increased co-curricular participation. This has helped me showcase our student community to numerous prospective students over the years through various social media forums, building a broader student community. Programs like Emerging Ethnic Leaders have given me a chance to interact with freshmen and sophomores and share my experiences with the emerging leaders.

The United States is often called "Melting Pot of the World" and the cultural diversity here is like nowhere else. For some of us international students who come from racially homogenous countries, the value of this diversity and inclusion is an alien concept. All we know as kids is what the media shows us, and its perspective on certain cultures and communities in the United States is often skewed. UC has played a major role in my learning diversity and inclusion. My involvement with the Racial Awareness Program at UC was such an eye-opening experience and contributed a great deal toward my understanding of life in the United States. Through my involvement with UC's first TEDx team, I learned that "Diversity

Is Being Invited to the Party; Inclusion Is Being Asked to Dance." I have been sharing these experiences, the knowledge I have learned with fellow students and encouraging involvement ever since. Programs like TEDxUCincinnati, have provided a platform to students, staff, faculty, and the community to share ideas and inspire each other, and experience the intellectual adrenaline rush of simply imagining a significant accomplishment through these ideas.

My time at UC has helped me understand, value, and embrace the spirit of discovery. As I said, studying at an American university is more than just getting a degree. To me, UC has been a place that encourages creativity, innovation, collaboration, and entrepreneurship. The university has offered me several opportunities for applied learning and engagement with real-world problems, one of which is the Hyperloop. Transportation is at the cusp of transformation. Human travel as we know is about to change in the near future, and our lives will change for the better along with it. Imagine living in Cincinnati and going to Chicago for work in half an hour. Students from Cleveland could commute to the University of Cincinnati for their classes in twenty minutes. Sounds too ambitious? It sounds very doable for a group of students at Hyperloop UC.

In August 2013, the founder, CEO/CTO of SpaceX, and CEO/product architect of Tesla Motors, Elon Musk, put forth an idea called Hyperloop, a conceptual high-speed transportation system—a fifth mode of transportation, after rail, road, water, and air. Hyperloop will be "a cross between a jet plane, a rail gun, and an air hockey table." Fast-forward two years to June 15, 2015, SpaceX announced that it will sponsor a Hyperloop Pod Design Competition and would build a one-mile test track near its headquarters in Hawthorne, California.

There were over 1,200 teams in the earlier stages of this competition in October 2015. After design review rounds, the University of Cincinnati Hyperloop team, Hyperloop UC, was invited by SpaceX to Texas A&M University for their "Design Weekend" event in late January to present the design to the entire world.

In all, 124 worldwide teams including Hyperloop UC were invited to this event with U.S. Secretary of Transportation Anthony Fox, Elon Musk, and several other big names. After initial judging, twenty-two teams were selected to go to the final round and build their prototype pods to be tested in California later this year. Hyperloop UC, the only team from Ohio to have qualified, is one of the finalists along with MIT, UCLA, and Delft University among others. Eight other teams were later added to pool of twenty-two, making it a total of thirty teams in the final round. Long story short, Hyperloop UC has a one in thirty chance of changing the way people will travel.

Working on this project, I have learned that life does not get better by chance, it gets better by change. UC has given me an opportunity to be a vehicle for change and have a positive impact on the students who are a part of the team and we hope, many positive impacts on humankind.

Everybody has good things to say about our project on social media. ANSYS Inc. conducted an interview of our team to put it up on its social media. Our success there was noticed by TIME.com and it reached out to feature our designs. Our team was invited for a thirty-minute podcast interview by 10x labs, a European podcast giant, to talk about our project and our university; this interview was later made available all over Europe. Other media coverage that Hyperloop received includes *Popular Science, The Verge, Bloomberg, Fortune,* and others. We continue to make news. This has done a great deal of good for the students who are a part of the team and coming this far wouldn't have been possible without the support of our university. Over 100 years ago, Ohio became "the birthplace of aviation." Today, as the only team from Ohio, having beaten the likes of Stanford University, Hyperloop UC continues to work toward its primary goal. While envisioning the future is exciting, we continue to work in the present toward making "Ohio—The Birthplace of Hyperloop."

This project stands testimony to the fact that UC provides its students with opportunities to:

- Enhance learning, professional development, communication skills, and leadership qualities in ways that cannot be realized in coursework alone.
- Apply knowledge from class to groundbreaking real-life context while still in school.
- Team up with people from various educational and cultural backgrounds to get an idea of a diverse workplace.
- Network with university administration and professionals off campus.

I believe that the world should be a better place because I'm here. I want my efforts, my work, and my time to mean something. I believe that I am wasting my time if I am not making whatever little difference I can make in changing somebody's life for the better. UC has encouraged me to purse this desire.

I joined UC knowing very little about my future as a person, as an individual. My time at UC has been an amazing time for self-discovery. I have had to encounter stressors inherent to being a student leader, in addition to the stress faced by graduate students who spend more time in their labs than at home. But life on campus has helped me strike a balance between my primary role as a student and that of a student leader; in fact, it has made the experience more enjoyable.

I can surely say that I've transformed for the better as a person when I compare myself with Sid, the international student who came to Cincinnati in 2012. UC has guided me through this transformation. I gave up offers of admission from four other universities from California, Illinois, New York, and New Jersey. Looking back, coming to UC was the best decision of my life. I have had a great time at UC and I am sure thousands of students share the sentiment. I was just an international student from India and now I am a proud "#BearcatForLife."

Vignettes from a Corner of Café Momus

by Vidita Kanniks

C lose your eyes. Take a second to visualize the quintessential university coffeehouse.

You may see various tables and chairs, maybe a squishy armchair or two, a large number of MacBooks and the occasional PC. You may smell the wafting aroma of freshly brewed coffee or a toasted croissant. You may hear the furious scuttling of fingers over laptop keyboards, a classic jazz standard or that go-to coffeehouse soundtrack lingering in the background, featuring some new alternative artist who has not yet been discovered. You may sense the buzz of different conversations surrounding you, maybe even in languages foreign to you. This atmosphere, this undeniably "hip," fresh setting is a haven for brief, midday respites, emergency caffeine-fixes, first dates, meetings and brainstorms, exam cram sessions, spontaneous run-ins with friends, and so many more inevitable college experiences. It is a place of familiarity, comfort, and solace that arguably keeps many of us sane as we navigate through our hectically wonderful student lives.

My safe haven and happy place for the past three years as a University of Cincinnati student has undeniably been the good old faithful CCM café, nestled in the heart of campus, conveniently connected to the conservatory where I study classical voice. With my insatiable need to constantly make music jokes, I've always playfully called this place our "Café Momus" (despite the fact that it is actually a Starbucks) in reference to a very famous setting in Giacomo Puccini's opera *La Bohème*, a well-loved and widely performed work in the standard repertory. Café

Momus, in the opera, exists as a symbol for the artistic and social environment in which the characters live and the drama unfolds, further romanticizing the Parisian bohemian lifestyle in the nineteenth century—a notable movement in the history of Paris, its art, and its classicism. The city's young, eccentric, talented-yet-struggling artists would gather at the Café Momus to explore ideas, share thoughts, create art, and observe the bourgeoisie. The act of sipping a coffee and having a conversation at the Café Momus developed into an identity, to be remembered and admired for its elegance and brilliance for years to come.

The CCM café is hardly evocative of a Parisian bohemian aesthetic. It's just your every-day coffee place. But for us students, especially those of us music students who are identified regulars and admitted café-bums, it is truly an identifiable example of a modern-day Café Momus in regard to its instrumental presence in our daily lives and its sentimental presence in the memories of our college years. UC's College-Conservatory of Music is known to be one of the best conservatories in the country, even one of the best in the world. With a selective audition process, an elite group of students, and highly rigorous demands, our student population is truly a connected community. Each day when I walk into the café, whether to grab a snack between classes or to sit down and journal, read, or work on an assignment, I see my friends, colleagues, peers, and teachers. We exchange friendly smiles, have quick conversations or sometimes surprisingly deep conversations about life and love and personal goals. I've found myself spending countless hours imprinted into those wooden chairs, hunched over stacks of books, studying with fellow students for our upcoming exams on Baroque instrumentation, French art song, or eighteenth-century counterpoint technique. I've found myself simply entering the café just in anticipation of running into someone I know, just for that social interaction to cast a pleasant glow upon my day.

I was sitting in my favorite armchair by the window at the CCM Café the other day, enjoying my coffee and watching people go by, when I realized how meaningful these small moments have been to me. My identity as a musician and student has grown and defined itself exponentially throughout my years studying at this stellar institution. But my identity as a person, a human being, an artist, has truly stemmed from my social environment and those by whom I am constantly surrounded.

My immediate circle, my musical colleagues and I at the College-Conservatory of Music, are in some ways the bohemians of a modern world. We are the pioneers of a new movement of progressive art and redefined classicism. In our daily lives, we experience ups and downs, and then come together at the Café Momus to share our respective experiences, which inspire us to create beautiful art, leaving a legacy for the future. As a population of young, aspiring musicians at CCM, we are a generation of vivacious, driven talent. And we are so incredibly lucky to be immersed and surrounded, 360 degrees, by such an enriching atmosphere to not only learn, but also make unforgettable memories and relationships with people. If you were to ask any CCM student to picture our conservatory without its infamous café, full of past laughs, tears, hugs, and so many more cherished memories, I'm sure he or she would tell you that it is simply not possible, for that is the sentimental effect of having a Café Momus.

DAAP Slapped

by Victoria Fromme

"You've been DAAP slapped." Quite perplexed by the graffiti on the bathroom stall, I wondered what the statement meant on my first day of undergrad at the College of Design, Architecture, Art & Planning (DAAP). Little did I know I would be "slapped" with a lifestyle that I reminisce about years after I graduated. DAAP is an intense but rewarding lifestyle. DAAP is a culture of passion, imagination, and creativity. DAAP broadened my perspective, built my character, and strengthened my work ethic through the rigorous coursework, and provided a network of friends that encouraged me along the way.

I grew to expect the unexpected at DAAP. The building's slanted angles and burst of colors gave the impression I was walking into a fantasy. Inside those walls, I never knew what I was walking into—what art installation protested boldly in the foyer or which music pulsed as voguing models strutted down a catwalk. I can only imagine that if the mannequin perched high above the atrium were real, how much creativity he's seen from all of the fashion, graphic, urban, and building design students over the years. DAAP expanded my perspective on the world, enabling me to embrace the eccentric and underappreciated details of life. Everything became art. I started noticing the way the sun cast shadows on the huddle of bikes outside, the swirls in my cappuccino, and the artful cracks in the brick wall. Even my clothes and accessories became my canvas and artful expression. DAAP encouraged me to think unconventionally, to tinker, to take prudent risks, and be imaginative in every aspect of my life. DAAP enabled the innovative thinking that pays dividends in my career today.

I fully expected DAAP to be academically rigorous, and it certainly was. My classmates and I often scrupulously worked on our projects throughout the night until the morning sun flooded the studio. We would scramble to incorporate last-minute edits before final critique. This was not because we procrastinated but because we aspired for excellence. I remember spending two weeks selecting a font for my design portfolio that adequately depicted my personality. I wanted it to be perfect. Early on in my studies, I realized the importance of hard work, attention to detail, and balancing multiple demands at once. These values laid the solid foundation for my future.

All the while, I built incredible friendships and memories. My classmates became my family. Our overnight work sessions were accompanied by late-night pizza deliveries, the occasional karaoke or dance break, and hide-and-seek through the maze of DAAP. Even outside of class, we spent countless occasions together. I remember sledding down McMicken hill on our makeshift sleds, shopping in the Gaslight District, or strolling down McMillan trying to decide which cuisine sounded best for dinner. We were a support system through the challenging times and celebrated in our successes. We still joke about our shenanigans and look back fondly on the memories we created.

DAAP was the most challenging experience of my life, but it prepared me to be successful. Every time I visit Cincinnati, I add the University of Cincinnati to my itinerary, so I can stroll through DAAP and relive my memories. It delights me that no matter what time I visit, I see the glow of studio lights and students creating—not only designs but priceless memories.

Embracing the Uncertainty of Life

by Faith Prince

When I began at the College-Conservatory of Music, exactly forty-two years ago, I couldn't have imagined the journey my life would take. I was from a small town in Virginia. One of my earliest memories was imagining myself in front of my classmates performing a musical number. I used to practice in the living room of our home using a shelf of family photos as my attentive audience. This passion for performing realized itself through church choir, school show choir, to trying out and then starring in my high school musicals. My chorus teacher, Mr. Harries, then steered me to a college in the Midwest that had a BFA program for musical theater.

No one in my family had ever been in show business. It seemed as far away as an exotic land. Once this passion had entered my body, I no longer felt like the only one in control of my destiny. It was as though I had signed a contract with this inner voice. I remember not having the confidence, yet. However, my need to push through the fear, to follow this yellow brick road, was overwhelming.

After I received my joyous letter of acceptance, I remember a neighbor asking, "Faith, where are you going to college?" I proudly answered, "I've been accepted to the College-Conservatory of Music at the University of Cincinnati!" She exclaimed, "What? You aren't going to a Virginia state school? Where is Cincinnati?" I said, "OHIO!!!"

So if we go with this *Wizard of Oz* theme, Cincinnati was my Oz. I remember my heart racing as my parents and I drove across the Ohio River. Cincinnati, "The Queen City." Since I was a Prince, somehow that felt like an omen...then continuing around by the river, we caught a quick glimpse of Riverfront Stadium. My dad was thrilled that I was part of the town whose Reds might win the World Series, and they did that fall!

Little did I know that my pulse rate would continue to be at a steady fast pace for the next four years and beyond. That's how passion works. CCM was thrilling, scary, and exhilarating all at once. My knees felt wobbly every time I walked into the building. I remember praying hard just to let me push beyond the fear and stay—no going home like so many of my friends had done in their first quarter.

I found out I had very little knowledge of the musical theater canon, and even less experience compared to the other students there. I decided that that could be my wild card. I would simply be a sponge for the next four years, and I secretly called myself a turtle. (You know, the Tortoise and the Hare.) It was a slow road at the beginning, many boards, auditions, trials, and grueling lessons of putting oneself out there only to get critiqued, and judged, over and over and over again! My mentors at the time were the illustrious Worth Gardener, Oscar Kosarin, Earl and Stephanie Rivers, and Beverly Rinaldi. They pushed, prodded, lectured, challenged, and whipped me into proper shape for the world that was to come.

The education I received at the university was one of the defining moments in my life. Almost forty years go by quickly. I moved from CCM to New York City and did lots of regional theater throughout the country, lots of Off Broadway and Off-Off Broadway, and a few out-of-town Broadway wannabes. It took ten years for me to land my first Broadway show and it was a doozy: *Jerome Robbins' Broadway*. Then came Miss Adelaide in *Guys and Dolls*, *The King and I*, twenty years of shows, television roles, films, concerts, and my own one-woman shows, all with CCM at my center.

As an artist, I learned early on that it is a given to live day to day with the constant uncertainty of life. Embrace it! The Roman philosopher Tacitus rightly observed, "The desire for safety stands against every great and noble enterprise." Eckhart Tolle wrote, "If uncertainty is unacceptable to you, it turns to fear. If it is perfectly acceptable, it turns into increased aliveness, alertness, and creativity." It's a lot to ask, but consider the alternative.

The measure of success is tricky. In my profession, it could be awards, or landing that big film or TV series. But I believe success is really measured by how connected you are, how loved you are, and how you do what you do. If you look, you'll find these principles within every religion. At almost sixty, I realize the more

I know, the more I don't know. I still feel like a graduate student, but there are a few things I've learned along the way I would love to share with each of you as you embark down your own yellow brick road.

- Stay in your own lane. All you have to do is cross the finish line. It's your finish line. The cars in the other lanes don't matter.
- Love and be loved.
- Don't be afraid to ask for help.
- Invest in good linens.
- Be good to people. Not because it's going to get you something. Just do it.
- Be relentless!
- When in doubt, bake.

I truly believe that in this texting, twittering, insular culture of communication we navigate through today, we are losing the actual energy that transpires between people who share the same space. Be present. Don't forget to be a part of something bigger than yourself. I've learned from a life in the theater that collaboration is key. Your wealth is in your connective relationships. I realize I am no longer Dorothy, but your Fairy Godmother, here to tell you that "you've had it all along." So, click your heels and be on your way. I'll be here, living in the unknown, full of passion, looking for the signs to my next adventure, with big thanks to CCM and the University of Cincinnati from the start.

The Ultimate UC Trivia Quiz

by Kevin Grace and Greg Hand

QUESTIONS

01 The University of Cincinnati traces its origins to 1819. How many public universities in the United States can claim an older founding date?

02 What is the monumental sculpture built in Burnet Woods by University of Cincinnati students, and from where did they get the stones?

03 At University of Cincinnati commencement ceremonies, each college is announced with the same musical fanfare, with one exception. Which college gets special treatment?

04 Who is the only person to play on NCAA, NBA, and ABA championship teams?

05 In the early 1960s, who was the person largely responsible for giving the political and funding push to build two-year colleges in Ohio, leading to what is now UC Blue Ash and Clermont College at the University of Cincinnati?

06 Who was the UC history graduate who went on to become one of the major figures in the American counterculture of the 1960s?

07 Who was the University of Cincinnati president, a global guru in management studies, who enfranchised many underrepresented segments of UC during his tenure?

08 What was the name of the on-campus summer theater series at the College-Conservatory of Music from 1980 to 2004?

09 Which Cincinnati school principal was the first African American woman to earn a PhD at the University of Cincinnati?

10   Before the University Pavilion was built on the main campus of the University of Cincinnati, Beecher Hall occupied that site. For whom was that building named and what other name was used for the building?

11   UC's first Bowl game was the 1947 Sun Bowl played in El Paso, where the Bearcats beat Virginia Tech 18–6. However, there was much more to that game than football. What was the controversy that stirred up UC and the Cincinnati community?

12   What University of Cincinnati alum won the Nobel Peace Prize?

13   As dean of the College of Engineering at the University of Cincinnati from 1906 to 1939, Herman Schneider instituted a practice called "Hobby Hour." What was this?

14   When did the University of Cincinnati football team first play in a postseason game?

15   How many colleges are there at the University of Cincinnati?

16   There are a number of sculptures on the University of Cincinnati campuses, but what is the only living sculpture?

17   University of Cincinnati football player Leonard "Teddy" Baehr is generally credited as being the inspiration for UC's teams being named "Bearcats." After graduation, Baehr played for a professional football team for a short time. What was that team?

18   In May 1970, students at the University of Cincinnati briefly took over administrative offices to protest the war in Vietnam, and some of their signage said "SDS." What was "SDS"?

19   On the main campus of the University of Cincinnati, why is the entrance floor of different buildings variously on the first, second, third, or fourth levels, etc., rather than uniformly on the first?

20   What other animal besides the Bearcat do we employ as a sports mascot at the University of Cincinnati?

21   At the University of Cincinnati, where will you find Egyptian hieroglyphics?

22   Eight decades ago, University of Cincinnati students responded to a natural disaster in the city by organizing food and clothing drives and helping with communication stations. What was that disaster?

23   The original dome on Van Wormer (the first library building at UC and now an administration building) was removed in 1930 during renovation. A new dome was put on the building during additional renovations in 2006. Now,

colored lights can rotate within the dome. Within a million, guess how many colors are possible.

24 This former University of Cincinnati football coach was one of the pioneers in the use of video to break down game study. He also instituted the long forward pass instead of the traditional short passes near the line of scrimmage. Later he went on to coach professional football and is in both the Pro Football Hall of Fame and the College Football Hall of Fame. Who is he?

25 Where was the University of Cincinnati/Cincinnati College's first observatory located?

26 When did women begin playing basketball at the University of Cincinnati?

27 Where at the University of Cincinnati will you find carved words advocating the freedom of expression and opposition to book censorship?

28 How many college and departmental libraries (not library buildings, libraries) are there at the University of Cincinnati?

29 Who was the University of Cincinnati College of Law dropout who went on to develop household appliances, a lightweight economy automobile, and one of the most powerful radio stations in the world?

30 Within twenty-five, how many University of Cincinnati students had a study-abroad experience in 2015–16?

31 Who was the legendary University of Cincinnati coach named "Socko" and why was he/she called this?

32 On the main campus of the University of Cincinnati is Rieveschl Hall, named for George Rieveschl. What was his major contribution to science?

33 Where will you find a giant nautilus on the University of Cincinnati main campus?

34 What is the newest college at the University of Cincinnati and when was it formed?

35 What was the University of Cincinnati student magazine in the last quarter of the twentieth century that featured fiction, poetry, politics, fashion, social commentary, and photography? And, where can you find a copy of every issue?

36 What is the biggest margin of victory in University of Cincinnati football history?

37 Who is the youngest graduate in University of Cincinnati history?

38 In 1925, three University of Cincinnati graduates held three important federal government posts, thus greatly influencing national affairs. Who were they and what were their jobs?

39 In 1968 and 1969 this newly formed organization used the University of Cincinnati's Nippert Stadium for its meetings. What is this organization and what is its business?

40 At the University of Cincinnati there is a monument to the sacrifices of UC students and faculty during World War I. What and where is it? (Think broadly.)

41 Who can be credited with being the founder of both the University of Cincinnati's College of Education, Criminal Justice & Human Services, and the College of Nursing?

42 On the main campus of the University of Cincinnati there is a statue of a figure from classical mythology. Who is the figure and where is it?

43 This college, chartered in 1850 and incorporated in 1853, became a part of the University of Cincinnati in 1954. Its "round table" discussions were literally that: students and faculty sat around a round table and discussed the instructional material. What college was it?

44 Has anyone from the University of Cincinnati ever been commemorated on a postage stamp?

45 A part of the University of Cincinnati abuts an old cemetery. Where is it and what goes on there now?

46 The University of Cincinnati played its first football game in 1885 and its first intercollegiate game—against Miami University—in 1888. But at the time, UC was located in the original university building on the Clifton hillside, hence, had no campus football field. Where did the team play its home games?

47 What was the name of the University of Cincinnati summer theater venue on the banks of the Ohio River from 1967 to 1988?

48 What University of Cincinnati alum wrote the most famous and most widely used textbook in American history on how to write clearly and effectively? What is the book?

49 Name the University of Cincinnati president who served as a general in the Civil War.

50 In 1935, University of Cincinnati alum and bridge engineer Joseph Strauss took bricks from his alma mater to place in a pylon of San Francisco's Golden Gate Bridge. Some think these bricks came from the first McMicken Hall on UC's present campus, but they did not. From where did UC give up the bricks, and why was Strauss anxious to use them?

51 On October 2, 1973, the University of Cincinnati welcomed this franchise eatery, the first one ever on a college campus. What was it and where was it located?

52 On December 21, 1981, the University of Cincinnati basketball team entered the NCAA record book for a very specific reason. What was special about that game and what team did the Bearcats play?

53 In 1905, this now-traditional piece of music was played for the first time at a university commencement ceremony, and it happened at the University of Cincinnati! What was the music and who was the composer?

54 Taking into account all the University of Cincinnati's campuses—main campus, east campus, UC Blue Ash, and Clermont College—what is the university's oldest building and for whom is it named?

55 In what year did the University of Cincinnati achieve full status as part of Ohio's state colleges and universities system rather than remaining a municipal university?

56 Mick and Mack are just two of the many copies around the world of these famous lions. What name is generally used to refer to these lions?

57 The University of Cincinnati marks its bicentennial in 2019 because of two educational institutions founded in Cincinnati in 1819. What were those two institutions?

58 What UC professor is credited with launching the United States Weather Bureau?

59 Among the online tools used constantly by doctors and medical researchers, *Medline*, an online service of the US National Library of Medicine, is among the most trusted and prestigious. What UC alumnus is credited with creating the analog predecessor to *Medline*?

60 What annual honor, conferred by UC's College of Nursing, recognizes outstanding nurses in the Greater Cincinnati region who go above and beyond expectations to provide exceptional patient care?

61 What Cincinnati doctor wrote both UC's Alma Mater and Xavier University's fight song?

62 At one time, UC's maintenance department had authority to fine campus neighbors for what specific infraction?

63 The University of Cincinnati once had a campus in Mason, Ohio. What was it called?

64 Of the two sundials located on UC's campus, which one is reasonably accurate?

65 Where will you find a set of Magdeburg hemispheres displayed on campus?

66 Where does UC house a substantial collection of snow globes?

67 Today, UC's student media include an online radio station named Bearcast. Back in the day, UC once held the licenses for two radio stations. What were they?

68 In 1819, where did the students of Cincinnati College attend classes?

69 When did UC adopt red and black as school colors?

70 Who started the UC Marching Band?

71 What do writer Jorge Luis Borges, poet Gwendolyn Brooks, Congressional Representative Shirley Chisholm, astronaut John Glenn, comedian Bob Hope, civil rights activist Jesse Jackson, advice columnist Ann Landers, Chief Justice Earl Warren, and pioneer aviator Orville Wright have in common?

72 What popular UC sport was abandoned because of all the injuries sustained by student participants?

73 On December 10, 1890, the Cincinnati Zoo brought in a firing squad to execute an elephant. What does that bizarre incident have to do with UC?

74 What is UC alumnus Abe Bookman known for?

75 Can you name two UC Engineering alumni from the 1930s who laid the foundations for rock 'n' roll music?

76 Who is the *Cincinnati Times-Star* reporter who bequeathed almost $250,000 to UC in 1946 to create a poetry foundation?

77 What was the name of the gospel choir organized at UC in 1972?

78 Among the first instructors in art and design at UC was Benn Pittman, who was responsible for Cincinnati's becoming a center for fine woodcarving. Pittman had another career outside the university, though. What was it?

79 On summer evenings, the brilliant red star Antares dominates the southern sky. What did UC astronomers discover about this star?

80 Who is the sculptor who created the statue of Oscar Robertson located outside the Lindner Athletic Center?

81 Perhaps you think this quiz has been a pain in the butt. Who was the UC alumnus who could offer you some relief?

82 Who is the only UC president to graduate from UC?

ANSWERS

01 UC is tied with the University of Virginia, which shares the founding date of 1819. There are thirteen public universities with earlier origins, namely William & Mary (1693), the University of Delaware (1743), Rutgers, the State University of New Jersey (1766), the University of Georgia (1785), the University of Pittsburgh (1787), the University of North Carolina (1789), the University of Vermont (1791), the University of Tennessee (1794), the University of South Carolina (1801), the US Military Academy at West Point (1802), Ohio University (1804), Miami University (1809), and the University of Michigan (1817).

02 The sculpture, unofficially dubbed "Richardson's Rocks," was designed and constructed from 1968 to 1970 by students and faculty at the College of Design, Architecture, Art & Planning to honor iconic architect H. H. Richardson (1838–1886), who, among other masterpieces, designed the old Cincinnati Chamber of Commerce building. When that building was destroyed by fire in 1911, surviving stones were carted off to western Hamilton County, to be used in building an astronomical observatory that was never finished.

03 The exception is the College-Conservatory of Music, whose graduates are greeted with a greatly extended fanfare. The reason? The ceremonial orchestra is composed of CCM students who are honoring their colleagues.

04 The only person to play on NCAA, ABA (American Basketball Association), and NBA (National Basketball Association) championship teams was the University of Cincinnati's Tom Thacker. Wearing #25, Thacker was a guard/forward on the Bearcats' NCAA championship team in 1961 and 1962. In 1968, he was a member of the NBA champion Boston Celtics, and in 1970 Thacker was on the Indiana Pacers squad when they won the ABA championship. After his playing career was over, Tom Thacker coached the Bearcat women's team from 1974 to 1977.

05 In 1962, James A. Rhodes was running for Ohio governor and issued a position paper entitled "Blueprint for Brainpower." Recognizing that the Baby Boomer generation would soon reach college age, Rhodes anticipated growth in higher education and believed that Ohio's universities should establish branch campuses and two-year colleges. As governor, he pushed the funding through and in the following two decades the University of Cincinnati created UC Blue Ash (Raymond Walters College) and Clermont College, as well as University College on the main campus.

06 Jerry Rubin (1938–1994) graduated from UC in 1961 and was an antiwar activist who co-founded the Youth International Party (the Yippies) with Abbie Hoffman and Paul Krassner. He agitated for social change and an end to the war in Vietnam. His most notable writing was *Do It! Scenarios of the Revolution.*

07 International management expert Warren Bennis served as UC's president from 1971 to 1977, leading the successful effort to make the University of Cincinnati a full state university while also empowering women and African Americans on campus through administrative posts and academic programs.

08 The campus summer theater series at the College-Conservatory of Music was "Hot Summer Nights." This musical theater repertory program gave CCM students the opportunity to showcase their talents as actors and singers while providing Cincinnati residents with some wonderful productions.

09 The first African American woman to earn a PhD at the University of Cincinnati was Cincinnati public school principal Jennie Davis Porter. In 1928 when she earned her doctorate, Porter headed the Harriet Beecher Stowe School in the West End. Her motto was "Take what you have and make what you want."

10 Beecher Hall was named for the nineteenth-century educator Catharine Beecher (1800–1878). The sister of Harriet Beecher Stowe, Beecher lived in Cincinnati for several years, arriving in 1832 with her father, the Rev. Lyman Beecher. She considered the teaching profession a vitally important one, and she promoted the benefits of kindergarten, physical education, and the benefits of reading aloud. Beecher also strongly believed in the education of women, and in fact, Beecher Hall, built in 1915, was also called the Women's Building for its coed-oriented classrooms and gymnasium for women. Today, some of the architectural remains of Beecher Hall can be seen between Swift Hall and the Steger Center.

11 The 1946 University of Cincinnati football team finished with an 8–2 record and were invited to play in the Sun Bowl on January 1, 1947. However, there was a stipulation from the Bowl committee: star wide receiver and World War II veteran Willard Stargel could not play because he was black. Earlier in the season, Stargel had to sit out the game against the University of Kentucky because the Wildcats refused to take the field against an African American player. For the Sun Bowl, UC president Raymond Walters told the university's board of directors to turn down the invitation for "ethical and pa-

triotic reasons" but the board and the athletic department accepted anyway because they were enthralled with the idea of the University of Cincinnati playing in its first Bowl. Despite UC's 18–6 victory over Virginia Tech, that decision created a firestorm of protest from outraged community members. For Stargel's part, he completed his degree and for decades was one of the most respected teachers in the Cincinnati public schools.

12   The University of Cincinnati alum who won the Nobel Peace Prize was Charles G. Dawes. An 1886 graduate of the Cincinnati Law School (now the College of Law), Dawes was a banker and diplomat who helped create the Dawes Plan after World War I to ease reparations for Germany and provide short-term economic benefits for that country in the aftermath of the war's devastation. For this, Dawes was the co-winner of the 1925 prize with Sir Austen Chamberlain. That same year, Dawes became vice president on the Republican ticket with Calvin Coolidge.

13   Herman Schneider created "Hobby Hour" as a designated time of the day in which students were strongly encouraged to put aside their engineering studies briefly and follow other pursuits. His idea was that students should become well-rounded citizens by spending this time on art, journalism, literature, music, volunteer work, or anything other than their major.

14   The first time the University of Cincinnati football team played in postseason competition was in January 1898. The 1897 squad was a great one, winning every game except the final one of the regular season against the Carlisle Indians. They even had a 34–0 victory over Ohio State! On January 1, 1898, the 8–1 football team traveled to New Orleans and beat the Southern Athletic Club, 16–0, in its first-ever postseason battle. Louisiana State University pooh-poohed the Cincinnati win, so on January 3 UC went upriver to Baton Rouge and manhandled LSU 28–0.

15   There are fourteen colleges at the University of Cincinnati: Allied Health Sciences, Arts & Sciences, Business, College-Conservatory of Music, Design, Architecture, Art, & Planning, Education, Criminal Justice & Human Services, Engineering & Applied Science, Graduate School, Law, Medicine, Nursing, Pharmacy, Blue Ash, and Clermont.

16   Of the various sculptures on the campuses of the University of Cincinnati, the only living one is, of course, *Live*. This privet hedge sculpture was created in 1976 by land art sculptor Gary Rieveschl. and for the past four decades it

has been lovingly maintained by UC's landscape maintenance crew. *Live* is located on the slope on Clifton Avenue below the College of Art, Architecture, Design & Planning.

17   After his collegiate years, Bearcat Teddy Baehr briefly earned some money playing football for the Cincinnati Celts in 1915. The Celts were formed in 1910 by graduates of Miami University and soon they were joined by other former college players, including Baehr. The Celts played in the so-called Ohio League but went up against Indiana semipro teams as well. By 1923 they were done.

18   "SDS" stood for the national organization Students for a Democratic Society. Founded in Ann Arbor, Michigan, in 1960, SDS was an activist movement with a focus on participatory democracy, defense budget reductions, the end of the war in Southeast Asia, and direct protest action against racism and inequalities in American life.

19   The reason the main campus of the University of Cincinnati has buildings with entrances on different floors is topographical. Built on a series of small hills and valleys, the campus undulates from Calhoun Street to Martin Luther King Boulevard, so if your spatial imagination is strong enough, you can see that all the first floors of buildings are on the same geographical level, but not necessarily at street level. Why this is necessary or practical, we do not know. *But*, we're sure there is a logical answer out there.

20   UC Clermont's athletic teams are called the Cougars. The nationally recognized athletes at UC Clermont compete in men's and women's soccer and basketball, women's volleyball, women's softball, and men's baseball.

21   You'll find Egyptian hieroglyphics at the University of Cincinnati on a chandelier in Blegen Library lobby. Supposedly a quotation from the ancient Egyptian vizier Ptahhotep (2500 BC), taken from his instructions to young men on proper behavior, it reads: "Be not proud because of thy knowledge; be not puffed up because of thy manual skill. No art can be wholly mastered; no man can attain perfection in manual skill."

22   In January of 1937, a massive Ohio River flood covered Cincinnati. Fifty thousand people evacuated their homes as the river rose to nearly eighty feet. Classes were cancelled at the University of Cincinnati and co-op students provided communications over their amateur radio station atop Swift Hall while others assisted the Red Cross throughout the city.

23   Though the dome on Van Wormer at the University of Cincinnati is commonly lit with white light and sometimes with red, blue, and green, it is possible to program 16.7 million color variations!

24   That pioneering University of Cincinnati football strategizer was Sid Gillman, who coached at UC from 1949 to 1954. Gillman played college ball at Ohio State and then professionally for the Cleveland Rams in 1936 before coaching at several Ohio universities. After UC, Gillman coached the Los Angeles Rams, the San Diego Chargers, and the Houston Oilers. He was inducted into the Pro Football Hall of Fame in 1983.

25   The first observatory at the University of Cincinnati was affiliated with the Cincinnati College and dedicated by former president John Quincy Adams in 1843. Located at the top of Mount Ida, the Cincinnati Observatory's home was renamed Mount Adams after the dedication ceremony. The observatory moved to its current home in Mount Lookout in 1873.

26   Women began playing basketball at the University of Cincinnati in 1897, wearing their full-length dresses with "UC" stitched on the bodice. Male students were forbidden from watching the women's games. As the decades passed, the uniforms became a little more suited to moving up and down the court.

27   The carved words at the University of Cincinnati against book censorship and advocating the freedom of expression are found on Blegen Library, constructed in 1930. In 1644, the English man of letters John Milton (1608–1674) published a tract on education called *Areopagitica*. The quotation from this work on the library wall reads: "For books are not absolutely dead things, but do contain a potencie of life in them to be as active as they whose progeny they are."

28   There are fifteen college and departmental libraries at the University of Cincinnati: Archives & Rare Books, Clermont College, UC Blue Ash, Classics, CCM, Geology-Math-Physics, the Elliston Poetry Collection, Law, Engineering & Applied Science, Health Sciences, DAAP, Langsam, Winkler Center for the History of the Health Professions, Business & Economics, and Chemistry-Biology.

29   Powel Crosley Jr. dropped out from the University of Cincinnati College of Law and went on to create the "Shelvador" refrigerator, the Crosley automobile, radios, WLW radio station, and he owned the Cincinnati Reds from 1934 to 1961.

30 In 2015–16, 1,915 University graduate and undergraduate students took part in a study-abroad experience! And the number is growing every year.

31 John "Socko" Wiethe coached basketball at the University of Cincinnati from 1946 to 1952, compiling a record of 106–47 and bringing the Bearcats into the big time in college basketball. It was the Xavier University grad's fearless and tough reputation that gave the nickname to a guy who umpired, boxed, played pro football with the Detroit Lions, swam, golfed, and ran the Hamilton County Democratic Party.

32 George Rieveschl, a University of Cincinnati alum (1937) and professor of engineering, invented Benadryl, the world's first effective antihistamine, in 1946. During his career, Rieveschl also chaired the UC Foundation board of trustees.

33 You will find the giant nautilus at UC embedded in the plaza that connects Langsam Library, Rhodes Hall, and Zimmer Auditorium. Designed in 1997, the nautilus is intended to symbolize the symmetry of nature.

34 The newest college at the University of Cincinnati is the College of Allied Health Sciences, established in 1997.

35 Created in 1972 as the replacement for UC's yearbook, *The Cincinnatian*, and a literary magazine called *The Profile*, *Clifton Magazine* published quarterly until 1994. A complete set of all issues of *Clifton Magazine* can be found in the Archives & Rare Books Library at UC.

36 The biggest margin of victory in the history of University of Cincinnati football came in 1912 when UC played Transylvania in its first game that season. It was a bloody mess, with UC winning 124–0. The rest of the season? Not so good. UC finished 3–4–1, including a 45–7 loss to Ohio State.

37 The youngest graduate in University of Cincinnati history is Darwin Turner, class of 1947, who earned his bachelor's degree at the age of sixteen. Turner later earned a master's at UC and a doctorate at the University of Chicago, and over the course of his career became a renowned literary scholar.

38 In 1925, three University of Cincinnati graduates held influential positions in national government: William Howard Taft as chief justice of the United States, Charles Dawes as vice president of the United States, and Nicholas Longworth III as Speaker of the House of Representatives.

39 That organization was the Cincinnati Bengals. The Bengals played their first two seasons in Nippert Stadium while their permanent home, Riverfront Sta-

dium, was constructed downtown. They moved into Riverfront (later Cinergy Field) in the 1970 season.

40 The University of Cincinnati's monument to the sacrifices of World War I is Memorial Hall, designed by Harry Hake and opened in 1924. It served first as a men's dormitory, then as a general dormitory, and now is part of the CCM village. The carvings on the building emphasize learning and education, but several depict the horrors of war in memory of those who served and died.

41 Annie Laws can be credited with being the founder of both the University of Cincinnati's College of Education, Criminal Justice & Human Services (CECH), and the College of Nursing and was also an instrumental figure in the Cincinnati Women's Club and the Cincinnati Board of Education in the late nineteenth and early twentieth centuries. She established the Cincinnati Kindergarten Association, which over the past 100 years has evolved into CECH, and the Cincinnati Training School for Nurses, which eventually became the UC College of Nursing.

42 The sculpture of a mythical figure on campus is of the Greek god Pan, god of the wild and of rustic music. He is usually portrayed playing the flute. The statue is located in the CCM Alumni Garden and is formally known as the Clara Baur Memorial Fountain. Created by sculptor Clement Barnhorn in 1914, the Pan statue was commissioned by Conservatory of Music students and alumni as a tribute to founder Clara Baur, who died in 1912. The statue was originally located on the Conservatory campus on Oak Street.

43 The Cincinnati College of Pharmacy became a college of the University of Cincinnati in 1954. Women enrolled for the first time in 1880 and one of the first was Cora Dow, who went on to build a chain of drug stores.

44 William Howard Taft, Albert Sabin, and Neil Armstrong have all had United States postage stamps issued in their honor.

45 The part of the University of Cincinnati next to an old cemetery is the UC Blue Ash Art Gallery in the old Plainfield School building. Since the early 1800s there have been three elementary schools on that property, the last of which is the current building constructed in 1936. The school closed in 1975, was the Sycamore Senior Center for a brief time, and is now the UCBA Annex. The cemetery? Carpenter's Run Pioneer Cemetery, established in 1797 and now bisected by Plainfield Road.

46   When the University of Cincinnati football team first began play in 1885 and had its first intercollegiate game in 1888 (playing Miami U in Oxford), there was no on-campus field. So, the team played at League Park in the West End, then home of the Cincinnati Reds.

47   The summer performance venue for the University of Cincinnati on the Ohio River was the showboat *Majestic*. Built in Pittsburgh in 1923, the *Majestic* was the last of the great showboats that traveled up and down the Ohio River. The City of Cincinnati purchased the boat from Indiana University in 1967 and leased it to UC, which operated it as a summer repertory house for its CCM students and professional actors. The lease expired in 1988, and a few years later the *Majestic* was purchased by Cincinnati Landmark Productions, which continued to operate as a theater until 2013, when it closed.

48   William Strunk, born in Cincinnati in 1869 and a graduate of the University of Cincinnati in 1890, was an English professor at Cornell University. In 1918, he wrote a small guide for his students called *The Elements of Style* to help them write more clearly. In 1959, writer, editor, and Strunk's former student E. B. White revised the book and in the decades since it has often been re-ferred to simply as "Strunk and White." More than ten million copies have been sold, it is updated regularly, and there have been numerous parodies and even an opera based upon this seminal work.

49   The University of Cincinnati president who served as a general in the Civil War was Jacob Dolson Cox. As a major general, Cox was involved in several major battles, including Antietam. He later served as governor of Ohio, US secretary of the interior, and a congressman. Cox was dean of the Cincinnati Law School from 1881 to 1897 and during that time he was also UC's president from 1885 to 1889.

50   The bricks Joseph Strauss took from his alma mater, the University of Cin-cinnati, and placed in the Golden Gate Bridge came from the original Uni-versity Building constructed in 1875 on the Clifton Avenue hillside. Alerted in 1935 that the building was to be demolished, Strauss arranged for some bricks to be sent to him so that a piece of UC would forever be in his signa-ture creation.

51   The popular fast-food franchise restaurant on the University of Cincinnati campus in 1973 was McDonald's! It was not only the first McDonald's on a college campus, but the largest McDonald's in the country at the time. Locat-

ed in Tangeman University Center, the home of the Big Mac and the Hamburglar was deleted from UC when TUC underwent renovation in 2001.

52   The University of Cincinnati played Bradley University in that December 21, 1981, game. The match went to seven overtimes, still a record. That game featured sixth man Doug Schloemer as the hero: with a layup, he tied the sixth overtime and in the seventh period, Schloemer hit a game-winning jumper with three seconds left on the clock. The Bearcats won 75–73.

53   On May 27, 1905, the University's College of Law commencement ceremony featured "Pomp and Circumstance" by Edward Elgar as the recessional. Yale University has always claimed it was the first university to play this music, also as a recessional, but that institution was more than a month behind UC when it incorporated the tune into its June 28, 1905, ceremony. How do you like them apples, Yale?

54   The oldest building at the University of Cincinnati is Van Wormer Hall. Built in 1899 at a cost of $64,000, Van Wormer was the first library building at UC and now serves as an administration building. It was named for Asa Van Wormer, who was a local businessman with little education of his own but who had a great appreciation for its possibilities and promises.

55   The University of Cincinnati became a full state university in Ohio in 1977 after serving over a century as a municipal university. Following approval of the necessary bond issues by the voters, on July 1 of that year, UC and Ohio officials signed the conversion paperwork.

56   Mick and Mack are copies of what are known as the Medici Lions, which were originally placed at the Medici palace in Rome but for centuries have been in the Loggia dei Lanzi in Florence. There are copies and variations around the world, from Lithuania and Florida to India to one underwater at the bottom of the harbor in Alexandria, Egypt.

57   Cincinnati College and the Medical College of Ohio were founded in 1819. Around 1900, both institutions merged with UC, which had been founded in 1870, and UC adopted their founding dates.

58   Cleveland Abbe was director of UC's Observatory and professor of astronomy. Because Cincinnati's skies were often too cloudy for stargazing, Abbe turned to meteorology and initiated a program in which trained observers around the country telegraphed weather data to him at the university. His activities attracted the attention of the US Congress, and Abbe's program

was transferred to Washington, DC, where it became the National Weather Service. Cincinnati's telegraph messengers were delighted. Not happy with the extra work Abbe had caused them, they referred to him as "Old Probs" (Probabilities).

59 John Shaw Billings. Billings graduated in 1860 from the Medical College of Ohio, predecessor to UC's College of Medicine. Following military service in the Civil War, Dr. Billings was appointed as the director of the Library of the Surgeon General's Office, which later became known as the National Library of Medicine. In this role, he began compiling a card catalog for every medical article published, and eventually published his catalog as the *Index Medicus* in 1879. *Index Medicus* would eventually go online as *Medline.*

60 The Florence Nightingale Awards for Nursing Excellence recognize exceptional nurses in the Greater Cincinnati region. The University of Cincinnati College of Nursing, founded in 1889 as the Cincinnati Training School for Nurses, with a curriculum modeled after the Nightingale Training School for Nurses in London.

61 Otto Juettner, an 1888 graduate of UC's College of Medicine, is the composer of UC's Alma Mater, originally titled "A Varsity Song." Juettner also composed the Xavier University fight song, "Xavier for Aye." He earned his undergraduate degree from Xavier in 1885.

62 When UC first moved from the downtown "basin" area of the city to its present hilltop location in the Clifton neighborhood, the area was still rural. UC's grounds crews were instructed to take into custody any cows that wandered onto campus and to charge a fee before returning the animals to their owners.

63 Beginning in the late 1960s, UC operated the Tri-County Academic Center out of leased space in Mason, Ohio. In 1975, UC transferred responsibility for the center to Southern State Community College, which merged the center's programs into Southern State's curriculum.

64 One sundial is located at the west end of Schneider Quadrangle. It was presented to UC by the Class of 1955, and was designed by Ron Rosensweig and Hans Muller, set on a base by Ray Ogle—all three members of that class. Known as an analemmic sundial, it requires a little astronomical knowledge to operate, but is reasonably accurate if Daylight Savings Time is ignored. The other sundial, in front of the old Holmes Hospital building, designed by Ernest Bruce Haswell, is a traditional horizontal sundial would be fairly

accurate if oriented toward the north. The Holmes sundial, alas, is pointed to the west.

65   In Braunstein Hall, display cases fill the walls near the main entrance. Within these cases is an exhibit of antique classroom demonstration equipment, including a set of Magdeburg hemispheres that were once used to illustrate the power of atmospheric pressure. Erstwhile UC faculty employed the hemispheres to replicate the experiment performed in 1654 by Otto von Guericke, in which teams of draft animals could not separate the spheres once he had pumped all the air out of them and created a vacuum.

66   The DAAP library began collecting snow globes almost accidentally in 1983 when a staff member brought one back from vacation. There are now hundreds on display in the library, arranged (Of course they are arranged! It's a library!) by state and country of origin.

67   Classical music radio station WGUC-FM is still on the air, owned and operated since 2002 by Cincinnati Public Radio Inc. WGUC began broadcasting in 1960 under the auspices of the University of Cincinnati. From the 1960s into the 1980s, UC students operated what was known as a "carrier current" station with the call letters WFIB. Only radios plugged into campus electric outlets and tuned to 800 AM could receive the student broadcasts.

68   Cincinnati College was located on the east side of Walnut Street, a little north of Fourth Street, downtown. The old College Hall had been constructed in 1815 for a secondary school known as the Lancastrian Seminary.

69   In April 1892, a committee of students recommended red and black as official university colors. The first student organization to adopt the new colors was the Canoe Club. (Just three years earlier, students attending an athletic field day were encouraged to wear blue and brown to show UC spirit.)

70   Ralph A. Van Wye returned in 1920 to his engineering studies at UC following a tour of duty during World War I. A requirement that all male students participate in ROTC had just been initiated, and Ralph, fresh from two years of military service, saw no good reason to take ROTC classes. Commandant Major Sydney H. Guthrie thought otherwise. He saw that Ralph had been an army bandsman, and told Ralph that he was just the man they needed to organize an ROTC band. It was from this ROTC band that the University of Cincinnati Bearcat Marching Band claims its origins. Van Wye later worked as a co-op placement officer at UC for almost fifty years.

71   All these eminent persons have received honorary degrees from the University of Cincinnati.

72   For nearly forty years, until 1913, the most popular sport at the University of Cincinnati was Flag Rush. Here is how it worked: the freshmen posted a flag somewhere on campus and mounted guards to protect it. The sophomores attempted to steal the flag and burn it. Both classes endeavored to beat the living daylights out of each other in the process, and often did.

73   The elephant, known as Old Chief, was so cantankerous that he was sent to the zoo after a long career with the Robinson Circus, during which he had killed at least two men. At the zoo, his tantrums threatened other animals and so he was dispatched. His mounted skin and skeleton were donated to UC. The hide disappeared but the bones of Old Chief, for almost a century on display in UC's Geology Museum in the Old Tech building, are now at the Cincinnati Museum Center.

74   Abe Bookman (1898–1993) patented the Magic 8 Ball fortune-telling toy. Although the basic mechanism was developed by his brother-in-law, Alfred Carter, Bookman redesigned the novelty to enable mass production.

75   Theodore "Ted" McCarty, who graduated from UC's College of Engineering in 1933, developed the solid-body electric guitar endorsed by Les Paul, which earned the nickname "Hammer of God" when played by Led Zeppelin guitarist Jimmy Page. One of the first electronic keyboard instruments was invented by Winston Kock, who earned his bachelor's (1933) and master's (1933) degrees in engineering from UC. He developed the keyboard as his electrical engineering undergraduate thesis.

76   George Elliston, who, despite the first name, was a woman, wrote for the *Cincinnati Times-Star* for more than forty years. Unlike most women journalists of her era, she avoided the society pages and covered crime and politics. No one knew that she had invested in real estate and amassed a considerable fortune, planning to invest it in support of poetry.

77   The choir was the Hanarobi Contemporary Gospel Ensemble, which performed all over the United States.

78   Benn Pittman promoted his brother Isaac's system of shorthand through books, lectures, public demonstrations, and classes.

79   In July 1845, astronomer Ormsby MacKnight Mitchel at the Cincinnati Observatory on Mount Adams discovered that Antares was actually a double

star, with a small green companion circling the red giant star seen with the naked eye from Earth.

80   Blair Buswell was commissioned to depict "The Big O" in bronze. Buswell has also sculpted Jack Nicklaus, Doak Walker, "Bear" Bryant, and more than ninety-five busts of inductees to the Pro Football Hall of Fame.

81   George Sperti graduated from UC's College of Engineering in 1923 and was invited to remain at UC to continue a number of research projects he began as a student. The university organized the Basic Sciences Laboratory for Sperti to experiment in and it was there that Sperti's research team developed the famous hemorrhoid ointment, Preparation H.

82   Henry R. Winkler, president of UC from 1977 to 1984, earned his bachelor's degree in 1938 as well as his master's degree in 1940 from the University of Cincinnati.

Our Contributing Authors

CLARK BECK was one of the first two African American graduates of the University of Cincinnati College of Engineering when he earned his bachelor's degree in 1955. He followed this with a master's degree in aerospace engineering, and enjoyed a thirty-one-year career at Wright-Patterson Air Force Base and became the first black president of the Dayton Engineers Club. The recipient of a kidney transplant, Beck is a Donate Life Ambassador for Life Connection of Ohio and also serves on several community boards. UC awarded Beck an honorary doctorate in 2003.

JOHN BRYANT earned three degrees from the University of Cincinnati: a bachelor's degree in 1960, a master's in 1967, and a doctorate in 1971. While an undergraduate, he was a member of the 1958–59 and 1959–60 basketball teams that participated in the Final Four NCAA Basketball Tournaments. He returned to the University of Cincinnati in 1968 where he served as an assistant basketball coach until the end of the 1970–71 season. Bryant was honored by the University of Cincinnati College of Education as one of its outstanding alumni. He retired in 2002 after serving more than forty years in various areas of education. Postretirement, he remains active by serving as a member of the Board of Directors of the National Underground Railroad Freedom Center in Cincinnati.

JULIALICIA CASE is a PhD student in fiction at the University of Cincinnati. Her fiction and creative nonfiction have appeared in *Crazyhorse*, *Willow Springs*, *Witness*,

Water-Stone Review, The Pinch, and other journals. She has received a Fulbright Fellowship to Germany, a University of New Orleans Writing Award for Study Abroad, and a Tennessee Williams Scholarship to the Sewanee Writers' Conference. She graduated from the master's program in creative writing at the University of California–Davis.

JAY CHATTERJEE is dean emeritus of the College of Design, Architecture, Art & Planning at the University of Cincinnati. Educated at Harvard and at the University of North Carolina, he worked as the regional designer at the East Massachusetts Regional Plan before joining the faculty of University of Cincinnati. As dean he completely reorganized DAAP from a departmental to a school structure to deliver more effective educational services for students. The college has introduced a lecture program titled Chatterjee-Global in his honor. During his time in Cincinnati, Chatterjee participated and led numerous civic and professional organizations. In the early 1980s, he assumed the leadership of the Association of Collegiate Schools of Planning and followed up with a complete reorganization and introduced an annual national conference, a national journal, and the start of an accreditation process. The association has initiated a distinguished award in his name. His leadership at the university led to a complete revitalization of the campus, which was hailed by *Forbes* as one the most beautiful campuses in the world. Critic Herbert Muschamp of the *New York Times* wrote, "Jay Chatterjee…has earned himself a place in history as one of the century's most enlightened patrons."

JIM CUMMINS was born in Columbus, Ohio, and grew up in Cleveland and Indianapolis. He received his BA in English from the University of Cincinnati and his MFA from the University of Iowa Writer's Workshop. He has published six books of poems, the most recent of which is *Still Some Cake*, from Carnegie Mellon University Press; and he has published individual poems in many journals and anthologies, including the *American Poetry Review*, the *Kenyon Review*, the *New Republic*, and several *Best American Poetry* annuals. Cummins has worked at UC since October of 1975; he is the curator of the Elliston Poetry Collection and professor of English. Though he is getting up in years, he is still able to get up and down the stairs, thank you very much, and intermittently remembers he is married to the poet Maureen Bloomfield, also a UC grad. They have two daughters, Katherine and Margaret.

JANICE CURRIE is emerita professor, Murdoch University (Australia) and an alumna of University of Cincinnati. Her grandfather, grandmother, mother, father, and numerous aunts and uncles also attended UC. Currently she is a member of the Board of Friends of UC's Women, Gender, and Sexuality Studies and historian on the board of UC's Women's Club. Recently, she audited creative nonfiction writing courses at UC with a view to writing a memoir about her mother based on a diary she wrote in 1927 as a UC student, excerpts of which appear in this book. She is a coauthor of three books: *Academic Freedom in Hong Kong*; *Global Practices and University Responses*; and *Gendered Universities in Globalized Economies: Power, Careers, and Sacrifices*, and numerous articles on globalization and its impact on universities, gendered universities, and pay equity in higher education.

JACK L. DAVIS arrived as a graduate student in classics at the University of Cincinnati in 1972, one year after Carl Blegen's death. In 1993, he returned to UC to occupy the Carl Blegen Chair in Greek Archaeology. Davis has written extensively about Blegen's contributions to archaeology, as well as his political and philanthropic career. He and Sharon Stocker currently direct excavations at the Palace of Nestor at Pylos, discovered by Blegen in 1939. Davis is a member of the Society of Antiquaries of London and recently been honored for his scholarship by the president of Albania and the Giuseppe Sciacca Foundation of Vatican City. He is an occasional contributor to the blog "From the Archivist's Notebook."

VICTORIA FROMME, a 2011 graduate of the Urban Planning Program in the College of Design, Architecture, Art & Planning (DAAP), currently serves as a civil servant in the US government in Washington, DC. She obtained a master's degree in science and technology in 2017.

Several summers ago, on a charter to France with the University of Cincinnati, STEVEN LAWRENCE GILBERT got off the beaten path and hitchhiked from Paris to Geneva. At the youth hostel near Montreux a couple of guys asked him a question. Gilbert misunderstood so he said, "Please?" These guys shoved each other and exclaimed, "He's from Cincinnati!" They were soccer coaches at Miami University, in Oxford, Ohio. As a broadcast professional who's traveled all over the globe, Gilbert always lets people know he's from Cincinnati. The work he's collaborated on has collected a variety of distinguished awards for print, radio, television, and film. Beginning in 1980 as an art director at Leo Burnett, Chicago, he has ascended through the ranks to creative director and producer. Stepping to the film side of life, Gilbert entered the most rewarding time of his career at Colossal Pictures, San Francisco, where he wrote, directed, and produced work with the greatest collection of creative minds ever assembled in a giant sandbox. He continues to create and consult with anyone who aspires to shatter the mundane and elevate the audience to sit up and say, "whoa." All this he attributes to doodling, and a creative, musical family in Cincinnati, where "what if" was a question often entertained. And if you didn't understand, you asked, politely, "Please?"

KEVIN GRACE is the head of the Archives & Rare Books Library and the university archivist. He also teaches courses in the University Honors Program, with a focus on multicultural approaches to rare books and manuscripts, the history of books and reading, world folklore, and Shakespeare in the modern world.

TERRY GRUNDY has held the position of adjunct associate professor in the UC School of Planning in the DAAP for many years and, more recently, has been lecturer in the UC Department of Political Science. In addition, he directs popular seminars in intellectual history for undergraduate students in the UC Honors Program. He was for many years director of community impact at United Way of Greater Cincinnati, where he organized coalitions and partnerships for community development and directed United Way's social research efforts. Grundy has long been an advocate for the Urbanist approach to bringing vitality back to older American cities, including Cincinnati. In recognition of his work in this area, he has been named resident urbanist at UC's Niehoff Urban Studio.

GREG HAND, proprietor of the "Cincinnati Curiosities" blog, retired in 2014 as associate vice president for public relations at the University of Cincinnati. Since 1978, he filled various capacities at the university, including science writer, news bureau manager, university spokesperson, and public relations instructor. He is coauthor, with Kevin Grace, of three books on UC. A 1974 graduate of UC's McMicken College of Arts & Sciences, Hand was editor of the *Western Hills Press* in suburban Cincinnati before his employment by the university. In addition to his blog, Hand is a freelance writer and consults on public relations planning and crisis communication. He contributes regularly to *Cincinnati* magazine's "City Wise" blog.

MEG HANRAHAN is an adjunct instructor at UC Blue Ash in the Electronic Media Department. She is an award-winning filmmaker, media producer, and writer with credits that include two Emmy award winners: *Sacred Spaces of Greater Cincinnati* (2008) and *Cincinnati Parks: Emeralds in the Crown* (2009). Additional media credits include museum installations at the Dayton Aviation Heritage National Historical Park, the National Underground Railroad Freedom Center, Cleveland Health Museum, and the Fort Worth Zoo. She also regularly produces video for Procter & Gamble and other corporations and nonprofit organizations. Extending her reach in the community, Hanrahan is vice president and trustee of Voyageur Media Group, Inc., a nonprofit whose mission is to create media about science, history, and culture. Hanrahan is currently producing the documentary *A Force for Nature: Lucy Braun*.

JON HUGHES, UC professor emeritus, is a founding faculty member of the nationally recognized Department of English Writing Program, journalism major, and Department of Journalism. He is the author, editor, or major contributor to eleven books (including a novella and two radio plays), former president of the Radio Repertory Company where he was executive producer and artistic director of the public radio "Dimension Radio Theatre" drama series (supported in part by National Endowment for Arts), and founding staff member of *CityBeat*, Cincinnati's alternative newspaper. Hughes is a self-taught photojournalist who has been on assignment and documentary projects around the world, most recently Alaska, Tanzania, and Kenya. His work has been exhibited internationally and his publications include the *New York Times*, the *Christian Science Monitor*, the *Village Voice*, the *Los Angeles Times*, the *LA Review of Books*, the Associated Press, and the *Sun Magazine*. He is director of photography for the award-winning documentary *The Intimate Realities of Water*. Hughes is in the Cincinnati Chapter of the Society of Professional Journalists Hall of Fame, the Ball State University Journalism Hall of Fame, and the University of Cincinnati Journalism Hall of Fame.

EDNA S. KANESHIRO graduated from Hilo High School in Hawaii, and began her higher education at the University of Hawaii at Hilo for two years. She received her BS and MS (science education) from Syracuse University, and after teaching at the junior high school level for two years, she obtained her PhD at Syracuse. She finished her postdoctoral research positions at the University of Chicago and then at Bryn

From the Temple of Zeus to the Hyperloop

Mawr College. She joined the Department of Biological Sciences at UC in 1972, advanced up the ranks, and is now a University Distinguished Research Professor. She spent over ten summers taking courses and conducting research at the Marine Biological Laboratories in Woods Hole, Massachusetts, and is a member of the Society/Corporation. She has an extensive list of scientific publications and served as editor-in-chief of the *Journal of Eukaryotic Microbiology* and as associate editor and on editorial boards of several professional journals. She received a medal from the University of Lille in France for her leadership role in a microbiological field, and is a fellow of the American Association for the Advancement of Science and the American Academy of Microbiology as well. At UC, she was elected a fellow of the Graduate School, and served on various key committees. She is a recipient of a Faculty Achievement Award, the Rieveschl Award for Distinguished Scientific Research, the George Barbour Award for outstanding contributions and excellence in faculty-student relations, and the University Distinguished Research Professorship Award.

VIDITA KANNIKS is a graduate of the College-Conservatory of Music, with degrees in vocal performance as well as music history, along with a minor in French. She is currently pursuing a professional career in classical vocal interpretation. A native of Cincinnati, she finds the University of Cincinnati to be much like a second home. She is grateful for the incredible opportunities made possible through her university experience, including first-class training and education in her degree area as well as the chance to travel and build a new and vast global network. She will most certainly cherish the memories from her alma mater for years to come.

JAMES J. KELLARIS is the James S. Womack/Gemini Corporation Professor of Signage and Visual Marketing at the University of Cincinnati Lindner College of Business. Kellaris joined the marketing faculty in 1989. He holds a PhD degree in marketing from the J. Mack Robinson College of Business, Georgia State University. Additionally, he holds MS (marketing research) and AB (French and music composition) degrees. He has taught as a visiting professor at the École Supérieure de Commerce et de Management (ESCEM), Tours, France; the École Superieur de Commerce (ESC), Toulouse, France; Bond University, Queensland, Australia; and has lectured at the University of Liverpool, UK and the HEC Montréal, École de Gestion. He has won the EXCEL and Dornoff teaching awards, and is a Lindner Teaching Fellow. His research interests include the influence of music on consumers (e.g., auditory branding), marketing ethics and ethical decision-making, and signage-related topics. His work on the "earworm" phenomenon (songs stuck in your head) has received wide attention from the popular media and resulted in the introduction of the term into the Webster-Merriam dictionary. In addition to top academic journals, Kellaris's research has been reported in the *New York Times*, the *Los Angeles Times*, NPR, *CNN Headline News*, *CBS Sunday Morning*, *MSNBC Today Show*, *Forbes*, *BusinessWeek*, and numerous other media outlets in the United States and abroad. As a former professional musician and currently active composer of classical chamber music, Kellaris has won prestigious international competitions, served residencies with large orchestras, and his music is widely performed on three continents.

JUDY McCARTY KUHN is the author of *The Other UC and Me: Editing the Sixties*, a book chronicling her *News Record* experiences as reporter, section editor, and 1966–67 editor-in-chief. "I edited the *News Record* for one year, but the *News Record* edited my life," says Kuhn, a retired English, history, and journalism teacher. At Aiken High School, she advised the yearbook, the *Peregrine*. At Walnut Hills High, where she taught for twenty-seven years, she advised *The Gleam*, a literary magazine, and *The Chatterbox*, the school newspaper. Kuhn coauthored the journalism curriculum for Cincinnati public schools. When cable television arrived in Cincinnati, she worked with students to produce community programs. She has served as a guest speaker in the UC History Department and the School of Journalism. Kuhn, class of 1967, comes from a long line of UC graduates going back to the nineteenth century when one ancestor played UC football. Her parents, Ruth and Ray McCarty, and her uncle, Ted McCarty, graduated in the 1930s. Kuhn's husband, son, aunts, cousins, sister, and niece all hold UC diplomas. Every year, Kuhn and her sister, Beverly McCarty Waitz, sponsor a scholarship for a Walnut Hills High graduate.

MARIANNE KUNNEN-JONES is an editor and writer with nearly four decades of experience in strategic communications, publication writing and management, speechwriting, news and feature writing, video scripting, web content management, and special event planning. A Cincinnati native and 1981 graduate of Northwestern University, she wanted to work in a place she could care deeply about and identified the University of Cincinnati as a possibility. UC gave her the opportunity, and she devoted the bulk of her career to it. She started in the Office of Public Information in 1991 as an associate public information officer. In 2003, she moved to the Office of the President, becoming a special assistant for communication to six consecutive presidents. She has served as a coeditor for two UC books—*The Future of Learning: Addressing Issues of Diversity*, published by the Office of the President and the Just Community Initiative, and *The University of Cincinnati: Soaring into Our Third Century*, a photo history. Prior to UC, Kunnen-Jones worked as a freelancer for the *Cincinnati Enquirer*, reporter for the *Fairfield Sun* and *Western Hills Press*, and reporter and managing editor for the *Catholic Telegraph*.

HELEN LAIRD came to the College-Conservatory of Music at the University of Cincinnati by way Harrisburg, Illinois, Sheridan Wyoming, the University of Nebraska, Columbia University, the Julliard School of Music, and some of the great opera houses in Europe. Laird was recruited by Dean Jack Watson in 1965 as the merger between the College of Music and the Conservatory of Music was being finalized as a professor of voice and artist in residence. Almost immediately she began to understand the need for broadening the curricula for voice students, and, with the arrival of Jack Rouse at CCM, the nation's first musical theater program was born. As a performer and teacher, Laird has sung more than eighty operas, judged many voice and opera competitions, and provided personal and professional guidance to hundreds of performers. Laird left CCM in 1978 to assume the position of dean at the Esther Boyer College of Music at Temple University in Philadelphia. She is now retired and living in Haddonfield, New Jersey.

MITCHEL D. LIVINGSTON retired from the University of Cincinnati in 2013 as vice president for student affairs and chief diversity officer emeritus. He was tenured as professor of educational studies in 1994. Highlights of his eighteen-year career at UC include the Just Community program; the concept of Main Street, to advance the co-curricular experience of students; development of enrollment management system; and, the Five-Year University Diversity Plan. A two-degree graduate of Southern Illinois University, Livingston received his PhD in higher education administration from Michigan State University, and served five public universities before capping his career at UC. Complementing his academic work, Livingston provided leadership on several corporate and community boards. In 2016, he was selected a Great Living Cincinnatian for outstanding community leadership and service by the Cincinnati USA Regional Chamber. Currently adjunct professor of educational studies at UC, he is an organizational consultant for Marathon

Petroleum Company, serves as mentor for adult and youth organizations, and is a frequent speaker in the Cincinnati area.

RUSSELL E. MCMAHON is a faculty member in UC's School of Information Technology and has been teaching IT subject matter for over thirty-five years. His undergraduate degree is from UC's McMicken College of Arts & Sciences in 1976 and his master's from the College of Education. He has been teaching full-time at University of Cincinnati since 1999 and helped create the information technology BS degree, which started in 2004. His wife's family are all Bearcats and his father-in-law taught accounting at UC for nearly forty-eight years. His son and daughter graduated from UC as well. He is very active in the IT user group community and helped create TechLife Cincinnati for those who want to get involved in the local IT scene. Prior coming to UC he has taught at several area high schools and spent more than eight years in the IT world. In 2008, he organized a conference to recognize the fiftieth anniversary of the arrival of the first computer on UC's campus. He currently maintains a blog on UC's computing history writing about alumni, faculty, and staff whose work in this field reflects their dedication to advancing knowledge and innovative usage of computers.

ROBERT EARNEST MILLER earned his PhD in American history from the University of Cincinnati in 1991. Since then, he has taught in many capacities for several of its colleges. He currently teaches full time at Clermont College. Miller specializes in twentieth-century US social and political history. His interest in presidential history is reflected in the essay in this book. Miller is the author of three books on different aspects of Cincinnati history, including *Cincinnati: The World War II Years* (2004), *Hamilton County Parks* (2006), and *World War II Cincinnati: From the Front Lines to the Home Front* (2014). He is currently working on a biography of Raymond Walters, UC's longest tenured president. Miller also works as a public historian for local and national organizations. He served as a project historian for the Cincinnati Museum Center's long-running, award-winning exhibit entitled *Cincinnati Goes to War: How a Community Responds to Total War, 1941–1945* (1991–2016). More recently he wrote the text for *Treasures of Our Military Past: 1788 to the Present* (2015) for the Museum Center.

JULIA MONTIER-BALL, MEd, is manager of international student services in the Division of Experienced-Based Learning and Career Education at the University of Cincinnati. She has served as an assistant director, marketing/communications manager, adjunct and career coach in career services since 2002. She developed career programs for students, and published the e-book, *Career Champions Playbook: Career Planning & Job Search Student Guide*. Her research includes "Assessing Career/Professional-Development Course Effectiveness" and "Equalizing Access to Online Career Resources: Supporting Mid-Life Women Career Changers." In the seven years prior to joining UC, she was director of development, fundraising, and building community and corporate relationships for two local nonprofit agencies. Initially, with a BA in interior design from UC, for seventeen years she ran a commercial interior design business serving regional corporate and healthcare clients. Having served on numerous professional, civic, and community boards, she now admits to just being a "job junkie," who may just ask you—"What do you do?"

BILL MULVIHILL, president of the Mulvihill Advisory Group, retired in the spring of 2016 from the University of Cincinnati after forty-four-plus years of service. A proud 1970 graduate of UC's Lindner College of Business, he started his career at UC in the fall of 1970, and except for a two-year hiatus earning a master's degree at Ohio University, he dedicated the entirety of his professional career to boldly pursuing the best for his beloved alma mater. He held positions in Student Affairs, the Office of the President, Public Affairs, Alumni Affairs, Bearcat Athletics, the UC Foundation, and the UC Bicentennial. Among his many achievements was serving as campaign director of the UC's $1 Billion Proudly Cincinnati Campaign. He has served on numerous nonprofit boards including the Arthritis Foundation (national chair), the Lupus Research Alliance, Saint Xavier High School, and the NIAMS Council of the NIH. He was a coeditor of *Soaring into Our Third Century*. In 2016 the university awarded him the President's Award of Excellence Medal.

A 1972 graduate of the UC College of Law, BUCK NIEHOFF practiced at Peck, Shaffer & Williams for forty years, specializing in municipal bond law. He was active in politics, serving as chair of the Hamilton County Republican Party in 1999. In 2000, he was a delegate and in 2004 he was an alternate delegate to the Republican National Convention. At UC, he established the Niehoff Urban Studio, a multidisciplinary, experiential academic center focused on urban issues. He was chair of the UC Board of Trustees in 2009 and was co-convener of the Proudly Cincinnati Capital Campaign, which raised $1.1 billion for the university. He is the author of four books. He and his wife, Patti, have a son, Peter, who is working toward a PhD in history at UC.

Celebrated actor and producer in television, film, and theater, SARAH JESSICA PARKER is an alumna of the University of Cincinnati's College-Conservatory of Music Preparatory Department. She performed at age five as a member of Kay King's Mini-Mummers, a theatrical troupe in the department. At the age of eight, she began taking lessons in the department, and was taught by one of the first dancers to receive his MA in dance from CCM, David Blackburn. Parker is the star and executive producer of the HBO original series *Divorce*. This dark comedy premiered more than a decade after the finale of her long-lived HBO hit, *Sex and the City*. Parker has won four Golden Globes, three Screen Actors Guild awards, and two Emmy awards. Parker currently serves as a vice chairman of the board of directors for the New York City Ballet and is a UNICEF ambassador. In November 2009, the Obama administration elected her to be a member of the President's Committee on the Arts and the Humanities. Parker also recently launched her own imprint, SJP for Hogarth, in partnership with Crown and Hogarth. In this new role, she acquires and curates works of fiction that reflect her own taste as a reader. She is also serving as the American Library Association's honorary chair of Book Club Central.

PAULETTE PENZVALTO studied computer science while a student at Columbia University and is a program manager in the Corporate Engineering department at Google. She is passionate about diversity and inclusion, leads the Google Prison Elders Project, Autism Programs at Google, and she is active as a leader in the Google Disability Alliance. Penzvalto sits on the San Francisco Mayor's Council for People with Disabilities and presents nationally on issues pertaining to autism and employment in tech. She received an artist diploma in opera from the University of Cincinnati College-Conservatory of Music, completed an internship at the Juilliard School, and is currently studying with Suzanne Mentzer at San Francisco Conservatory of Music. Penzvalto also enjoys writing for an international audience as a "Scribbler" for Google Doodles.

FAITH PRINCE has been dazzling Broadway audiences since winning the Tony, Drama Desk, and Outer Critics Circle awards for her performance as Miss Adelaide in *Guys and Dolls*. As one of Broadway's best-loved leading ladies, Faith most recently starred on Broadway in *Disaster! The Musical* for which she received rave reviews. In 2008, she was nominated for Tony, Drama Desk, and Outer Critics Circle awards for *A Catered Affair*. Other Broadway credits include *The Little Mermaid, Bells Are Ringing, Nick & Nora, Jerome Robbins' Broadway, Little Me, The Dead*, and *Noises Off*. Prince currently has a recurring role on the ABC hit series *Modern Family*. She also appeared as Joey Lawrence's mother on ABC Family's long-running series *Melissa & Joey* and wrapped her five-season run as Brooke Elliott's mother on Lifetime's popular series *Drop Dead Diva*. She is a 1979 graduate of the University of Cincinnati's musical theater program. In June 2009, Prince received an honorary doctor of performing arts and addressed UC's graduating students as commencement speaker.

HOLLY PROCHASKA is a 1993 graduate of UC's School of Social Work and began her library career as a student worker in the Geology-Physics Library. After a few years of wandering the Pacific Northwest looking at its geology, Holly returned to the university in 1999 working at the libraries in various positions, including head of the Geology-Mathematics-Physics Library and coordinator of renovations. Currently, Prochaska is preservation librarian for the University of Cincinnati Libraries and the co-manager of the Preservation Lab, a collaboration between the University of Cincinnati and the Public Library of Cincinnati and Hamilton County.

JACK ROUSE came from the University of Wisconsin to CCM at the University of Cincinnati in 1969 to develop and head what was to become the Department of Musical Theater, Opera, Broadcasting, and Technical Theater. During his short stay at CCM (he left academia for the business world in 1975) he founded the first musical theater program in the United States. He was the founding chair of the Port of Greater Cincinnati Development Authority, and an original board member of 3CDC and the Music Hall Revitalization Company. In 1987, he established Jack Rouse Associates, a global experiential design firm based in Cincinnati. He serves on the board of trustees for the Cincinnati Symphony Orchestra, Playhouse in the Park, ArtsWave, and the Lake Dillon Theatre Company (Silverthorne, Colorado). Currently Rouse is an adjunct professor at Columbia University's Graduate School of the Arts in New York where he teaches leadership.

ANNE DELANO STEINERT's parents met in 1965 in Old Chem where her father was her mother's chemistry TA. Her mother earned a BS in medical technology and her father got a PhD in chemistry (he also now holds an MBA from UC). They married in 1968 and in 1970 they brought her home to their apartment on Joselin Avenue (now the Phi Kappa Theta house). Steinert grew up in gaslight Clifton, walking distance to UC's campus, but it took forty-three years before she took her first class at UC. After attending Walnut Hills High School, she moved to Baltimore where she earned a BA in historic preservation from Goucher College, and then to New York City where she earned an MS in historic preservation from Columbia University. After twenty years of work in preservation and education, Steinert earned an MA from UC in American and public history in 2013. She is now working toward her PhD and teaching in the History Department. Steinert is proud to be descended from her great, great, great aunt, Elizabeth Antoinette Ely, who became the second woman to earn a graduate degree from UC when she received her MA in 1892 (she also earned a normal degree in 1885 and a BA in 1887). Steinert currently serves as the board chair of the Over-the-Rhine Museum and has curated two recent local history exhibits, *Look Here!* and *Schools for the City*. Her proudest accomplishment is her work raising her delightful seven-year-old son, Seneca.

BOB TAFT began his career in public service as a Peace Corps volunteer, working as a schoolteacher in Tanzania right after graduating from college. He went on to get a master's degree in government from Princeton and a law degree from the University of Cincinnati. His first job in government was with the Bureau of the Budget in the State of Illinois. He has served as an elected official in Ohio for thirty years, as a member of the state legislature, a county commissioner, Ohio secretary of state, and, most recently, as governor of Ohio (1999–2007). In his role as governor, he focused on improving schools, reforming Ohio's tax system, attracting advanced, high-paying jobs, and helping communities clean up polluted sites and provide better recreational opportunities for their citizens. Former governor Taft is currently a Distinguished Research Associate with the University of Dayton, teaching political science courses and working with state and federal internship programs.

SID THATHAM, a graduate student from Chennai, India, earned two master's degrees at the University of Cincinnati, an MBA and a master's in chemical engineering, in 2017. Thatham's passion for helping other international students quickly led to being elected president of the Indian Students' Association at UC, as well as being an international ambassador for UC International and president of the Environmental and Chemical Engineering Graduate Students' Association. While juggling the roles of a business and chemical engineering graduate student, Thatham served two terms as the vice president of the graduate student body at UC and as the business-lead for "Hyperloop UC," one of the final 30 out of 1,200 global competitors in the SpaceX competition for which he later delivered a talk for TEDxCincinnati. During his time at UC he was the recipient of the first ever Presidential Medal for Graduate Student Excellence, the International Spotlight award, the Who's Who award, a two-time recipient of the International Graduate Student award, and the Exemplary Service award.

JERRY P. TSAI, 2008 graduate of UC's McMicken College of Arts & Sciences, was the 2006–07 student body president and 2005 homecoming king. Throughout his collegiate career, Jerry was dedicated to contributing to the UC community as a student leader who ensured his fellow Bearcats felt their voices were heard and appreciated. He is the special contributor to a UC children's book written by fellow UC alum, Joel Altman, called *Bearcat's Journey Through UC!* Jerry works at Acceptd, a start-up company connecting artists and arts opportunities, founded by two UC alumni, and continues to be active with UC as an alumnus.

DONALD L. VIETH earned Met. Eng. (1963) and PhD (1972) degrees from the University of Cincinnati. While in graduate school he was also an instructor in the College of Engineering. He was recognized as a Distinguished Alumnus in 1985. Vieth's professional career of thirty-three years included service at the National Bureau of Standards, the Energy Research and Development Administration, and the Department of Energy. His primary areas of interest were measurement science, nuclear energy, and disposal of the nation's high-level radioactive waste. He served as the US representative to the International Atomic Energy Agency's Committee on Underground Disposal. During that time, he managed the Yucca Mountain Project, leading to its selection by Congress as the single site to be considered for the nation's first high-level radioactive waste repository. Pursuant to his government service he was a consultant at the Los Alamos National Laboratory and at the Rocky Flats Plant during its final remediation. Vieth is coauthor of the book *Waste of a Mountain: How Yucca Mountain Was Selected, Studied, and Dumped*, a political and technical history of the federal government's turbulent and chaotic programs for disposing of high-level radioactive waste.